APPLIED BEHAVIOUR AND HUMAN CONSTRUCT

THE GLIMPSE AND GLANCE INTO HUMAN PSYCHOLOGY

DR.A.JANAKI RANI, DR.M.RAMASUBRAMANIAN, DR.C.KARTHIKEYAN, MS.JUNO.A.M

Copyright © Dr.A.Janaki Rani, Dr.M.Ramasubramanian, Dr.C.Karthikeyan, Ms.Juno.A.M
All Rights Reserved.

This book has been self-published with all reasonable efforts taken to make the material error-free by the author. No part of this book shall be used, reproduced in any manner whatsoever without written permission from the author, except in the case of brief quotations embodied in critical articles and reviews.

The Author of this book is solely responsible and liable for its content including but not limited to the views, representations, descriptions, statements, information, opinions and references ["Content"]. The Content of this book shall not constitute or be construed or deemed to reflect the opinion or expression of the Publisher or Editor. Neither the Publisher nor Editor endorse or approve the Content of this book or guarantee the reliability, accuracy or completeness of the Content published herein and do not make any representations or warranties of any kind, express or implied, including but not limited to the implied warranties of merchantability, fitness for a particular purpose. The Publisher and Editor shall not be liable whatsoever for any errors, omissions, whether such errors or omissions result from negligence, accident, or any other cause or claims for loss or damages of any kind, including without limitation, indirect or consequential loss or damage arising out of use, inability to use, or about the reliability, accuracy or sufficiency of the information contained in this book.

Made with ♥ on the Notion Press Platform
www.notionpress.com

Contents

Contents

Foreword

Human behaviour is a multifaceted and evolving subject that has intrigued scholars for centuries. It extends beyond psychology, encompassing the internal and external influences that shape our decisions, interactions, and daily experiences.

In today's evolving world, understanding behaviour is more critical than ever. This book serves as an essential resource for students and professionals, offering insights into behavioural awareness that can enhance both personal and professional relationships.

Through its exploration of behavioural science, the book delves into motivation, decision-making, leadership, and interpersonal dynamics. By uncovering the principles that drive human behaviour, readers will gain valuable tools to inspire, influence, and communicate more effectively—essential skills for success in any field.

I believe this book will not only support academic inquiry but also serve as a practical guide for those seeking a deeper understanding of human behaviour. It provides a meaningful framework for navigating complex social interactions with greater awareness and purpose.

Dr.P.P.Murugan
Director of Extension Education

Preface

Understanding human behaviour is fundamental across various disciplines, offering key insights into how individuals think, feel, and act. By examining behavioural patterns, we can make informed choices, refine products and services, and develop a deeper awareness of the world around us. Businesses, for instance, benefit from studying consumer behaviour, enabling them to enhance customer experiences and achieve market success.

Beyond commerce, behavioural insights are valuable in numerous fields. Farmers can leverage psychological principles when adopting new agricultural technologies, managing labour, or navigating market dynamics. Similarly, students can optimize learning through cognitive strategies that improve focus, memory, and problem-solving skills. Professionals in healthcare, education, and management can apply behavioural science to foster teamwork, leadership, and workplace efficiency.

This book explores the intricate mechanisms of human behaviour, beginning with sensory inputs—the foundation for cognitive functions such as perception, attention, and memory. Sensory signals processed by the brain shape our reality, influencing decision-making and learning.

In an era of rapid societal change, understanding behaviour is crucial for fostering positive relationships and resolving conflicts constructively. This book examines personality development, including traits shaped by thoughts, values, emotions, and beliefs, while also emphasizing the role of Emotional Intelligence (EI) in communication, leadership, and workplace dynamics.

Designed as a comprehensive resource, this book bridges psychological theory with real-world applications. It aims to equip students, scholars, and professionals with the knowledge and skills needed to navigate complex human interactions and build fulfilling careers.

Dr.C.Karthikeyan
Professor and Head
Department of Extension Education
and Rural Sociology

Acknowledgements

THIS BOOK IS A COMPILATION OF VARIOUS CONTENT FROM VARIOUS SOURCES. NONE OF THE CONTENT IS OWNED BY THE CONTRIBUTORS. COPYRIGHTS ARE REESERVED FOR THE RESPECTIVE CREATORS

CHAPTER ONE

MEANING IMPORTANCE AND FACTORS INFLUENCING HUMAN BEHAVIOUR

BEHAVIOUR:

Behaviour refers to the actions or reactions of an object or organism, usually in relation to the environment. Behaviour can be conscious or unconscious, overt or covert, and voluntary or involuntary.

HUMAN BEHAVIOUR:

Human behaviour is the collection of activities performed by human beings and influenced by culture, attitudes, emotions, values, ethics, authority, persuasion, and/or coercion.

DEFINITION OF HUMAN BEHAVIOUR

Human behaviour refers to the way humans act and interact. It is based on and influenced by several factors, such as genetic makeup, culture and individual values and attitudes.

Human behaviour refers to the range of actions, reactions, and interactions exhibited by individuals in response to internal or external stimuli. It includes physical actions, emotional responses, social interactions, and cognitive processes. Understanding human behaviour helps in predicting and explaining why people act in certain ways in different situations.

IMPORTANCE OF HUMAN BEHAVIOUR

1. Social Interactions: Understanding behaviour allows people to navigate social interactions and build relationships more effectively.

2. Personal Development: It aids individuals in improving their emotional intelligence, decision-making, and self-awareness.

3. Conflict Resolution: Recognizing the factors influencing behaviour helps in resolving conflicts and improving communication.

4. Mental Health: Insight into human behaviour can lead to better mental health care and therapeutic practices.

5. Workplace Efficiency: In organizational settings, understanding employee behaviour can optimize performance, motivation, and team dynamics.

6. Sharpening and refinement of common sense: Through experiences, social interactions, emotional intelligence, and problem-solving, individuals continuously adjust their behaviour, leading to a deeper and more practical understanding of the world.

7. Development of people skills: From cognitive abilities and emotional intelligence to social skills, leadership, and coping mechanisms, behaviours that involve interaction, learning, adaptation, and reflection enable individuals to hone their skills over time.

8. Enhancement of organization and individual effectiveness: On an individual level, behaviours such as self-discipline, emotional intelligence, motivation, and stress management lead to improved productivity and success. On an organizational level, fostering positive behaviours related to communication, leadership, collaboration, and adaptability can create an environment where both individuals and teams thrive.

1. <u>Understanding people's behaviour can help us create better products and services:</u> Companies and businesses can <u>improve their products and services</u> by <u>analyzing customer behaviour</u>. For example, by understanding <u>the buying habits</u> of their customers, companies can create products that meet their needs and expectations.

2. **<u>Improving communication:</u>** Effective communication is essential in every aspect of life. By studying <u>human behaviour</u>, we can learn how to communicate better with others, which can lead to <u>stronger relationships</u> and better outcomes in different areas of life.

3. **<u>Enhancing mental health:</u>** Studying human behaviour can help us understand the causes of mental illnesses and develop better treatments. By analyzing the behaviour of <u>people with mental health</u> issues, <u>healthcare professionals</u> can provide better care and support.

4. **<u>Creating safer environments:</u>** Understanding <u>human behaviour</u> can help us create <u>safer environments</u>, whether it's in the workplace, schools, or public spaces. For example, by analyzing the behaviour of criminals, <u>law enforcement</u> can develop strategies to prevent crimes and keep communities safe.

Studying human behaviour is crucial in various fields and can help us create a better world. By analyzing human behaviour, we can <u>gain valuable insights</u> into how people think, feel, and behave, which can <u>lead to better decision-making</u>, <u>improved products and services</u>, and <u>a deeper understanding</u> of the world around us.

FACTORS INFLUENCING HUMAN BEHAVIOUR

• ATTITUDES: The degree to which the person has favourable or unfavourable evaluation of the behaviour in the question.

• SOCIAL NORMS: This is the influence of social pressure that is perceived by the individual (normative beliefs) to perform or not perform a certain behaviour

• PERCEIVED BEHAVIOURAL CONTROL: This construct is defined as the individual's belief concerning how easy or difficult performing the behaviour will be.

OTHER FACTORS

1. BIOLOGICAL FACTORS: Genetic predispositions, brain chemistry, hormonal levels, and physical health can all influence behaviour. For instance, genetics may contribute to temperament or mental health conditions.

2. PSYCHOLOGICAL FACTORS: Cognitive processes (thoughts, attitudes, beliefs), emotional states, personality traits, and past experiences shape behaviour. An individual's mindset or mood can determine how they react in different scenarios.

3. SOCIAL AND ENVIRONMENTAL FACTORS: Culture, family upbringing, peer influence, societal norms, and environmental conditions significantly affect how people behave. For example, people may act differently in public versus private settings due to social expectations.

4. SITUATIONAL FACTORS: Immediate contexts, such as stress, perceived threats, or specific circumstances, can trigger particular behaviours. The way a person reacts in a crisis or under pressure often depends on the situation at hand.

5. LEARNING AND CONDITIONING: Past experiences, including rewards, punishments, and observational learning, play a crucial role in shaping human behaviour. Classical and operant conditioning are key psychological concepts that explain how people learn behaviours.

6. CULTURAL AND SOCIETAL INFLUENCES: The norms, values, and practices of a particular society or cultural group influence the actions of its members. Behaviours acceptable in one culture may be seen as inappropriate in another.

CHARACTERISTICS OF HUMAN BEHAVIOUR

Personality is the sum total of one's experience, thoughts and actions.

• It includes all behaviour patterns, traits and characteristics that make up a person.

• A person's physical traits, attitudes, habits and, emotional and psychological characteristics are all parts of one's personality

BIOLOGICAL BASES OF HUMAN BEHAVIOR – NERVOUS SYSTEM, BRAIN, ENDOCRINE SYSTEM AND GENES

INTRODUCTION

The term "biological bases of human behavior" describes the physiological processes that underlie and mold our reactions, thoughts, and feelings, mostly in the brain and nervous system; in other words, how our biology including hormones, neurotransmitters, genetics, and brain anatomy contributes to our behavioral patterns. This field of study investigates how environmental factors and genes passed down from our parents combine to produce observable behaviors. It looks at things like how different parts of the brain process information, how neurotransmitters like dopamine affect motivation and mood, and how behaviors can change throughout life due to hormonal fluctuations.

RECEPTORS
SENSE ORGAN

- Sense organs are the specialized organs composed of sensory neurons, which help us to perceive and respond to our surroundings. There are five sense organs – eyes, ears, nose, tongue, and skin.
- Specialised sensitive cells called receptors, which are connected to the termination of sensory nerve fibres, make up sense organs. The following sensory defects or disorders result from malfunctioning receptors: visual, auditory, cutaneous, olfactory, gustatory, kinaesthetic, and static disorders. These receptors are triggered by both internal and external stimuli.

EFFECTORS

The term "organs of responses" refers to effectors.

• The majority of our behavioral patterns are influenced by the hormones generated by the ductless gland, which are responsible for physiological reactions and motor activities carried out by muscles

Hormonal secretion is either insufficient or excessive when these glands are overactive or underactive.

• This has an impact on the person's whole personality.

• MUSCLES

Different bodily parts move as part of our behaviour and activities.

• The body uses muscles to perform motor functions so that it can react to different input. There are primarily three kinds of muscles: skeletal, cardiac, and smooth muscles.

• GLANDS

Human behaviour is significantly influenced by glands, which also help with food digestion, waste product removal, emotion formation and prolongation, and body metabolic management.
  • Two categories of glands exist:

○ **Duct glands**
○ **Endocrine or ductless glands.**

Duct glands

• **Examples**: Sweat glands and salivary glands
• **Function**: Secrete substances onto body surfaces

Endocrine glands

• **Examples**: Pituitary gland, thyroid gland, adrenal glands, parathyroid glands, and pineal body
• **Function**: Secrete hormones into the bloodstream

  • They have an impact on the body's development, general metabolism, brain growth, secondary sex traits, and emotional behaviour.
  • These are the endocrine glands: the pituitary, thyroid, parathyroid, and adrenals.

CONNECTERS
Connectors or adjustors aid in coordinating, regulating, or modulating receptor

• Muscle coordination is necessary to hit a tennis ball, drive a car, and play the piano
• The body must communicate with the muscles in order for them to coordinate.
• Neurones are specialised cells that carry messages. Neurones
  The smallest unit of the nervous system is the neurone. We must first comprehend the types, structures, and functions of neurones before moving on to the major nervous system. Neurones are responsible for converting various stimuli into electrical impulses.
• Three structural components make up a neurone:

○ Axon
○ Cell body
○ Dendrite

• Dendrites receive signals from other neurons. Spines are leaf-like structures that extend from the cell body. Are typically thin and restricted to a short area surrounding the cell body.
• Cell Body Also known as the soma, this section comprises the nucleus and cytoplasm Controls neuron activity and produces necessary proteins for other neuron components to function
• Axon Sends messages from the cell body to other neurons or bodily tissues. Can be significantly longer than dendrites. Typically keeps a consistent radius. Often gives rise to many smaller branches before ending in nerve terminals. Many axons are coated with a myelin coating, which speeds up the passage of electrical signals

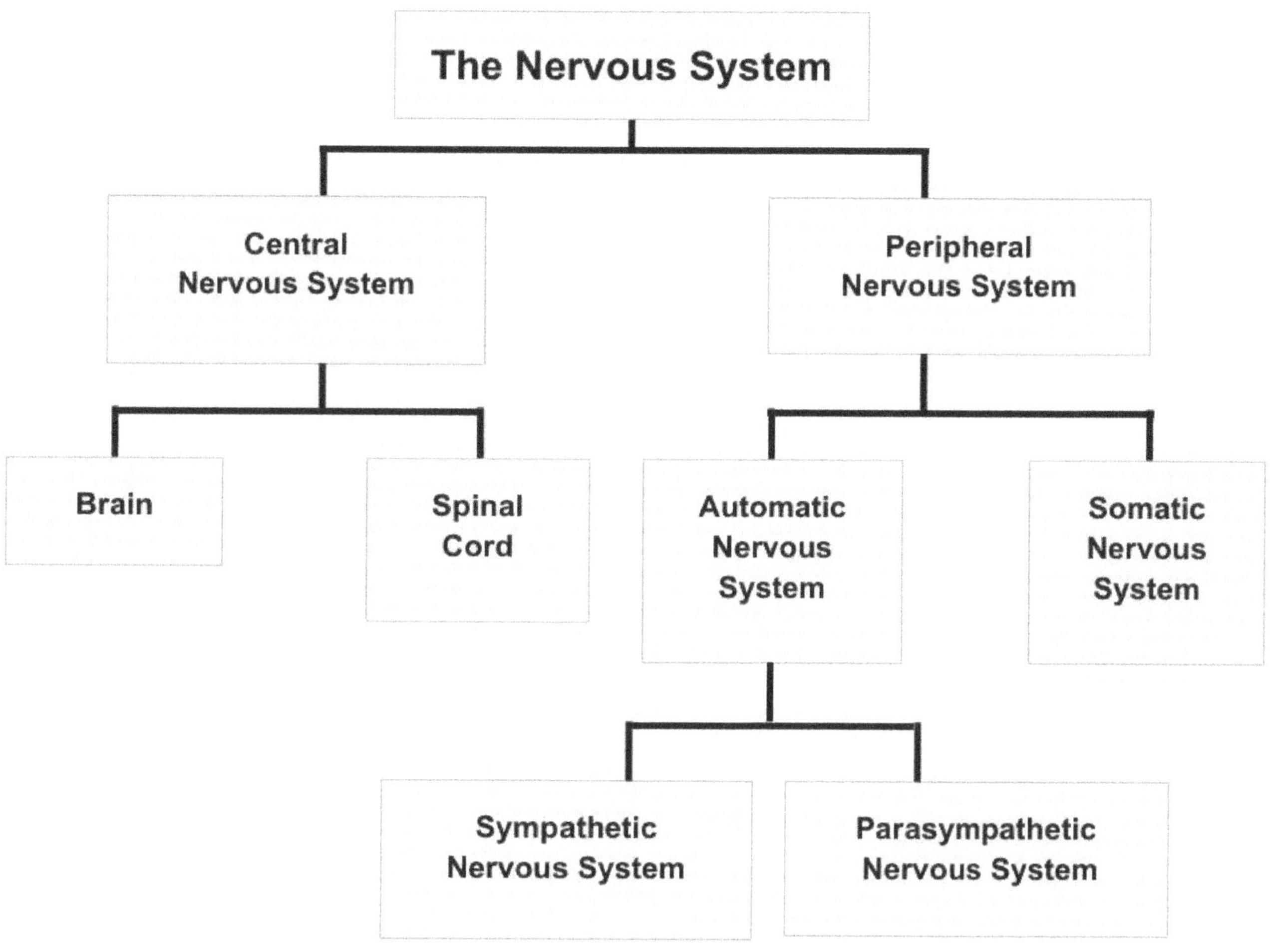

CLASSIFICATION AND TYPES OF NEURONS

1) **Sensory neurones**: They are in charge of transmitting nee impulses from the sense organ to the cortex and brain.

2) **Motor neurones**: They are in charge of sending nerve impulses to effector muscles from the brain and spinal cord so that the body can react to stimuli

3) **Association neurone**: Located exclusively in the brain and spinal cord, these neurones are also referred to as interneurons. These neurones primary jobs are to take in sensory data, process it, and determine how to react to it.

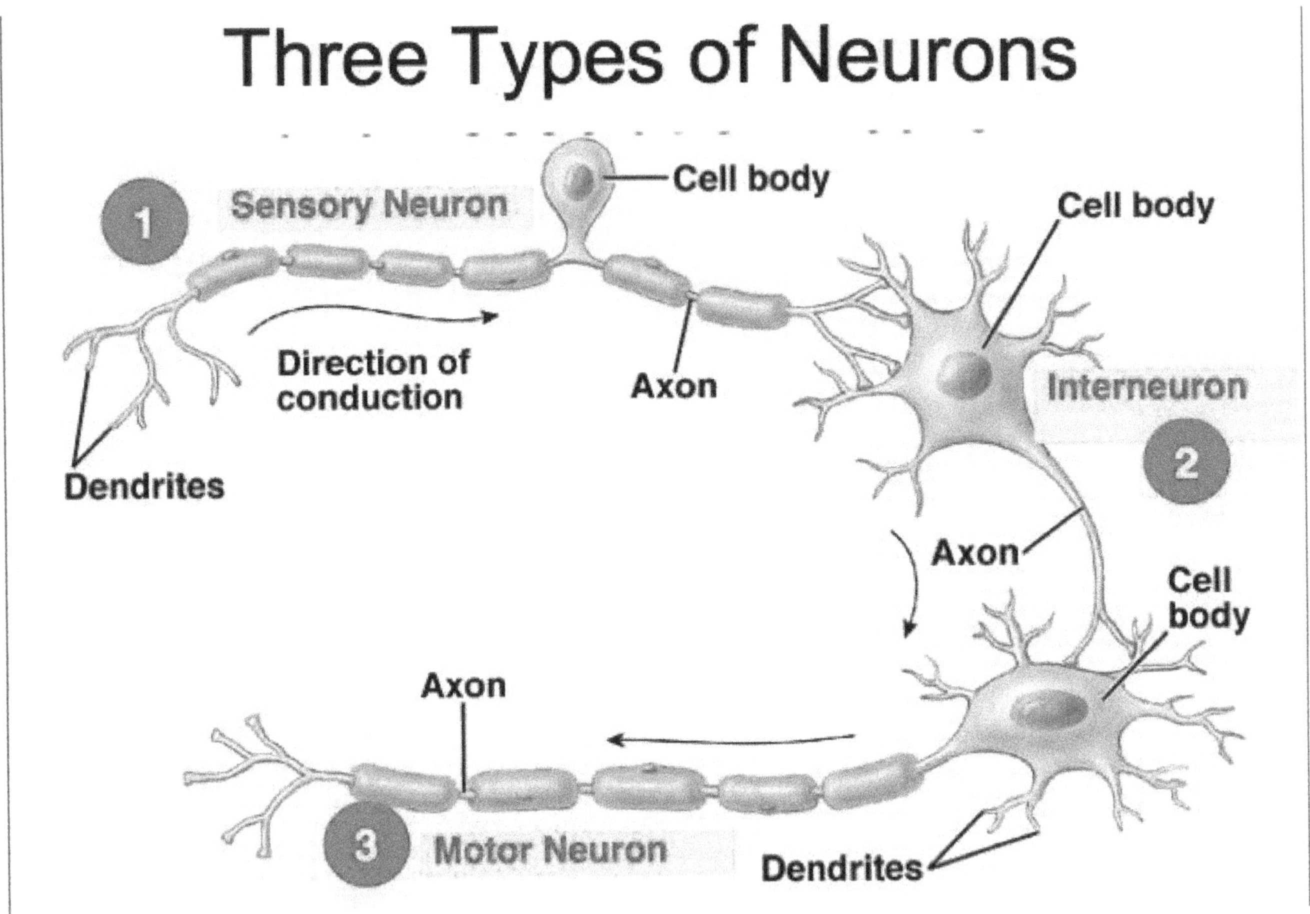

CENTRAL NERVOUS SYSTEM

It extends from the end of the waist to the cervix. It contains a fluid that has meninges covering it. At regular intervals, pairs of spinal nerves emerge from its thirty-one divisions. It is an excellent nerve impulse conductor. Here, all sensory data from the body's numerous portions is received before being transmitted to the brain's higher regions. The spinal cord receives all of the brain's motor information before it is transmitted to the various body parts for action. In addition, the spinal cord serves as the focal point for reflex actions. Because of its significance, it is also known as the automatic machine.

1. Brain
2. Spinal cord

The brain controls higher functions such as thinking, learning, and memory, while the spinal cord connects the brain to the body's peripheral nerves. The function of the nervous system is to receive sensory information from the body, process it in the brain, and generate motor responses. The skull protects the brain, while the spinal cord is contained within the vertebrae. Both are further covered by layers of membranes known as meninges and cerebrospinal fluid.

BRAIN

- Fore brain (thalamus, hypothalamus and cerebrum).
- Mid brain (situated between forebrain and hind brain)
- Hind brain (medulla, pons, cerebellum and reticular formation

1.FOREBRAIN

The limbic system, the cerebrum, the thalamus, and the hypothalamus are its key components.

• Every sensory impulse travels to the higher centres via the thalamus.

• The regulation of sleep and alertness is influenced by the thalamus. **Hypothalamus**

It is located beneath the thalamus and has a significant impact on motivational and emotional behaviour of all kinds.

The hypothalamus contains centres that regulate vital bodily functions like eating, drinking, sleeping, and controlling body temperature

- It is made up of thalamic, hypothalamic, and cerebrum components that surround the bottom portion of the forebrain in a ring.
- The limbic system, sometimes referred to as the emotional brain, is involved

in emotional elements of behaviour, including memory, smell, pleasure and pain, anger and aggression, and survival.

Cerebrum

It is the biggest and most intricate area of the brain.

- The cerebral cortex is a dense layer of closely spaced neurons that covers the cerebrum.
- It is separated into the left and right hemispheres

Thalamus

The thalamus responsible for processing and transmitting sensory data to the brain including vision hearing and pain.

2.MIDBRAIN

The midbrain is a part of the brain that controls motor movement, vision, hearing, and more. It's located at the top of the brain, below the cerebral cortex.

Midbrain functions

- **Motor control:** The midbrain controls movement of the eyes and head, and is involved in reflexes.
- **Vision and hearing:** The midbrain processes visual and auditory signals.
- **Pain modulation:** The midbrain helps distinguish between expected and perceived pain.
- **Sleep and wake cycle:** The midbrain is involved in the state of consciousness and the waking and sleeping rhythms.

3.HINDBRAIN

1.Medulla Oblongata: This structure connects the brain to the spinal cord and controls essential autonomic processes, including blood pressure, heart rate, and respiration. Instant death may result from medulla damage

2. Pons: It houses sensory and motor neurones and is situated above the medulla. It connects upper and lower brain regions, controls facial expressions, eye movements, and jaw action, and processes sensory input from the face and head, including touch, pain, and temperature.

3. Cerebellum: Located below the hindbrain, this structure consists of an inner white matter and an outer grey matter. Damage to it causes uncoordinated motions, like a disorganised gait, as it coordinates motor activities

SPINAL CORD

The spinal cord is a structure that resembles a rope and is composed of long, circular nerve fibers. It serves as a conduit for communication between the brain and the body and is also an organ for efficient reflex actions, such as the withdrawal of the hand when something is hot. These reflex actions are nearly automatic.

FOUR LOBES OF THE BRAIN

- **Frontal lobe**

Resides in the motor cortex and is in charge of controlling voluntary movements, decision-making, and behavior planning. Damage: incapacity to make wise decisions and acknowledge the consequences; heightened anger; mood swings; and impaired behavior regulation

- **Parietal lobe:**

Involves processing bodily sensory data, including touching, limb location, temperature, and discomfort.
Damage: Reduce or abolished multitasking abilities, left and right recognition Neglectful damage

- **Temporal lobe:**

The primary auditory region location, which incorporates the appreciation of spoken words and sounds, is in charge of learning, memory, and hearing.
Damage includes the inability to focus on what they see and hear, as well as the incapacity to understand language Memory loss, Disturbance in emotions, Prosopagnosia.

- **Occipital lobe:**

Involves processing visual information, such as appreciating colors and identifying and identifying things, people, and animals
This Loss of vision is the damage
Incapacity to recognize color
The hallucination

PERIPHERAL NERVOUS SYSTEM

1. **Somatic Nervous System**: Send signals from the central nervous system to muscles, which regulates voluntary movements.
2. **The Autonomic Nervous System (ANS)** plays a crucial role in controlling involuntary physiological functions such blood pressure, breathing, digestion, and heart rate. It is essential for preserving the body's equilibrium

ENDOCRINE SYSTEM

By producing hormones that control a number of body processes and affect mood, emotions, and physical reactions, it plays a significant part in the biological underpinnings of behaviour

The endocrine system controls the way your body functions.it produces hormones that travels to all parts of your body to maintain your tissues and organs.

The chemical communication network that sends messages throughout the body via the blood stream

1. **Hypothalamus**: Controls emotional reactions and basic urges including hunger, thirst, and tension.
2. **Pituitary Gland**: Often referred to as the "master gland," it regulates growth, reproduction, and emotional responses.
3. **Thyroid Gland**: Controls metabolism, which impacts mood, energy levels, and cognitive abilities.
4. **Adrenal Glands**: Release cortisol and adrenaline, which regulate energy, stress reactions, and emotions like aggression and anxiety.
5. **Gonadal organs** (ovaries and testes): Generate sex hormones that control emotional reactions and sexual behaviour.
6. **Pancreas**: Regulates blood sugar levels, which affect energy, mood, and focus.

7. **Pineal Gland:** Generates melatonin, which controls emotional stability and sleep cycles.

8. **Thymus:** Promotes immunological function, which influences stress levels and mental wellness.

9. **Parathyroid Glands:** Control calcium levels, which affect mood and mental ability

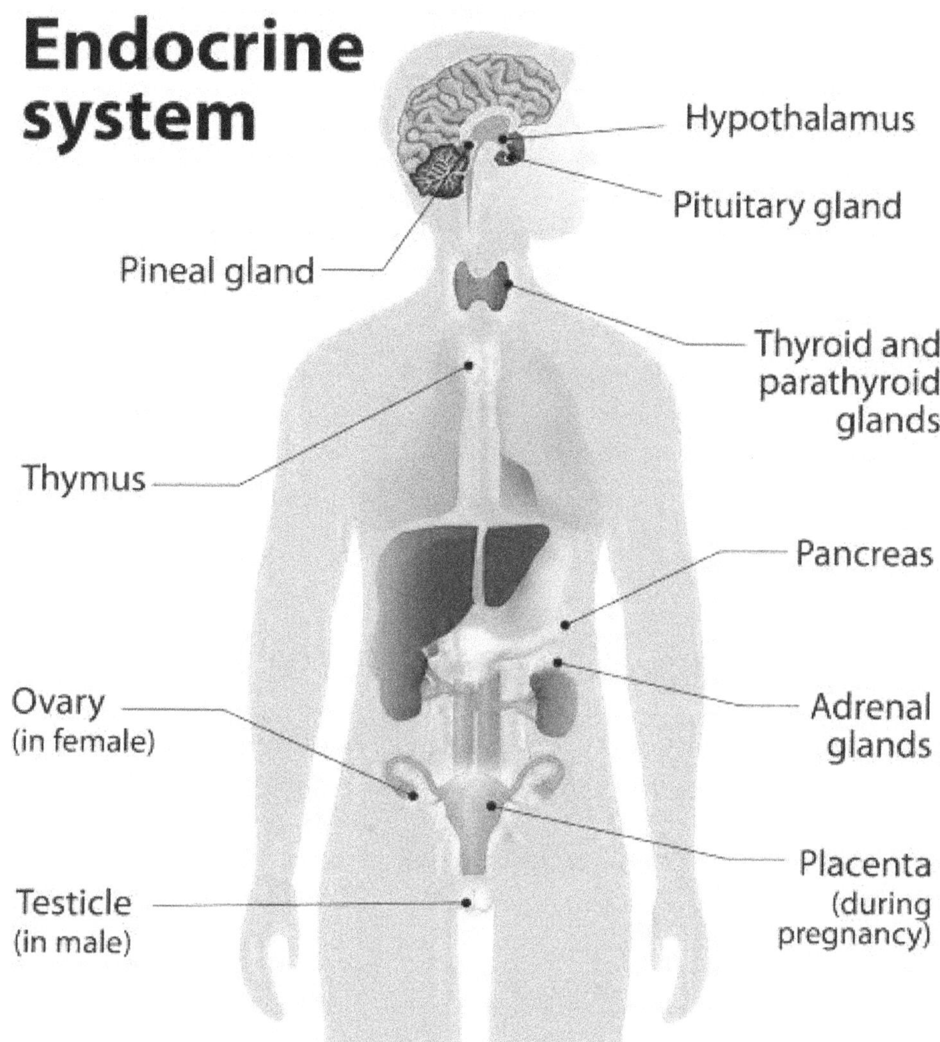

GENES

Human personality development is based on heredity. A person's genetic endowment influences many facets of their behaviour and development, from physical traits like height, weight, and skin and eye colour to intricate patterns of social and intellectual behaviour. Chromosomes-strands of DNA carrying genetic information .Human cells contain 46 chromosomes in pairs.Each chromosome-thousands of genes, also in pairs

THE INDIVIDUAL FUNCTIONS AT THREE LEVELS:

1. Conscious level

2. Preconscious level

3. Unconscious level

CONSCIOUS LEVEL

- Consciousness level is a measure of a person's awareness and understanding of their surroundings. It can range from a coma to full wakefulness
- There are three components to every conscious experience: cognitive (knowing), affective (feelings and emotions), and conative (doing).

PRE-CONSCIOUS LEVEL

- It is part of the mind that contains thoughts and feelings that are not currently being used, but can be easily brought into consciousness

- Another name for pre-conscious mental processes is subconscious mental processes.

UNCONSCIOUS LEVEL

- It can influence conscious activity.
- It can store information that is not currently in focal awareness, but can be retrieved later.
- It can contain unacceptable or unpleasant thoughts, feelings, or urges, such as feelings of pain, anxiety, or conflict

Freud's View of the Human Mind:
The Mental Iceberg

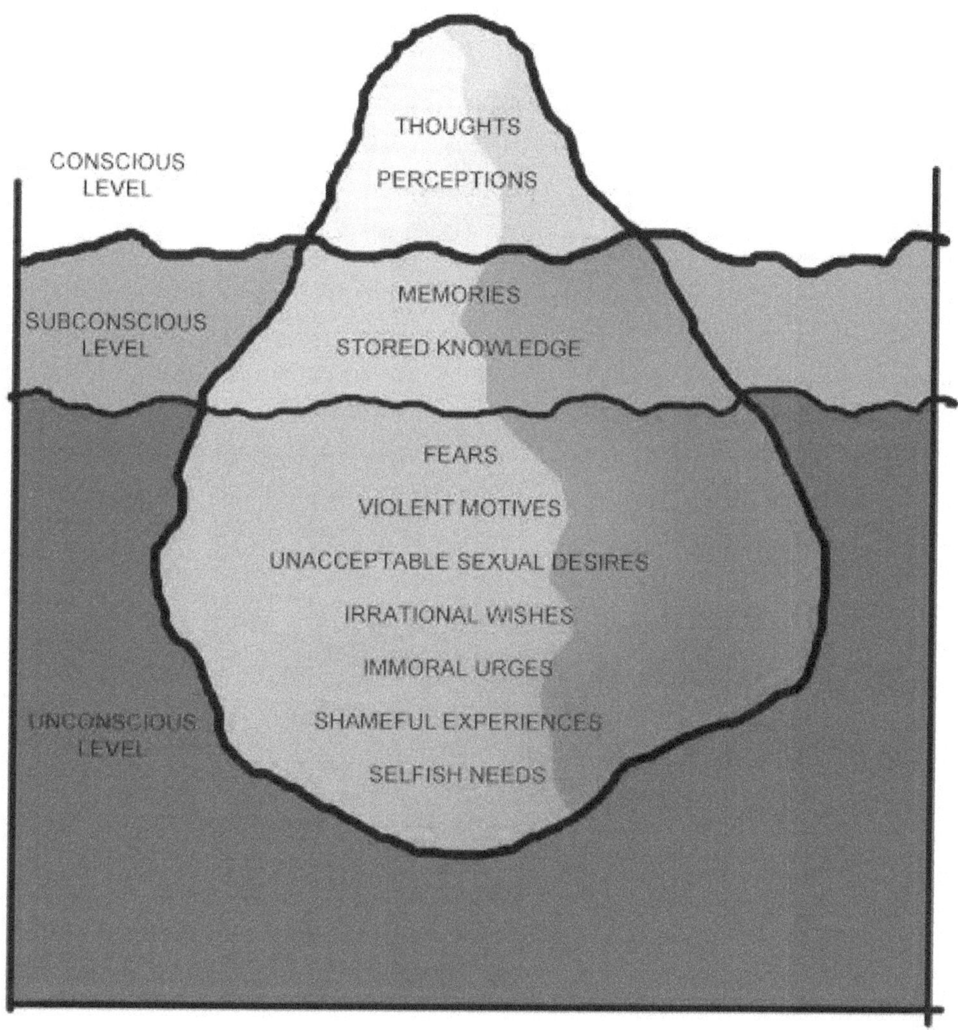

INDIVIDUAL VARIATIONS INTELLIGENCE, ABILITY AND CREATIVITY FOUNDATIONS AND THEORIES

Individual variations refer to the differences in physical, psychological, and cognitive traits between individuals. These variations can be observed across a wide range of attributes such as intelligence, personality, abilities, interests, creativity, and behaviour. The study of individual variations seeks to understand why people differ and how these differences emerge and manifest.

1. Intelligence

Intelligence is traditionally defined as the capacity for learning, reasoning, problem-solving, and adapting to new situations. Several theories have been developed to explain individual differences in intelligence:

Intelligence:

Learn: This includes all kinds of informal and formal learning via any combination of experience, education. And training

Pose problems: this includes recognizing problem situations and transforming them into more clearly defined problems

Solve problems: this includes solving problems, accomplishing tasks, fashioning products, and doing complex projects

Spearman's Two-Factor Theory: Charles Spearman proposed that intelligence consists of a general factor (g) and specific factors (s). The general intelligence factor (g) underlies all cognitive tasks, while specific abilities (s) are task-specific.

- **General Intelligence (g-factor):** A core ability influencing performance across all cognitive tasks.
- **Specific Intelligence (s-factor):** Abilities unique to particular tasks (e.g., mathematical ability, verbal skills).

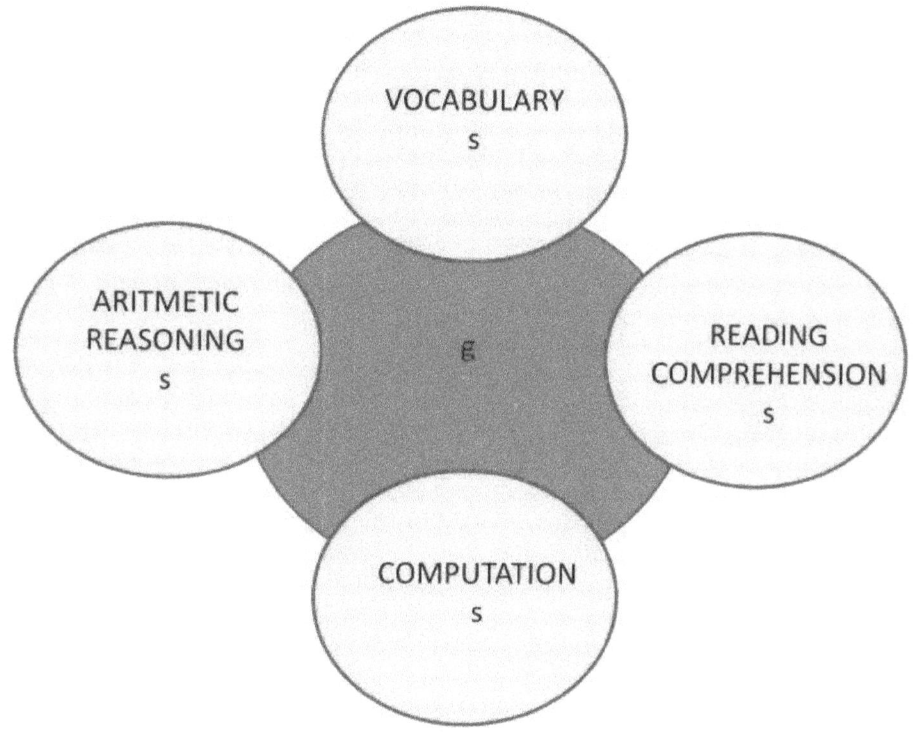

- **Thurstone's Primary Mental Abilities:** Louis Thurstone rejected the idea of a single general intelligence and proposed that intelligence consists of multiple primary abilities, such as verbal comprehension, numerical ability, spatial relations, and memory.
- Verbal comprehension
- Word fluency
- Numerical ability
- Spatial visualization
- Associative memory
- Perceptual speed
- Reasoning

Gardner's Theory of Multiple Intelligences: Howard Gardner introduced the concept of multiple intelligences, suggesting that intelligence is not one-dimensional but includes various domains such as linguistic, logical-mathematical, musical, spatial, bodily-kinesthetic, interpersonal, intrapersonal, and naturalistic intelligences.

- **Linguistic** – Verbal ability
- **Logical-Mathematical** – Analytical reasoning
- **Spatial** – Visual and spatial thinking
- **Musical** – Sensitivity to sound patterns

- **Bodily-Kinesthetic** – Coordination and movement skills
- **Interpersonal** – Understanding others' emotions
- **Intrapersonal** – Self-awareness and reflection
- **Naturalistic** – Recognizing patterns in nature
- **Existential (proposed later)** – Philosophical and spiritual thinking.

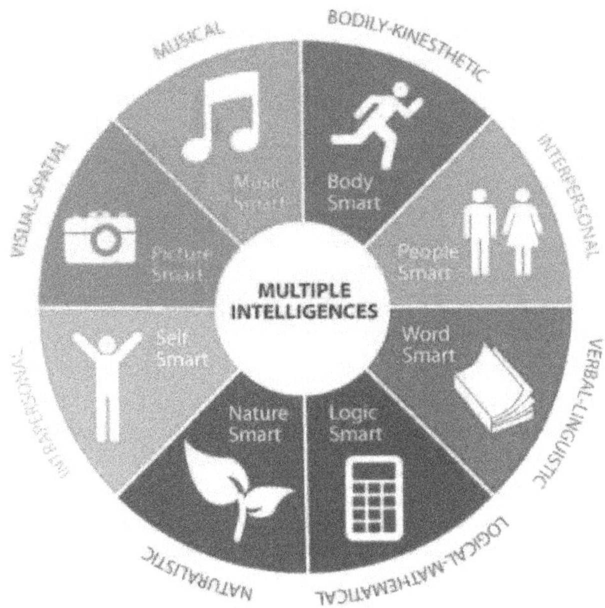

Sternberg's Triarchic Theory of Intelligence (1985)

- Robert Sternberg identified **three types of intelligence**:

1. **Analytical Intelligence:** Logical reasoning, problem-solving (measured by IQ tests).
2. **Creative Intelligence:** Innovation and adaptability in new situations.
3. **Practical Intelligence:** Applying knowledge to real-world tasks (also called "street smarts") **Cattell-Horn-Carroll (CHC) Theory:** This theory is one of the most widely accepted models of intelligence today. It combines Raymond Cattell's fluid and crystallized intelligence with John Carroll's three-stratum model, proposing a hierarchy of intelligence, from broad general abilities to narrow, specific ones.

Three-Stratum Theory:

- **Stratum I:** Narrow abilities (e.g., reading speed, short-term memory).
- **Stratum II:** Broad abilities (e.g., fluid and crystallized intelligence, processing speed).
- **Stratum III:** A single **g-factor** at the top.

Emotional Intelligence (EI) – Daniel Goleman (1995)

- This theory, based on Peter Salovey and John Mayer's work, suggests intelligence includes emotional awareness and management.
- Four main components:

1. **Self-awareness** – Recognizing one's emotions.
2. **Self-regulation** – Controlling emotions and impulses.
3. **Social skills** – Managing relationships effectively.
4. **Empathy** – Understanding others' emotions.

INDIVIDUAL INTELLIGENCE TESTS:
The Binet Tests:-

- Mental age: an individual's level of mental development relative to others
- Intelligence quotient: mental age/chronological age x 100
- Normal distribution: a symmetrical distribution, majority of the scores falling in the middle, few scores in the extremes.

The Wechsler Scales: -

- Age-related versions provide an overall IQ and also yield both verbal and performance Iqs

- (WPPSI-P) Wechsler Preschool and Primary Scale of Intelligence-revised ages:4 to 6 ½
- (WISC-R) Wechsler Intelligence Scale for Children- revised ages:6 to 16
- (WAIS-R) Wechsler Adult Intelligence Scale-revised

1. **Ability**

Ability refers to the specific skills or competencies an individual has in performing particular tasks. These abilities are often seen as part of the broader construct of intelligence, but they can be more domain-specific. Theories on abilities typically highlight the relationship between innate potential and skill development.

Emotional Intelligence (EQ): Proposed by Daniel Goleman and others, emotional intelligence refers to the ability to recognize, understand, and manage one's own emotions, as well as the emotions of others. It is considered a separate form of intelligence that contributes to overall cognitive functioning.

Theories of Aptitude: An aptitude is a specific ability to perform well in a particular domain. Theories about aptitude focus on the genetic, environmental, and educational factors that shape specific skills. For example, mathematical or musical aptitude theories examine how individuals can excel in specific disciplines.

Theories of Expertise: These theories suggest that high-level abilities in certain domains (like chess or music) are primarily the result of deliberate practice, not innate talent. The "10,000-hour rule," proposed by Malcolm Gladwell, argues that expertise comes through extensive practice, though recent research highlights the role of cognitive abilities and early talent as well.

Physical abilities:

- Types of physical abilities
- Strength-capacity to exert physical force
- Flexibility-capacity to move one's body in an agile manner
- Stamina-capacity to endure physical activity for prolonged periods
- Speed-the ability to move quickly
- Many jobs require blend of physical and intellectual abilities
- Companies are introducing measures to promote the health and well-being of the employees performing physical tasks.

3.Creativity

Creativity refers to the ability to produce novel and valuable ideas, solutions, or products. Theories of creativity emphasize the importance of both cognitive processes and environmental factors.

Guilford's Structure of Intellect (SI) Model: J.P. Guilford proposed that creativity involves a range of cognitive processes, including divergent thinking (the ability to generate multiple solutions to a problem) and convergent thinking (the ability to narrow down these possibilities to one best solution).

Key Elements of Guilford's Creativity Model:

1. **Divergent Thinking vs. Convergent Thinking:**

   - **Divergent Thinking:** Generating multiple unique solutions to a problem.
   - **Convergent Thinking:** Finding the single best solution to a problem.
   - Creativity is mainly associated with **divergent thinking**.

2. **Four Abilities of Creative Thinking:**
   Guilford identified four main components of creative thinking:

   - **Fluency:** The ability to generate many ideas quickly.
   - **Flexibility:** The ability to think in different ways and adapt perspectives.
   - **Originality:** The ability to produce unique and unusual ideas.
   - **Elaboration:** The ability to expand on ideas by adding details.

3. **Structure of Intellect Model:**

   - Intelligence is not a single factor (IQ) but consists of multiple abilities.
   - The SOI model includes **150 intellectual abilities**, categorized into:

     - **Operations (mental processes)** – e.g., problem-solving, memory.
     - **Contents (types of information processed)** – e.g., words, numbers, symbols.
     - **Products (the outcomes of thinking)** – e.g., ideas, solutions.

   - Creativity involves using these different abilities to develop original solutions.

Vygotsky's Sociocultural Theory of Creativity (1978)
Lev Vygotsky, a Russian psychologist, believed that creativity is a **socially and culturally influenced** process rather than just an innate trait. His theory emphasizes the role of **environment, learning, and interaction** in creative development

Key Principles of Vygotsky's Creativity Theory:

1. **Creativity Develops Through Social Interaction:**

   - Creativity is shaped by interactions with parents, teachers, peers, and culture.
   - Language and social learning help individuals build creative ideas.

2. **Imagination and Creativity Emerge from Experience:**

   - People combine past knowledge with new ideas to create something original.
   - Childhood pretend play is an early form of creativity, influenced by the child's environment.

3. **The Role of Cultural Tools:**

   - Creativity depends on access to cultural tools (e.g., books, technology, art).
   - Exposure to different ideas helps individuals develop unique perspectives.

4. **Zone of Proximal Development (ZPD) in Creativity:**

   - Creativity improves when individuals are guided by more knowledgeable mentors.
   - Teachers, mentors, and collaboration help expand creative potential.

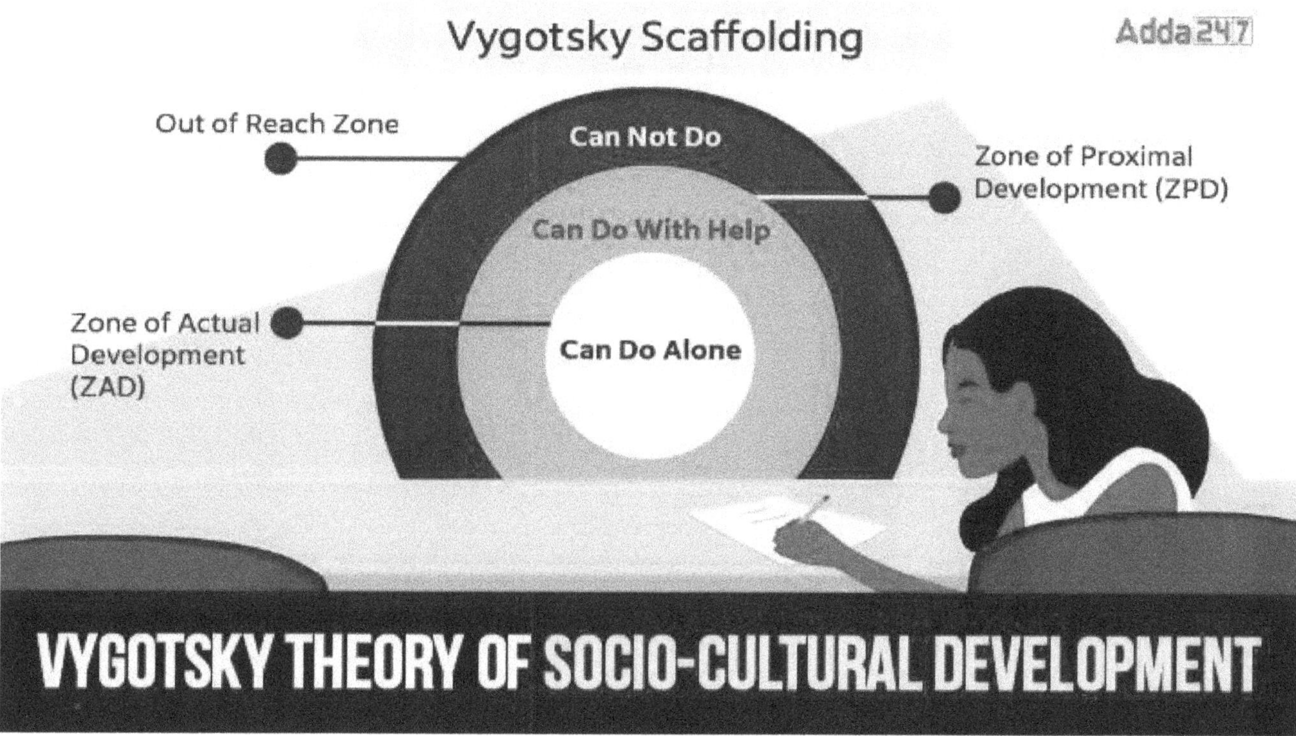

Torrance's Model of Creativity: E. Paul Torrance focused on creative thinking and developed a widely used test for measuring creativity. He proposed that creativity involves fluency, flexibility, originality, and elaboration, which are measurable in how individuals approach problems.

The Investment Theory of Creativity (Sternberg & Lubart): According to this theory, creative individuals are like investors in the stock market, taking risks by investing time and energy into novel ideas. They possess high levels of intelligence, knowledge, and creativity and also demonstrate persistence and an ability to overcome obstacles.

Csikszentmihalyi's Flow Theory: Mihaly Csikszentmihalyi developed the concept of "flow," a mental state of deep immersion in an activity. According to him, creativity arises when individuals are fully engaged in their tasks, leading to high levels of performance and innovation.

CHAPTER FOUR

PERSONALITY AND TEMPERAMENT – FOUNDATIONS, APPROACHES, THEORIES OF PERSONALITY, MEASURING PERSONALITY (TRAITS, LOCUS OF CONTROL, SELF-EFFICACY).

PERSONALITY:

The word personality is derived from the Latin word **persona** meaning "mask". J.P. Guilford (1952) defined personality as an integrated pattern of traits. It is the synthetic unity of all personal trait.

Personality is a person's characteristics and qualities that are acquired throughout life such as : thoughts , preferences, behaviours, traits, beliefs, interests, values and emotional patterns.

TEMPERAMENT:

A person's innate behavioural and personality traits, which are usually present early in life and are thought to be biologically determined. Temperament includes characteristics like: Energy life , emotional responsiveness , response tempo , behavioural inhibition , willingness to explore.

FOUNDATIONS OF PERSONALITY:

Personality is founded on certain structures.

1. Physiological structure of the organism
2. Psychic structure of the organism
3. Social and cultural structure

1. PHYSIOLOGICAL STRUCTURE OF ORGANISM:

The foundation of this structure is laid in the mother's womb. It is deeply influenced by certain internal as well as external agencies (heredity and social environment)

2. PSYCHIC STRUCTURE OF THE ORGANISM:

This consists of attitudes, traits, sentiments, feelings, emotions and values / ideals.

3. SOCIAL AND CULTURAL STRUCTURE:

The personality of an individual develops from socio cultural background. Differences can be seen in the behavior due to their sociocultural environment. Experiences also play a major role in personality and behavior.

APPROACHES TO PERSONALITY:

There are 6 major approaches of personality that provide insights into development and manifestation of personality:

- Psychoanalytic Approach
- Trait Approach
- Humanistic Approach
- Behavioral /Social Learning Approach
- Biological Approach
- Cognitive Approach

1. PSYCHOANALYTIC APPROACH:

Also called as psychodynamic theory, this approach lies in the belief in how crucial the unconscious and childhood memories are. According to **Freud**, many aspects of our thoughts, feelings, and actions are shaped by hidden motives and desires we aren't aware of. Freud categorized the mind's structure into three parts: the **id, ego, and superego**. The id reflects basic instincts, driven by seeking immediate pleasure. In contrast, the ego serves as a bridge between the id and the outside world, focused on practicality. Lastly, the superego embodies societal values turned into an internal moral guide. Freud believed that personality development hinges on psychosexual growth, which unfolds in five key stages: **oral, anal, phallic, latent, and genital.**

2.HUMANISTIC APPROACH:

Humanistic personality theories highlight the importance of personal choice and individual experiences in shaping one's character. Humanistic theories focus on the idea of **self-actualization**, which is the inner drive people have to achieve their full potential.

This drive motivates individuals to pursue personal growth by setting meaningful goals and participating in activities that reflect their values and interests. **Maslow** introduced the hierarchy of needs theory, outlining a sequence of fundamental needs that must be fulfilled for individuals to achieve their maximum potential.

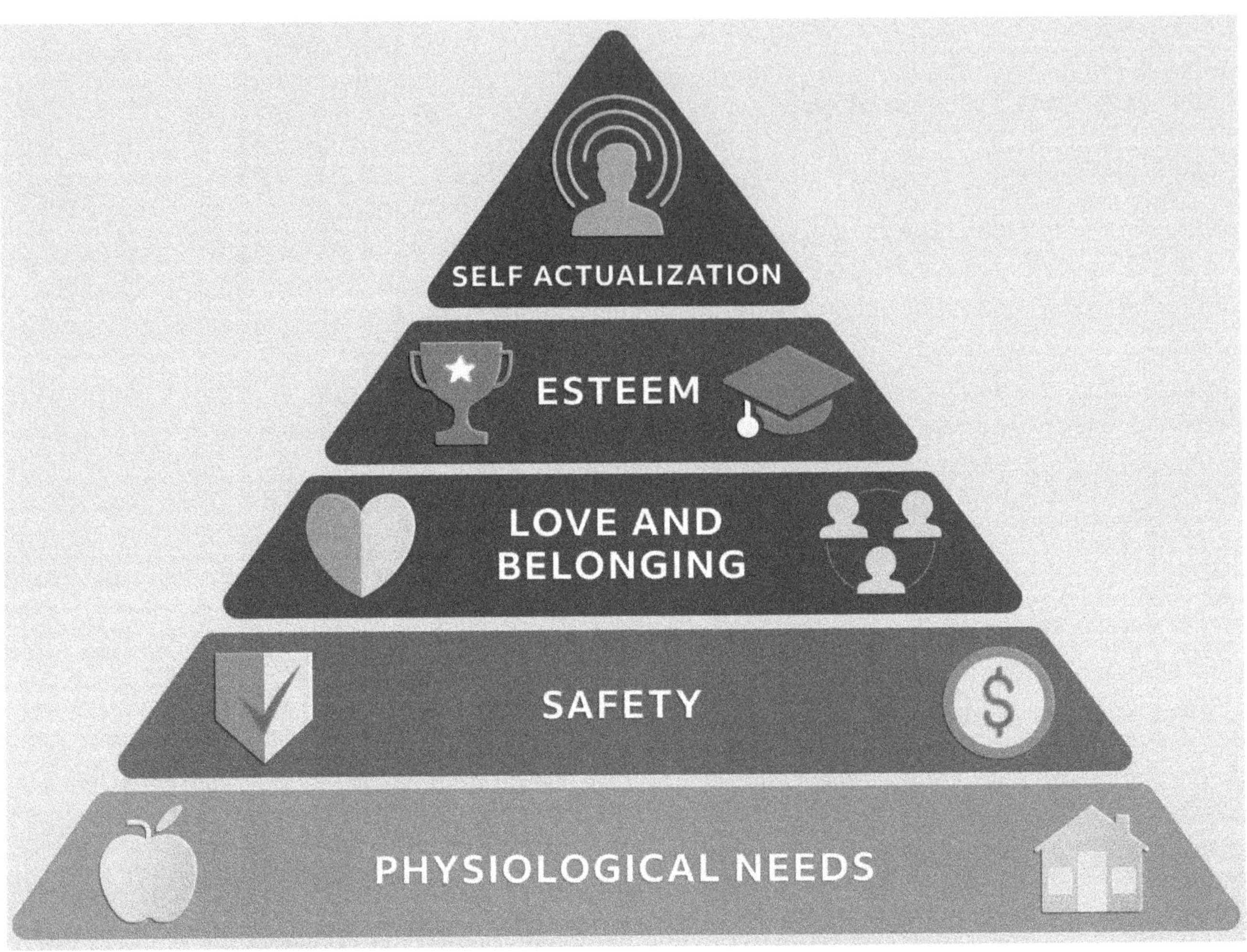

3.TRAIT APPROACH:

Personality theory, also known as trait theory, suggests that people have consistent traits that affect their behaviour in different situations. These traits are believed to stay the same over time and greatly influence how individuals act.

The Big Five model categorizes personality traits into five key groups:

Openness – embrace new experiences, creative, curious and imaginative.

Conscientiousness – strong self-discipline, organization and responsibility

Extroversion – socializing, energetic and outgoing nature.

Agreeableness – kindness, empathy and togetherness.

Neuroticism – anxious, doubtful and insecure.

4. BEHAVIOURIST APPROACH:

The behaviourist theory of personality, rooted in the principles of behaviourism, offers a distinctive perspective on how individuals' personalities are formed and expressed. Developed by psychologists such as **John B. Watson, B.F. Skinner and Ivan Pavlov** state that behaviourism emphasizes observable behaviours as the primary determinants of personality, with a focus on **learning processes and environmental influences**.

The behaviourist theory of personality offers valuable insights into how individuals' personalities are shaped by their interactions with the environment, conditioning and learning experiences.

5. SOCIAL COGNITIVE APPROACH:

This approach highlights how **internal thoughts and beliefs** shape individuals. They stress that personality isn't just influenced by external factors but also by how a person thinks and perceives the world. According to **Bandura**, individuals' thoughts about themselves in shaping their actions and personalities. Cognitive processes like attention and memory also play a key role in shaping one's personality by influencing how information is perceived and interpreted.

6. BIOLOGICAL APPROACH:

The biological theory of personality explores how biological factors, including genetics, neurobiology, and physiology, influence the development and expression of individual differences in personality. This perspective emphasizes the role of biological processes in shaping temperament, behaviour patterns, and psychological traits.

THEORIES OF PERSONALITY:

Also called the classification by various psychologists:

KRETSCHMER'S CLASSIFICATION:

According to the German psychiatrist Earnest Kretschmer, the personality were related to the physical makeup.

TYPE

CHARACTERISTICS

Pyknic (fat)

Jolly, sociable, popular.

Asthenic (tall and thin)

Controlled, idealist.

Hypoplastic (physically weak)

Suffers from inferiority, unsocial.

Athletic (strong)

Energetic, optimistic, normal.

SHELDON'S CLASSIFICATION:

Sheldon classified human beings into types according to their physical structure and their corresponding temperamental characteristics:

PHYSICAL CHARACTERISTICS

TEMPERAMENT

Ectomorph (straight and slender).

Weak, fearful, introvert, re- strained, pessimistic.

Mesomorph (strong and muscular)

Energetic, love risk and adventure.

Endomorph (Fat, soft and round)

Extrovert, affectionate, love physical comfort, easy going.

HIPPOCRATE'S CLASSIFICATION:

This classification is based on four temperaments / personalities associated with four bodily fluids called humors.

SANGUINE: People with this temperament are optimistic, social, and pleasure-seeking.

CHOLERIC: People with this temperament are ambitious, leader-like, and short-tempered.

MELANCHOLIC: People with this temperament are analytical, quiet, and reserved.

PHLEGMATIC: People with this temperament are relaxed, peaceful, and thoughtful.

JUNG'S THEORY:

He classified personality based on perspectives / where they get their stimulation.

INTROVERTS: The introverts are people whose interests **are turned inward upon themselves.** Introvert people are shy avoid people, like to be alone and self centered. **Eg:** Philosophers and scientists

EXTROVERTS: The interests of such people is **oriented towards the external world.** They are social and friendly: **Eg:** Politicians, salesmen and social workers.

Jung recognises four other functional types of personality:

(1) Sensing type: The sensing type depends on the evidence of their senses for their actions without exercising their reason upon it.

(2) Intuitive type: The intuitive type is also dominated by sense-perception, but he can discover the causes of the facts perceived and envisage what can be made of a situation.

(3) Feeling type: The feeling type is dominated by emotions. They have definite sentiments of right and wrong and they are governed by them in their behaviour

(4) Thinking type: The thinking type is dominated by reason and logic. This type initiates new ways of thought.

ALDER'S INDIVIDUAL APPROACH:

According to Adler, human beings cannot be divided into distinct types. Every person is unique in himself. People strive towards gaining superiority and power. Different people have different styles of life.

MEASURING PERSONALITY:

OBSERVATION:

Observation is the objective method of studying the behaviour of a person. There are two processes of observation. In **open observation**, the observer does not hide himself from the subject and in **closed method**, he observes the behaviour of his subject from behind a screen.

SITUATIONAL PERFORMANCE TESTS:

In situational tests, the behaviour of an individual is assessed in an **artificial situation**. They are asked to identify how they would respond to the situation. **Eg**: Honesty of a student in examination without invigilator.

INTERVIEW:

Interview is an important technique to elicit personal information from the subject in **face-to-face** contacts. Usually, a list of questions is prepared before-hand and all the subjects are to answer these **pre-planned questions.**

THE QUESTIONNAIRE METHOD:

This method is used to assess personality traits. The individual is asked a large number of crucial questions, which he has to answer by saying **yes or no**. The questions bring out **extroversion or introversion** of personality:

Eg: Do you like to talk before a group of people? Yes/No.

RATING SCALES:

Rating scales are used to evaluate a **single trait.** Teachers use this to classify their students on a particular trait like persistence, leadership or cooperation. The divisions of the scale are indicated by numbers **1-3, 1-5 or 1-7,** comprising a three-point, five-point or seven-point scale, respectively. Its options represent degrees of a particular characteristic.

CASE HISTORY:

From the case history of an individual we can have some idea of his personality. The case history includes a brief account of a person's family and neighbourhood, his behaviour in childhood, his school experiences, his physical and mental development, etc. Previously, this method was used in the treatment of mental diseases. At present, it is, however, used in determining personality of a normal person.

PROJECTIVE TESTS:

Projective tests attempt to reveal a person's unconscious repressed wishes. Projective tests attempt to study the totality of behaviour of a person. These includes:

THE RORSCHACH INK BLOT TEST:

The subject is shown a series of **10 (ten) standardised bilaterally symmetrical ink blots** one at a time. Five of the blots are black and white and five are multi- coloured. These ink blots are highly ambiguous and do not carry any specific meaning

The subject is allowed to look at the ink blot from different angles. Different persons see different things in these ink blots. The Rorschach test stimulates the **association of ideas** in the personality of an individual. An individual gives free expression to his reaction on seeing these ink blots.

SCORING: based on the content of the response, the location of the response, and the stimulus characteristic emphasized.

THEMATIC APPERCEPTION TEST:

This test consists of **30 cards of ambiguous character** pictures (that may include men, women, and/or children or scenes) and 1 blank cards.20 cards are used for an individual. This tool helps evaluate a person's inner thoughts and emotional responses. The person examining the card is then asked to tell a dramatic story.

SCORING:

The TAT is used to assess personality, behavior disorders, psychosomatic illnesses and more. Psychologists can reveal a person's personality based on the story they have told.

CHAPTER FIVE

PERSONAL, SOCIAL, MORAL DEVELOPMENT –MEANING, CONCEPT –SELF CONCEPT, SELF ESTEEM, SELF WORTH AND THEORIES

PERSONAL DEVELOPMENT MEANING

- Personal development or self-improvement consists of activities that develops a person's capabilities and potential, enhance qualities of life, and facilitate the realization of dreams and aspiration. Personal development may take place over the course of an individual's entire lifespan and is not limited to one stage of a person's life.
- It can include official and informal action for developing others in roles such as a teacher, guide, counsellor, manager, coach, or mentor, and it is not restricted to self –help.
- When personal development take place in the context of institution, it refers to methods, programs, tools, techniques, and assessment systems offered to support positive adult development at the individual level in organization.

DEFINITION

- Personal development as the process of achieving ones full potential by developing and improving various aspects of ones life, including but not limited to mindset , emotion , relationship health , and finances (Tony Robbines).
- Personal development can be defined as human development which can be closely relates to particular context of **Expanding Capabilities** (The abilities for individual to enhance their skill, education , and knowledge , which leads to better opportunities for employment , participation , and overall quality of life). **Improving Well Being** (Fostering the physical ,mental and social well being of individual to help them to reach their potential and improving their standard of living).**Empowerment** (Personal development involves equipping individual with the tools an confidence to take control their lives , make informed choices , and contribute to society , which aligns with the UNs focus on inclusivity gender equality , and human rights by (UNDG).
- Personal development as a sand alone concept , however in the context of frame work , personal development can be inferred through its focus on capacity building like abilities to improve their livelihoods , particularly in context of agriculture, food security, and rural development (FAO).

5 AREAS OF PERSONAL DEVELOPMENT
They are,

- Mental
- Social

- Spiritual
- Emotional
- Physical

MENTAL GROWTH

- As human ,our primary emphasis is often on physical development , which isn't wrong , but how we mold our mind makes a huge difference in our lives.
- Mental growth is thus the first area of personal development that I consistently put pressure on during my coaching sessions . Optimal development of your mind influences the way you think and learn . It also correlates to our congnitive function , including memory retention and perception of things.
- The best things about mental development is that it does not require you to do anything exponential. Reading a book or even watching a you tube video from the start till the end has the potential to improve our mental growth.

SOCIAL GROWTH

- Social growth development is key to clear communication skill. It allows you to connect with people outside , be it a group of friends or even your colleagues that you don't normally see outside of work.
- Learning and practicing social skills also help us overcome our fear of public speaking , which isn't limited to your school activities . They are equally important at work , where you have to give presentation or even walk into an office for a potential job interview.

SPIRITUAL GROWTH

- Quote from Roy T.Bennett "Belive in your infinite potential . Your only limitation are those you set upon yourself ".
- Foundational concept of spiritual growth is all about holistically connecting with yourself and finding that inner peace . Some of our spiritual growth is heavily influenced by our culture , beliefs and experience , but I feel spiritual growth is more about how we connect with our inner mind .
- Spiritual growth is extremely subjective . Some seek their true spiritual growth by believing in and practicing a certain religion , while others seek solace with meditative practice .

EMOTIONAL GROWTH

- Emotional development is the process in which an individual is able to experience , recognize , and express varying emotion .
- Emotion are an individuals subjective response or reaction to various situation . Often ,an individual is referred to as being emotional when expressing their reaction to a situation . Emotional means than an individual is experiencing intense feeling , such as happiness or sadness .
- The emotional description is often associated with a physical response , such as laughing or crying .

PHYSICAL GROWTH

- Physical growth in personal development refers to the process of improving ones physical well being and health , which in turn can support overall persona growth and self -improvement .
- While personal development is often associated with mental and emotional growth , physical health plays a crucial role in boosting energy ,focus and resilience .

- Here how physical growth connects to personal development is physical health , mental clarity , self discipline ,confidence and body language .

THE THINGS THAT PERSONAL DEVELOPMENT MAY INCLUDE THE FOLLOWING ACTIVITIES

- Social entrepreneurship or civic engagement
- Participating in festival conference etc
- Improving self knowledge
- Improving skill and or learning new ones
- Developing strengths or talents
- Improving a career
- Improving wealth or social status

SOCIAL DEVELOPMENT

- Social development is a process of change that improves the well being of individual and groups in society by addressing various aspects such as poverty , inequality , human rights , gender equality ,and environment sustainability.
- Social development plays a vital role in achieving sustainable development . It has been promoting the realization of human potential and dignity , fostering social inclusion and cohesion, enhancing social capital and innovation ,and contributing to economic growth and environmental protection

CHARACTERISTICS OF SOCIAL DEVELOPMENT

- It is the process of change involves the interaction of social cultural , political, and economic factors.
- It is a normative concept that reflects the values and aspiration of society, such as dignity, equity , diversity ,and participation.
- It is a holistic concept that considers the interrelatedness and interdependence of various aspects of human well being , such as health, education, work and security.
- It is a dynamic concept that adapts to the changing needs and contexts of society , such as globalization, urbanization , migration , and technology.
- It is a participatory concept that involves the active engagement and empowerment of all stakeholders, such as individuals , communities , civil society , government , and international organization

ROLE OF SOCIAL DEVELOPMENT

- Social development plays on vital role in achieving sustainable development for several reasons ,it addresses the root cause and consequence of poverty and inequality, which are major challenges for human development and social cohesion.
- It promotes the realization of human rights and human dignity, which are essential for potential and social progress.
- It fosters social inclusion and social cohesion , which are key for social stability and peace.
- It enhance the social capital and social innovation, which are important for social resilience and transformation.
- It contributes to economic growth and environment protection , which are necessary for social prosperity and sustainability.

IMPACT OF SOCIAL DEVELOPMENT

- **Individual:** Social development improves the quality of life and well being of individual by enhancing their access to basic services , opportunities and resources . It also strengthens their capabilities, skills, and confidence to participate in social economic activities .
- **Groups:** Social development supports the empowerment and participation of marginalized and vulnerable groups , such as women , children , youth, elderly, persons with disabilities , ethics minorities, indigenous people , refugees, and migrants. It also fosters the recognition and respects of their rights , identities, cultures, and contribution to society.
- **Society:** Social development enhances the social cohesion and harmony of society by reducing the gaps and disparities between different groups . It also promotes the values and principle of democracy , justice , solidarity , and cooperation among all members of society.

MORAL DEVELOPMENT

- Moral development refers to the process through which children develop the standard of right and wrong within their society , based on social and cultural norms , and laws.
- Moral development as a process of discovering universal moral principles , and is based on a child's intellectual development(Lawrence Kohlberg).
- Moral development as a constructivist process , whereby the interplay of action and thoughts builds moral aspects(Piaget).
- In general moral is Latin word "moralis" .Moral development focuses on the emergency , change , and understand of morality from infancy through adulthood .
- The theory states that morality develops across the life span in a variety. individual's experience , behavior and when they are faced with moral issues through different periods of physical and cognitive development .

MORAL DEVELOPMENT OFTEN EMPHASIZES THESE FOUR FUNDAMENTAL

- **Feeling or emotion aspects** : These theories emphasize the affective aspects of moral development and include several altruism theories.
- **Behavior aspects:** These theories mainly deal with moral behavior.
- **Cognitive aspects** : These theories focus on mora judgement and moral reasoning .
- **Integrated perspectives:** Several theorists have also attempted to propose theories which integrate two or three of the affective , behavioural , and cognitive aspects of morality.

STAGES OF MORAL DEVEOPMENT

Kohlberg's theory is broken down into three primary level . At each level of moral development there are two stages .Kohlberg's believed not everyone progress to the highest stages of moral development .

LEVEL 1. PRECONVENTIONAL MORALITY

- Preconventional morality is the earliest period of moral development . It lasts until around the age of 9 . At this age , children 's decisions are shaped by the expectation of adult and the consequence of breaking the rules .

There are two stages within this level :
Stage 1(Obedience and Punishment)

- The earliest stage of morality development , obedience and punishment are especially common in young children , but adults are also capable of expressing this type of reasoning .
- According to Kohlberg, people at this stage see rules as fixed and absolute . Obeying the rules is important because it is a way to avoid punishment .

Stage 2(Individualism an Exchange)

- At the individualism and exchange stage of moral development , children account for actions based on how they serve individual needs .
- In the Heinz dilemma , children argued that the best course of action was the chose that best served Heinz 's needs. Reciprocity is possible at this point in moral development , but only if it serves one's own interests.

LEVEL 2. CONVENTIONAL MORALITY

- The next period of moral development is marked by the acceptance of social rules regarding what is good and moral . During this time, adolescents and adults internalize the moral standards they have learned from their role models from society.
- This period also focuses on the acceptance of authority and conforming to the norms of the group. There are two stages at this level of morality.

Stage 3(Developing Good Interpersonal Relationship)

- Often referred to as good boy good girl orientation , this stage of the moral development is focused on living up of social expectation and roles .
- There is an emphasis on conformity, being " nice," and consideration of how choices influence relationship.

Stage 4(Maintaining Social Order)

- This stage is focus on ensuring that social order is maintained . At this stage of moral development , people begin to consider society as a whole when making judgement.
- The focus is on maintaining law and order by following the rules , doing ones duty , and respecting authority.

LEVEL 3. POSTCONVENTIONAL MORALITY
Stage 5(Social Contract and Individual Rights)

- The ideas of a social contract and individual rights cause people in the next stage to begin to account for the different values , opinion , and belief of the other people .
- Rules of law are important for maintaining a society , but members of the society should agree upon these standards.

Stage 6(Universal Principle)

- Kohlberg's final level of moral ethical principle and abstract reasoning . At this stage, people follow these internalized principle of justice , even if they conflicts with laws and rules.

CONCEPT OF SELF CONCEPT
WHY IS SELF- CONCEPT IS IMPORTANT?

- Knowing who are you help you feel that you have worth and values in this world. When you can accept yourself for who you are , it will be easier for others to accept you , too .
- Learning about yourself can help you develop lasting relationship with others as well as help you choice that will direct your life in the path you want to go.

DEFINITIONS

- It's is a fluid but consistent pattern of perception of the 'I' or 'me' in relation to the environment , personal , values , goals and ideals (Carl Rogers).
- Self -concept is the individual identity about how one think about himself or herself . It means how one think or how one feels about himself or herself (Dougles 1966).
- The "totality of the individual's thoughts and feelings having reference to himself as an object " (Rosenberg,1979).

THREE ASPECTS IN SELF- CONCEPT THEORY- Sincero
Self -concept is learned

- A person will soon develop this as he /she grows old. This means that self – concept can only be acquired as soon as the person earns how to mingle with others and so this indicates that self – concept is influenced by the person environment and can be a product of the persons socialization

Self –concept is organized

- This stresses out that one's perception towards himself/herself is firm. This means that a person may hear other people's point of view regarding himself /herself but will keep on believing that what he/she thinks of himself/ herself is always right one . Change on one's perception towards however, may also be possible but it takes time.

Self –concept is dynamic

- As an individual grows older , he /she continues to encounter problems or challenges that may reveal his/her self-concept in that particular time or situation. A person will responds to the scenario based on his/her own insights and how he/she perceives himself/herself in the situation .Thus self –concept undergoes development as the person goes through different experience.

TWO BROAD CATEGORIES OF SELF –CONCEPT
Actual self

- Is the one that you actually see. It is the self that has characteristics that you were nurtured or, in some cases , born to have.
- How you are yourself . Each individual 's self –image is a mixture of different attributes including our physical characteristics , personality traits, social roles .Self –image doesn't necessarily coincide with reality . The actual self is built on self –knowledge

Self – knowledge :

- Is derived from social interaction that provide insights into how others react to you . The actual self is who we actual are. It is how we think, how we feel, look, and act.

THE BENEFITS OF SELF- CONCEPT
Happiness

- You will be happier when you can express who you are. Expressing your desires will make it more likely that you get what you want.

Less inner conflict

- When your outside action are in accordance with your feeling and values, you will experience less inner conflict.

Better decision making

- When you know yourself , you are able to make better choices about everything , from small decision like which sweater you'll buy to big decision like which partner you'll spend your life with. You'll have guidelines you can apply to solve life's varied problem.

Self- control

- When you know yourself , you understand what motivates you to resist bad habits and develop good ones. You'll have the insight to know which values and goals activates your will power.
- Resistance to social pressure. When you are grounded in your values are preference you are likely to say "yes" when you want to say "no".

Tolerance and understanding of others

- Your awareness of your own foibles and struggles can help emphasis with others vitality and pleasure.
- Being who you truly are helps you feel more alive and makes your experience of life richer , larger and more exciting

SELF –ESTEEM
Introduction

- Self – esteem refers to one's general evaluates or appraisal of the self ,including feelings of self – worth . According to Oxford dictionary "Confidence in one's worth or abilities, self- respect " is the self- esteem.
- Individual with higher levels of self -esteem are better able to cope with stressful life events, whereas lower levels of self- esteem are associated with more loneliness. Peer rejection , aggression and psychopathology.

Self-Esteem and Psychology

- Self – esteem is an attractive psychological contract because it predicts certain outcomes such as academic achievement , happiness, satisfaction ,in social relation .
- Psychologists usually regard self- esteem as an enduring personality characteristics. They use synonyms like self-worth self- regards, self-respect or self –integrity for self- esteem.

Definitions of self-Esteem

- Self – esteem refers to an individual overall positive evaluation to the self. High self-esteem consists of an individual respecting himself and considering himself worthy(Rosenberg 1955).
- Self –esteem refers to individual 's perception or subjective appraisal of one's own self – worth, one's feelings of self – respect an self – confidence and the extent to which the individual holds positive or negative views about self (Sedikides and Gress 2003).
- " Self- esteem is satisfaction with oneself" , Self – esteem means "one's good opinion of one's dignity or worth".

Steps to improve your self –Esteem

- Practice self- compassion
- Challenge negative self- talk
- Set realistic goals
- Practice assertiveness
- Cultivate self- care habits
- Celebrate your accomplishment
- Surround yourself with supportive people
- Practice gratitude
- Embrace failure as learning opportunities

Seek professional help if needed
Maslow's Hierarchy of Needs

- Maslow's hierarchy of needs is a conceptualization of needs or foal that motivate human behaviour , which was propose by the American psychologist Abraham Maslow .
- According to Maslow's original formulation , there are five sets of basic needs of that are related to each in a hierarchy of prepotency or strength.
- Typically , the hierarchy is depicted in the form of a pyramid although Maslow was not himself responsible for the iconic diagram . The pyramid begins at the bottom with physiological needs and culminates at the top with self –actualization needs. In this later writing , Maslow's added a sixth level of 'meta-need' and metamotivation.

SELF WORTH

- Self- worth and self –value are two related terms that are often used interchangeable . Having a sense of self –worth means that you value yourself , an having a sense of self –value means that you are worthy . The difference between the two are minimal enough that both terms can be used to describe the same general concept.

- Self- worth is your overall sense of value and important as a person . It is how you see an appreciate yourself regardless of your accomplishment, failure, or the opinion of others. It is the inherent value we place on ourselves, influence our thought, action and relationship .
- In the context of the Bible, self –worth is intricately attached to one's relationship with God and the principles outlined in the scriptures. Having a healthy sense of self worth is essential for our individual mental, emotional and relational well being.

HOW TO DISCOVER YOUR SELF –WORTH
Explore Interest

- Being by exploring a variety of activities, hobbies , and subjects. Pay attention to what genuinely captures your attention an bring you joy that is things you derive pleasure in doing irrespective of the inconveniences you may have to go through. Identifying areas of interest often leads to discovering of strength and passions.

Reflects on Past Experience

- Consider past experience (these include activities, team work involvement , family engagement etc.) both positive and negative . What activities have you excelled in ? What tasks have energized and fulfilled you? Reflecting on these moments cab provide insights into your strengths and passions. This reflection reveals your uniqueness to you.

Seek feedback

- Ask friend , family, and colleagues for feedback on your strengths as to your involvement in any activities they have witnessed, and it could sometimes be based on the relationship or rapport you have had with them for a long time. Sometimes , others can see qualities in us that we might overlook . Their observation can offer valuable perspectives on your abilities and passions.

Experiment and Take Risks

- Be open to trying to things .Experimenting with different activities allows you to test your skills and interests . Taking calculated risks can uncover hidden strengths and ignite passions you may not have explored otherwise. Do not be too rigid not to explore opportunities that come your way that are not like your routine life style , they may be an avenue to unveil one or two hidden strengths in you.

Evaluate Values and Purpose

- Align your strengths and passions with your values and sense of purpose . Consider how your abilities and interests contribute to personal fulfillment and align with what you find meaningful. This alignment often leads to a more sense of strengths and passions.

CONCEPT OF THOERY

- Theories are explanation of a natural or social behavior, event , or phenomenon. More formally, a scientific theory is a system of constructs (concepts) and propositions (relationship between those constructs) that collectively presents a logical , systematic, and coherent explanation of a phenomenon of interest within some assumptions and boundary condition

Cognitive Learning Theory

- Cognitive Learning Theory is actually a set of theories that stem from the term <u>metacognition</u>. Cognitive Learning Theory asks us to think about thinking and how thinking can be influenced by internal factors (like how focused we are, or how distracted we've become) and external factors (like whether the things we are learning are valued by our community or whether we receive praise from others when we learn).
- Cognitive Learning Theory comes from the field of psychology and has roots going back to the beginning of Western philosophy. Important voices in this area include: Plato, Descartes, William James, John Dewey, and Jean Piaget.
- Cognitive Learning Theory is a well-developed area of educational theory, but here are two ideas that will get people started thinking about these ideas:

Social Cognitive Theory/Theories

- This perspective argues that learning is inherently social and happens in a social context. From this point of view, a learner's social interactions with their peers, instructors, and others impact learning directly. An instructor who works to provide a positive social experience with regular opportunities for students to see that learning is valued and that others around them are engaged in the process will be successful at encouraging learning.

Behavioral Cognitive Theory/Theories

- This perspective argues that a person's thoughts determines their actions and feelings, and ultimately their ability to learn and their enjoyment of learning. For example, students who believe they "don't like to read" will find reading more difficult, and students who believe they are "good at art" will try harder and enjoy art more.

Experiential Learning Theory

- Kolb Experiential Learning Theory, developed by David A. Kolb, is widely recognized and influential framework that describes how people learn through experience. Since learning is the primary process used to navigate life, people can use this process for all forms of learning, development, and change. Learning occurs in any setting and continues throughout life. The experiential learning process supports performance improvement, learning and development.
- David Kolb described the ideal process of learning in a four-step Experiential Learning Cycle:

Experiencing – Reflecting – Thinking – Acting.

1. Experiencing (Concrete Experience): Learning begins when a learner uses senses and perceptions to engage in what is happening now.
2. Reflecting (Reflective Observation): After the experience, a learner reflects on what happened and connects feelings with ideas about the experience.
3. Thinking (Abstract Conceptualization): The learner engages in thinking to reach conclusions and form theories, concepts, or general principles that can be tested
4. Acting (Active Experimentation): The learner tests the theory and applies what was learned to get feedback and create the next experience learning.

CHAPTER SIX

MOTIVATION- FOUNDATIONS, APPROACHES, THEORIES, MANAGING HUMAN NEEDS & MOTIVATIONS; PERCEIVING OTHERS-IMPRESSIONS, ATTITUDE, OPINIONS.

Motivation is goal-directed and need satisfying behaviour. It explains why people do the things they do. It influences a person to do a thing in a certain way. Motivation is a process of initiating a conscious and purposeful action.

Motivation makes a student interested in his studies and a farmer in his farming. It is a force which energizes a man to act and to make constant efforts in order to satisfy his basic motives.

The vital role of motivation in life and learning is indisputable success and achievement in life and learning depends on your motivation. Motivation is the most powerful director of all. It is true that motivation has inner and outer subjective and objective. The inner aspect is the tension which needs and desires create in the individual and which has to be relieved through activity and the outer aspect is the goal, the element in the environment, which he seeks.

MEANING AND DEFINITION:

Historically, the word 'motivation' comes from a Latin root **'moveers'** which means **to move**. Thus, we can say that in its literal meaning motivation is the process of arousing movement in the organism.

H.W. Bernard held "Motivation refers to all those phenomena which are involved in the stimulation of action towards particular objectives where previously there was little or no movement towards those goals.

Atkinson defined motivation as, the term motivation refers to the arousal of tendency to act to produce one or more effects.

Maslow defined motivation as, "Motivation is constant, never ending, fluctuating and complex and that it is an almost universal characteristic of particularly every organismic state of affairs".

D.O. Hebb said, "The term motivation refers (1) to existence of an organized phase sequence, (2) to its direction and content, (3) to its persistence in given direction or stability of content".

APPROACHES TO MOTIVATION

Motivation is the label we give to processes that energize (active) and direct behavior toward particular goals. Motivation affects the strength of behaviors, persistence of behavior and direction of behavior (direction = choosing which behavior to make) Motivation changes over time as conditions inside the body and in the external environment change, With these changes, behavior changes.

Motivation is very closely linked to <u>reinforcement.</u>A high level of motivation for something (food, social power, cigarettes, etc.) will make it easy to use it as a reinforcer. For example, a hungry pigeon will work very hard to get a bite of food, and smokers will expend a lot of effort to get cigarettes). This feature of motivation is the basis of

<u>Premack's (1959, 1965)and Allison and Timberlake's (1974) models of reinforcement.</u>

Motivation determines what will work as reinforcement. The more attractive something appears (motivation), the more likely someone will do something to get some (reinforcement). In fact, some psychologists claim that the only thing motivation does is to establish the conditions for reinforcement.

DIFFERENT APPROACHES TO MOTIVATION:

Traditional Approach:

Frederick W. Taylor's work was best represented by the traditional approach. His ideas were centered around the thought that everyone was primarily motivated by economic gain. He also believed that managers knew more about the jobs being performed than the who performed these jobs did.

Human Relations Approach:

Unlike the traditional approach the human relations approach is focused on the social environment of a company. It focuses on the role of the social processes and relationships. The human relations approach understands that employees have strong social needs and that economic gain can't always fill that gap. This approach is more concerned with the employees well being at work than the financial compensation the employees get for working.

Human Resource Approach:

The human relations approach tells us that employees want to contribute and make real contributions to something. Human religionists will tell you that the illusion of contribution and participation is enough to motivate employees. However, some employees need more than just an illusion of contribution and participation, but instead need to be actively involved in decision making and feel like they truly are contributing to the group. Managers need to figure out how to use all their human resources and encourage employees to participate. A way that managers can also make employees feel more involved is to create work teams that collaborate and make decisions.

Approaches to motivation:

Motivation is the label we give to processes that energize (active) and direct behavior toward particular goals. Motivation affects the strength of behaviors, persistence of behavior and direction of behavior (direction = choosing which behavior to make)Motivation changes over time as conditions inside the body and in the external environment change, With these changes, behavior changes.

Motivation is very closely linked to **reinforcement.**A high level of motivation for something (food, social power, cigarettes, etc.) will make it easy to use it as a reinforcer. For example, a hungry pigeon will work very hard to get a bite of food, and smokers will expend a lot of effort to get cigarettes). This feature of motivation is the basis of <u>Premack's (1959, 1965)and Allison and Timberlake's (1974) models of reinforcement.</u>

Motivation determines what will work as reinforcement. The more attractive something appears (motivation), the more likely someone will do something to get some (reinforcement). In fact, some psychologists claim that the only thing motivation does is to establish the conditions for reinforcement.

TYPES OF MOTIVATION THEORIES:

The study of motivation includes a variety of theories that explain why individuals are driven to do what they do. These theories can generally be categorized into two main types: <u>content</u> theories and process theories. Each category approaches motivation differently, focusing on the factors that motivate behavior or the cognitive processes that play a role in motivational dynamics.

Content Theories:

They focus on the specific factors that motivate individuals. These theories primarily aim to identify what needs or desires drive human behavior. The most well-known content theories include:

1. Maslow's Hierarchy of Needs: This theory proposes that humans are motivated by a hierarchy of needs. The most basic to higher-level needs include physiological, safety, love and belonging, esteem, and self-actualization.
2. Herzberg's Two-Factor Theory: According to Herzberg, certain factors in the workplace cause: job satisfaction, while a separate set of factors causes dissatisfaction. This theory divides motivational forces into 'hygiene factors' (which prevent dissatisfaction but do not motivate) and 'motivators' (which motivate individuals towards higher performance).

3. McClelland's Theory of Needs: This theory focuses on three key needs: achievement, affiliation, and power. Depending on their dominant need, individuals are motivated by a desire to excel, form <u>social</u> relationships, or control others.
4. Alderfer's ERG Theory: A modification of Maslow's theory, Alderfer proposed three categories of needs: existence, relatedness, and growth, suggesting that individuals can be motivated by needs at more than one level simultaneously.

Process Theories

Process theories of motivation focus on the psychological and cognitive processes that affect motivational levels. These theories explore how people choose to work hard or not based on their expectations, goals, and perceptions of fairness. Key process theories include:

1. Expectancy Theory (Vroom): This theory suggests that individuals are motivated to engage in behaviors depending on the expected outcomes of such behaviors. It is based on the belief that effort leads to performance, and performance leads to rewards.
2. Goal-Setting Theory (Locke): According to this theory, clear and challenging goals enhance employee <u>performance</u>. Motivation is influenced by the goals' specificity, difficulty, and feedback regarding progress.
3. Equity Theory (Adams): This theory posits that fairness motivates individuals. If workers perceive an inequity in their input-output ratio compared to others, they will be motivated to restore equity.
4. Reinforcement Theory: Based on behaviorist principles, this theory asserts that behavior is a function of its consequences. Positive and negative reinforcements are used to encourage or discourage behaviors.

IMPORTANT THEORIES OF MOTIVATION:

1. Maslow's Hierarchy of Needs

This theory suggests that humans have five levels of needs that dictate their behavior. These needs are often depicted as a pyramid, with the most basic needs at the bottom:

- Physiological Needs: These are fundamental biological necessities essential for human survival, such as air, food, water, shelter, clothing, warmth, and sleep.
- Safety Needs: Once physiological needs are met, security and safety become prominent.
- Love and Belongingness Needs: Social needs become important after safety, including relationships such as friendship and family.
- Esteem Needs: This includes self-esteem derived from personal achievement and recognition from others.
- Self-Actualization Needs: The highest level is fulfilling personal potential and self-fulfillment.

Theory of Human Motivation—Abraham Maslow | SpringerLink

Maslow's theory is widely influential in understanding human motivation, particularly in the workplace and educational settings. It helps structure rewards, recognition, and development opportunities that meet employee needs.

2. Herzberg's Two-Factor Theory

Developed by Frederick Herzberg in the 1950s, this theory distinguishes between motivators (factors that cause satisfaction) and hygiene factors (factors that prevent dissatisfaction but do not cause satisfaction). Herzberg's theory is particularly useful in the management of work and the design of jobs. Key aspects include:

- Motivators: These include challenging work, recognition, responsibility, and personal growth, which can lead to job satisfaction.
- Hygiene Factors: These include salary, work conditions, fringe benefits, and job security, which, if absent, can lead to dissatisfaction.

Organizations often use Herzberg's theory to design job enrichment programs and differentiate between job context and content to improve employee satisfaction.

Frederick Hertzberg's Two-factor Theory - Research Methodology

3. McClelland's Theory of Needs

David McClelland's theory, developed in the 1960s, focuses on three key needs: Achievement, Power, and Affiliation. People are motivated by:

- Achievement: The need to set, pursue, and achieve goals.
- Power: The desire to influence, teach, or encourage others.
- Affiliation: The desire for friendly and close interpersonal relationships.

This theory is often applied in leadership training and development. Understanding these needs helps managers motivate their staff more effectively by aligning tasks and rewards with individual motivational profiles.

4. Expectancy Theory

Victor Vroom's Expectancy Theory, formulated in the 1960s, is a process theory that addresses the mental processes regarding choice or deciding how to act. This theory suggests that:

- Expectancy: Individuals believe that more effort will yield better job performance.
- Instrumentality: The belief that if one performs well, then a valued outcome will be received.
- Valence: The importance that the individual places upon the expected outcome.

Expectancy Theory of Motivation - Explained

5. Equity Theory

Developed by John Stacey Adams in the 1960s, this theory focuses on the principle that fairness motivates individuals. If they perceive an imbalance in the input-output ratios compared to others, they will be motivated to restore equity. This can lead to changes in effort level, employment, or requests for higher compensation.

Equity Theory is crucial for understanding how employee perceptions of fairness affect motivation, satisfaction, and productivity. It has profound implications for pay scale, performance management, and employee retention strategies.

MOTIVATION PROCESS:

Motivation is a general term applying to the entire class of drives, desires, needs, wishes, and similar forces.

We are all motivated by different needs, depending upon circumstances and personality, but we will have certain basic needs, which have to be fulfilled. The fulfillment of these basic needs is what motivates people first of all. Once these have been achieved, they can set their sights higher. In 1943 Abraham Maslow has identified a hierarchy of needs.

THE NEED-WANT-SATISFACTION CHAIN:

Motivation involves a chain reaction: Felt needs give rise to wants or goals sought, which causes tensions (that is unfulfilled desires), which give rise to actions toward achieving goals, which finally result in satisfying actions. This chain is shown below:

Motivation refers to the drive and effort to satisfy a want or goal. Satisfaction refers to the contentment experienced when a want is satisfied.

The need want satisfaction chain goes like this: **Needs** give rise to **Wants,** which cause tension, that gives rise to action which results in **Satisfaction.**

The need want satisfaction chain theory is simple in its approach and it's easy to understand. It basically states that if you give people what they want (Need) they will be satisfied (Satisfaction). It works the other way around as well, if you take away what people need, they will become dissatisfied. The thing about this theory is that it explains how frustration can lead to unbalance and unproductivity within an organization or between employees and companies and vice versa.

Others like to refer to it as Maslow's hierarchy and state that people cannot reach self- actualization without the satisfaction of their physiological needs. The need want satisfaction chain theory is more flexible than that though, because certain organizations may require employees who care about ethical values and social responsibility (self-actualization). Every company has their own goals and expectations which leads them to design a specific set of needs for its employees.

Need -Want -Satisfaction Chain Examples

In order to understand the theory better, let's have a look at some examples from companies with different needs and resulting needs for their employees.

In theory, working in a financial institution means that your main need should be of financial nature, but if you work at a charity organization your main need might be helping others or making a difference in society. Depending on what kind of business you are running the satisfaction level will differ as well. All this makes it difficult to measure but that doesn't mean we should ignore it and not try to figure out what needs people have and how we can meet those needs.

The main reason why this theory is so valuable for companies is that they can use it to motivate their employees. If you think about <u>Super cell</u> or <u>Valve</u>, both companies are known for having happy and satisfied employees who like to work there. As a game developer, one of your needs might be creativity, so if your company can support that need you will be (more) satisfied. In case the company doesn't provide enough room for creative thinking this could result in an unsatisfied employee which means problems within the organization because this person would not be able to do his/her job properly anymore.

Need, Want and Desire

Needs are related to our physical and mental requirements. They are basic requirements in order for us to have a healthy life, grow, prosper and reproduce. They are not all equal though. Some needs are more important than others in the sense that if one is deprived, they would suffer more, but if some other need was deprived, they might not even notice it. This makes them different when they come into play in the need want satisfaction chain that exists between employees and organizations/companies

We all have needs that we need to satisfy in order to be happy. There are different levels at which we will want those things, for example:

- We need food to survive
- We might want a small house or a big one, but our real motive is to have shelter and somewhere safe for family members
- We want wealth which will allow us to acquire the things we need and also allows us the freedom to do the things that we really enjoy doing
- We need safety, security and freedom from fear

Maslow's Higher Order Needs:

There are some needs that don't really belong in the lower levels, these are called higher-order needs. They are known as self-actualization, esteem and friendship/love. Your company might also have goals that go beyond the satisfaction of their employees' basic needs. When this is the case you can use Maslow's hierarchy to motivate people within your organization to reach for goals they might not even know yet they wanted to achieve when you help them identify their own goals and why reaching them would be beneficial for both parties.

The more a person's needs are satisfied, the more they will move on to wanting more complicated things.

For example:

- Having shelter and food satisfies some of our basic needs which then makes us want safety from natural disasters or violence as well as freedom from war or oppression.
- Satisfying these two needs means that we might desire a lot of money so that we can have more security, buy things and invest.
- Having a high level of financial security lets us want other complicated things such as being famous and maybe even craving power and influence which is why people say that "money cannot buy happiness" because sometimes the higher up Maslow's Hierarchy you go, the more complicated things become and the more you realize that money cannot solve all of your problems.
- Satisfying needs at a high level, such as having a lot of power lets us want respect from other people or even just to be free from criticism.
- Finally, fulfilling these two last wishes lets some people have what they need which is freedom from the need to want anything. They are happy with what they already have and can stand back and reflect on their lives.

When you actually look at Maslow's Hierarchy, you realize that there are some basic needs that people cannot live without such as food, water, shelter etc. whereas other things like influence or respect cannot be seen as needs because you can live without them, but would feel even happier with them.

PERCEIVING OTHERS IMPRESSION, ATTITUDE AND MOTIVATION:

Perception is a fundamental aspect of organizational behavior that refers to how individuals interpret and make sense of the world around them. It involves the process of receiving, selecting, organizing, and interpreting information from the environment, which ultimately influences how individuals understand and respond to various stimuli. Here's a breakdown of the concept, nature, process, and importance of perception in organizational behavior:

Concept:

Perception is the cognitive process through which individuals perceive and interpret sensory information to give meaning to their experiences. It involves the interaction between the external stimuli and an individual's internal psychological processes, such as beliefs, values, attitudes, and past experiences. In an organizational context, perception influences how employees perceive their work environment, their superiors, colleagues, tasks, and overall organizational culture.

Nature:

Perception is a subjective and individualized process. It is shaped by the unique characteristics and experiences of each individual, leading to differences in how people perceive the same situation. It is influenced by factors like cognitive biases, stereotypes, emotions, and cultural backgrounds. Perception is also an ongoing and dynamic process that can be influenced by new information and feedback.

Process:

The process of perception can be divided into three main stages:

1. **Selection:** Individuals selectively attend to certain stimuli from the environment while ignoring others. This selective attention is influenced by factors such as the intensity, novelty, and relevance of the stimuli, as well as the individual's interests and expectations.

2. **Organization:** Once the stimuli are selected, individuals organize them into meaningful patterns and categories. This process involves grouping related stimuli together based on similarities, using perceptual filters and schemas to simplify and make sense of the information.
3. **Interpretation:** Finally, individuals interpret the organized stimuli, assigning meaning to them based on their existing knowledge, beliefs, and personal experiences. Interpretation can be influenced by cognitive biases, such as confirmation bias or stereotyping, which may lead to distorted or inaccurate perceptions.

IMPORTANCE:

Perception plays a crucial role in organizational behavior for several reasons:

1. **Decision making:** Perception affects how individuals gather and interpret information, which directly influences their decision-making processes. Different perceptions of the same situation can lead to varied judgments and choices, impacting individual and organizational outcomes.
2. **Communication and teamwork:** Perception influences how individuals understand and interpret messages from others. Diverse perceptions can lead to misunderstandings, conflicts, or effective collaboration within teams. Recognizing and managing different perceptions is vital for effective communication and teamwork.
3. **Employee behavior and motivation:** Individual perceptions shape employees' attitudes, beliefs, and behaviors within an organization. Positive perceptions of fairness, support, and opportunities can enhance employee motivation, job satisfaction, and engagement. On the other hand, negative perceptions may lead to demotivation, resistance to change, and lower organizational commitment.
4. **Organizational culture and climate:** Perception contributes to the creation of an organization's culture and climate. The shared perceptions and interpretations of employees regarding the organizational values, norms, and practices shape the overall culture. Managing perception effectively can help build a positive and inclusive organizational culture.

MANAGEMENT BEHAVIORAL ASPECT OF PERCEPTION

In the context of management, understanding the behavioral aspects of perception is crucial for leaders and managers to effectively interact with their employees, make informed decisions, and create a positive work environment. Here are some key behavioral aspects of perception in management:

1. **Selective perception:** Individuals tend to selectively perceive information based on their interests, needs, and expectations. In a management setting, this means that managers may focus more on information that confirms their existing beliefs or biases, while ignoring contradictory data. It is important for managers to be aware of their selective perception and actively seek out diverse perspectives and information to make objective decisions.
2. **Stereotyping:** Stereotyping refers to the tendency to assign certain traits or characteristics to individuals or groups based on preconceived notions or generalizations. In a management context, stereotyping can lead to biased judgments and decision-making. Managers should strive to avoid stereotyping and treat each employee as an individual, recognizing their unique abilities, skills, and contributions.
3. **Halo effect:** The halo effect occurs when a positive or negative impression of an individual influences perceptions of their other attributes or qualities. For example, if a manager has a positive impression of an employee based on their performance in one area, they may assume the employee is competent in all areas. This can lead to biased performance evaluations and promotion decisions. Managers should make an effort to evaluate employees based on objective criteria and avoid letting one aspect influence their perception of the individual as a whole.
4. **Attribution theory:** Attribution theory focuses on how individuals interpret and explain the causes of behavior. Managers may attribute an employee's behavior to internal factors (such as ability or motivation) or external factors (such as the task difficulty or resources available). Understanding attribution theory can help managers make more accurate judgments about employee performance and provide appropriate feedback and support.

5. **Emotional influence:** Emotions can significantly impact perception. Managers should be mindful of the emotional state of their employees and how it may affect their perceptions and behavior. Emotionally intelligent managers can effectively manage their own emotions and recognize and respond to the emotions of their employees, creating a more positive and supportive work environment.

6. **Perceptual biases:** Various cognitive biases can distort perception and influence decision-making in management. Some common biases include confirmation bias (favoring information that confirms existing beliefs), availability bias (relying on readily available information), and anchoring bias (relying too heavily on initial information). Managers need to be aware of these biases and strive to make objective and unbiased decisions.

Understanding and managing these behavioral aspects of perception can help managers make more accurate judgments, reduce biases, improve communication, and create a fair and inclusive work environment. By recognizing the subjective nature of perception and actively seeking diverse perspectives, managers can promote effective decision-making and enhance employee engagement and performance.

EFFECTS OF EMPLOYEE ATTITUDES:

Employee attitudes have significant effects on both individual and organizational levels. Here are some key effects of employee attitudes:

1. **Job satisfaction:** Employee attitudes, particularly their level of job satisfaction, significantly impact their overall well-being and motivation. When employees have positive attitudes towards their work, they are more likely to experience higher job satisfaction. This, in turn, leads to increased employee engagement, productivity, and commitment to the organization.

2. **Employee retention:** Positive employee attitudes can contribute to higher levels of employee retention. When employees are satisfied with their work and have positive attitudes towards their organization, they are more likely to stay with the company for a longer period. Conversely, negative attitudes, such as dissatisfaction or a lack of commitment, can result in higher turnover rates, leading to increased recruitment and training costs for the organization.

3. **Organizational commitment:** Employee attitudes also influence their level of organizational commitment. Organizational commitment refers to the extent to which employees identify with and are loyal to their organization. Positive attitudes, such as a strong sense of belonging and dedication, foster higher levels of commitment, resulting in increased employee loyalty, discretionary effort, and a reduced likelihood of turnover.

4. **Productivity and performance:** Employee attitudes can impact their productivity and job performance. When employees have positive attitudes towards their work, they are more likely to be motivated, engaged, and willing to go the extra mile. On the other hand, negative attitudes, such as disengagement, apathy, or cynicism, can lead to decreased productivity, poor performance, and a negative impact on overall organizational effectiveness.

5. **Team dynamics and collaboration:** Employee attitudes can affect team dynamics and collaboration within the organization. Positive attitudes, such as trust, respect, and cooperation, contribute to a harmonious and supportive work environment. This fosters effective teamwork, open communication, and the sharing of ideas and knowledge. Conversely, negative attitudes, such as conflict, distrust, or resistance, can hinder collaboration, create a toxic work environment, and impede team performance.

6. **Customer satisfaction:** Employee attitudes indirectly influence customer satisfaction and loyalty. Positive attitudes, such as enthusiasm, friendliness, and a genuine concern for customer needs, can enhance the quality of customer interactions and lead to increased customer satisfaction. On the other hand, negative attitudes, such as rudeness or indifference, can have a detrimental impact on customer experiences, leading to decreased customer satisfaction and potential loss of business.

It is important for organizations to recognize the effects of employee attitudes and take proactive measures to foster positive attitudes among employees. This includes creating a supportive work environment, providing opportunities for growth and development, recognizing and rewarding employee contributions, and promoting open communication and feedback channels. By cultivating positive attitudes, organizations can improve employee well-being, productivity, and overall organizational performance.

NATURE AND IMPORTANCE OF MOTIVATION

Motivation refers to the internal processes that drive and direct individuals' behavior towards achieving certain goals or fulfilling specific needs. Here are some key aspects of the nature of motivation:

1. **Individualistic:** Motivation is highly individualistic, as different people are motivated by different factors and have unique goals and desires. Individuals have diverse needs, values, interests, and aspirations, which influence what motivates them and how they are motivated.
2. **Dynamic:** Motivation is a dynamic process that can fluctuate over time. It is influenced by various factors, including personal experiences, external circumstances, and changes in goals or priorities. Individuals' motivation levels can vary, and it requires continuous attention and reinforcement.
3. **Complex:** Motivation is a complex phenomenon influenced by a combination of internal and external factors. It is not solely driven by one factor but rather by a multitude of factors, such as personal values, social norms, rewards, recognition, and the individual's perception of their abilities and the task at hand.
4. **Multi-dimensional:** Motivation can be categorized into different types or dimensions. Some common motivational factors include intrinsic motivation (internal drive based on personal interest and enjoyment), extrinsic motivation (external rewards or incentives), achievement motivation (desire for success and accomplishment), and affiliation motivation (desire for social interaction and belonging).

IMPORTANCE OF MOTIVATION:

Motivation plays a crucial role in individuals' personal and professional lives, as well as in organizational contexts. Here are some key reasons highlighting the importance of motivation:

1. **Enhanced performance and productivity:** Motivated individuals are more likely to exert effort, persevere in the face of challenges, and strive for higher levels of performance. They are driven to achieve their goals, which leads to increased productivity and improved performance at both individual and organizational levels.
2. **Goal achievement:** Motivation provides individuals with the drive and determination to pursue and accomplish their goals. It helps individuals set clear objectives, develop action plans, and maintain focus and persistence until the goals are achieved. Without motivation, individuals may lack direction and struggle to make progress towards their desired outcomes.
3. **Increased job satisfaction and engagement:** Motivation contributes to higher levels of job satisfaction and engagement. When individuals are motivated, they experience a sense of fulfillment, enjoyment, and meaning in their work. Motivated employees are more likely to be proactive, take ownership of their tasks, and actively contribute to the success of the organization.
4. **Employee retention and loyalty:** Motivation plays a role in employee retention and loyalty. When individuals are motivated and satisfied in their roles, they are more likely to remain committed to the organization and less likely to seek opportunities elsewhere. This reduces turnover rates, saves recruitment and training costs, and promotes stability within the organization.
5. **Innovation and creativity:** Motivated individuals are more inclined to think creatively, seek innovative solutions, and take calculated risks. They are not just focused on completing tasks but also on finding better ways of doing things. Motivation fosters a positive and proactive mindset that encourages individuals to generate new ideas and contribute to organizational growth and innovation.
6. **Positive work environment:** Motivated individuals contribute to a positive work environment. Their enthusiasm and drive can be contagious, inspiring and energizing others. A motivated workforce enhances teamwork, communication, and collaboration, creating a supportive and high-performing organizational culture.

Overall, motivation is crucial for personal fulfillment, goal achievement, and organizational success. By understanding the nature of motivation and recognizing its importance, individuals and organizations can take steps to foster and sustain motivation, thereby unlocking higher levels of performance, engagement, and satisfaction.

ACHIEVEMENT MOTIVE

The achievement motive, also known as the need for achievement, refers to an individual's desire or drive to set and accomplish challenging goals, excel in performance, and attain personal success. The achievement motive plays a significant role in motivating individuals to strive for excellence and accomplish meaningful outcomes. Here are some key points explaining the achievement motive:

1. **Definition and characteristics**: The achievement motive reflects an individual's desire to excel in tasks, solve problems, and meet high standards of performance. People with a high achievement motive are typically motivated by personal accomplishments, self-improvement, and mastery of skills. They have a strong drive to succeed and are willing to take on challenges and risks to attain their goals.

2. **Goal orientation**: Individuals with a high achievement motive tend to be more focused on mastery-oriented goals rather than performance-oriented goals. They are driven by a desire for personal growth and competence rather than solely seeking external rewards or outperforming others. They derive satisfaction from making progress, acquiring new skills, and achieving self-defined standards of excellence.

3. **Persistence and effort**: The achievement motive is associated with a high level of persistence and effort. Individuals with a strong achievement motive are willing to invest time, energy, and resources to overcome obstacles and achieve their goals. They exhibit a strong work ethic, a willingness to learn from setbacks, and a determination to improve their performance.

4. **Preference for challenging tasks**: Individuals with a high achievement motive are inclined to seek out and engage in challenging tasks. They actively pursue opportunities that provide a chance to demonstrate their abilities and achieve success. They thrive in situations where they can set ambitious goals, receive feedback on their performance, and experience a sense of accomplishment through their efforts.

5. **Feedback and recognition**: Individuals with a high achievement motive value feedback and recognition for their efforts and accomplishments. They seek constructive feedback to improve their performance and use it as a means to gauge their progress towards their goals. Recognition and acknowledgment of their achievements further motivate them to continue striving for excellence.

6. **Impact on performance and success**: The achievement motive has a significant impact on individuals' performance and success. Individuals with a high achievement motive are often high achievers who excel in their chosen domains, such as academics, sports, or professional careers. Their drive for achievement fuels their motivation to continuously improve and surpass their previous accomplishments.

7. **Cultivation and development**: The achievement motive can be cultivated and developed through various means. Providing individuals with opportunities to set challenging goals, offering feedback and recognition for their efforts, and fostering a supportive and growth-oriented environment can enhance the development of the achievement motive.

Understanding the achievement motive is important for both individuals and organizations. Individuals can leverage their achievement motive to set and pursue meaningful goals, enhance their performance, and experience personal fulfillment. Organizations can recognize and nurture the achievement motive in their employees to promote a culture of excellence, engagement, and continuous improvement

It is worth noting that the achievement motive is just one aspect of an individual's motivation, and other factors such as intrinsic motivation, extrinsic rewards, and social influences also play a role in driving behavior and performance

CHAPTER SEVEN

EMOTIONS: FOUNDATIONS, TYPES, FUNCTIONS, AND MEASURING EMOTIONAL INTELLIGENCE

INTRODUCTION

Emotions play a fundamental role in human cognition and behavior, influencing decision-making, social interactions, and overall well-being. Emotional intelligence (EI) has gained prominence in psychology and organizational behavior, highlighting the importance of understanding and managing emotions effectively. This chapter explores the foundations, types, and functions of emotions, along with the methodologies for measuring EI.

FOUNDATIONS OF EMOTIONS

Emotions are complex psychological states that involve physiological arousal, cognitive appraisal, and expressive behaviors (Ekman, 1999). They are triggered by external or internal stimuli and are essential for survival and adaptation. Several theories explain emotions:

1. **James-Lange Theory** - Emotions result from physiological responses to stimuli (James, 1884).
2. **Cannon-Bard Theory** - Emotions and physiological responses occur simultaneously but independently (Cannon, 1927).
3. **Schachter-Singer Two-Factor Theory** - Emotion arises from physiological arousal and cognitive interpretation (Schachter & Singer, 1962).
4. **Lazarus' Cognitive Appraisal Theory** - Emotions depend on personal appraisal of situations (Lazarus, 1991).
5. **Ekman's Basic Emotions Theory** - Universal emotions exist across cultures, including happiness, sadness, fear, anger, disgust, and surprise (Ekman, 1999).
6. **Plutchik's Psychoevolutionary Theory** - Emotions are adaptive and help in survival through their intensities and variations (Plutchik, 2001).

BIOLOGICAL BASIS OF EMOTIONS

Emotions are closely linked to brain structures such as the amygdala, prefrontal cortex, and hypothalamus. The amygdala plays a crucial role in fear and aggression, while the prefrontal cortex regulates emotional responses (LeDoux, 1996). Neurotransmitters like serotonin, dopamine, and oxytocin also influence emotional experiences (Davidson & Begley, 2012).

TYPES OF EMOTIONS

Emotions can be categorized into primary and secondary emotions:

1. **Primary Emotions** – Innate, universal emotions such as joy, sadness, fear, anger, surprise, and disgust (Ekman, 1999).
2. **Secondary Emotions** – Learned emotions influenced by culture and personal experiences, such as guilt, pride, jealousy, and embarrassment (Plutchik, 2001).

Plutchik (2001) proposed a wheel of emotions, suggesting emotions exist in pairs and intensities, ranging from basic to complex forms. For instance, anticipation and trust can combine to form optimism, while joy and trust create love.

FUNCTIONS OF EMOTIONS

Emotions serve various adaptive, social, and motivational functions:

1. **Adaptive Function** – Helps individuals respond effectively to environmental challenges (Darwin, 1872).
2. **Social Function** – Facilitates communication and relationship-building (Keltner & Haidt, 1999).
3. **Motivational Function** – Drives goal-directed behavior and decision-making (Izard, 2007).
4. **Cognitive Function** – Enhances memory and learning through emotional experiences (Damasio, 1994).

EMOTIONAL INTELLIGENCE (EI)

Emotional Intelligence (EI) refers to the ability to perceive, understand, manage, and regulate emotions (Salovey & Mayer, 1990). The main models of EI include:

1. **Ability Model (Salovey & Mayer, 1990)** – EI consists of perceiving, using, understanding, and managing emotions.
2. **Trait Model (Petrides & Furnham, 2001)** – EI is a personality trait involving emotional self-efficacy.
3. **Mixed Model (Goleman, 1995)** – EI integrates cognitive and behavioral skills for emotional regulation.

COMPONENTS OF EI

Goleman (1995) identified five core components of EI:

1. **Self-Awareness** – Recognizing one's own emotions and their effects.
2. **Self-Regulation** – Managing emotions and adapting to changing circumstances.
3. **Motivation** – Using emotions to pursue goals with persistence.
4. **Empathy** – Recognizing emotions in others and responding appropriately.
5. **Social Skills** – Managing relationships effectively.

MEASURING EMOTIONAL INTELLIGENCE

Various methods exist for measuring EI, including:

1. **Self-Report Questionnaires** – Measures individuals' perceptions of their emotional abilities (Schutte et al., 1998).
2. **Performance-Based Tests** – Assesses actual emotional abilities through tasks (Mayer-Salovey-Caruso Emotional Intelligence Test, MSCEIT; Mayer et al., 2003).
3. **Observer Ratings** – Evaluates EI through peer or supervisor assessments (Boyatzis, Goleman, & Rhee, 2000).

APPLICATION OF EMOTIONAL INTELLIGENCE

EI has significant applications in various fields, including:

Workplace and Leadership

- High EI contributes to better teamwork, leadership, and conflict resolution (Goleman, 1998).
- Leaders with strong EI foster motivation and productivity in organizations (Ashkanasy & Daus, 2005).

Education and Academic Success

- EI positively correlates with academic performance and stress management (Parker et al., 2004).

Mental Health and Well-being

- EI enhances coping strategies, reducing stress and anxiety (Zeidner, Matthews, & Roberts, 2004).

Social Relationships

- High EI individuals navigate social interactions effectively, fostering strong interpersonal connections (Bar-On, 2000).

SENSORY ORGANS AND THEIR ROLE COGNITION; COGNITIVE PROCESSES–ATTENTION, PERCEPTION, REMEMBERING AND FORGETTING, KNOWLEDGE AND EXPERTISE

What are the Sense Organs?

Sense organs are specialized organs that help to perceive the world around us. They are an integral part of our lives and it is the only way that enables us to perceive the environment.

Sense organs provide the required data for interpretation through various organs and a network of nerves in response to a particular physical phenomenon. These senses govern our association and our interaction with the environment.

ROLE COGNITION

- Sensory organs (such as the eyes, ears, nose, tongue, and skin) play a vital role in cognition by providing the brain with essential information about the external environment.

- These sensory inputs are the foundation upon which cognitive processes like perception, attention, memory, and knowledge are built. Each sense organ transmits signals to the brain, where they are processed, interpreted, and integrated to create our perception of the world and influence our decision-making, learning, and memory.

- **Eyes (Vision)**: Visual information is processed by the occipital lobe of the brain, contributing to spatial awareness, object recognition, and movement detection.
- **Ears (Hearing)**: Auditory signals are processed in the temporal lobe and are essential for language comprehension, environmental awareness, and communication
- **Nose (Olfaction)**: Smell is closely tied to memory and emotion, due to the olfactory system's direct connection to the limbic system, which governs emotions and memory formation.
- **Tongue (Taste)**: Taste perception is crucial for identifying food, and its integration with other senses (like smell) is important for flavor perception and food preference.
- **Skin (Touch)**: Tactile sensations provide information about pressure, texture, temperature, and pain. This feedback is essential for motor coordination and emotional regulation.

COGNITIVE PROCESS:

Cognitive processes refer to the mental activities and functions that allow individuals to acquire knowledge, make decisions, solve problems, and understand and interact with the world. These processes involve various stages such as perception, attention, memory, reasoning, and problem-solving, which work together to support thought, learning, and behavior.

TYPES OF COGNITIVE PROCESS

- **Attention**: The ability to focus on a specific stimulus in the environment.

- **Language**: Language and language development are cognitive processes involving the ability to comprehend and express concepts using spoken and written words. This permits us to communicate with others and is crucial in our thinking.

- **Learning**: Learning involves cognitive processes such as taking in new information, processing it, and integrating it with previous knowledge.

- **Memory**: Memory is a crucial cognitive function that allows people to encode, store, and retrieve data. It is an important part of the learning process because it allows people to remember information about the world and their own personal histories.

- **Perception:** The cognitive process that allows people to gather information through their senses and use that information to respond to and interact with the outside environment.

- **Thought**: Every cognitive process necessitates the use of thought. It enables people to engage in higher-order reasoning, problem-solving, and decision-making.

ATTENTION:

- Attention refers to the cognitive process of focusing mental resources on specific stimuli while ignoring others. It is a limited resource, so selective attention helps prioritize important information.

Theories of Attention:
Broadbent's Filter Theory: Suggests that attention acts as a filter that selects information based on physical characteristics (e.g., pitch, color) before further processing. (Eg: At a crowded party, you focus on one conversation while ignoring background noise.)
Treisman's Attenuation Theory: Proposes that unattended information is not completely blocked but attenuated (weakened).(Eg: In a crowded room, you focus on your conversation, but still hear your name mentioned in the background, demonstrating how unattended information is attenuated but not completely ignored.)
Kahneman's Capacity Model: Suggests that attention is a resource that can be divided among different tasks, depending on how much cognitive load each task requires. (Eg: Multitasking while driving and texting leads to slower reaction times due to limited cognitive resources.)
Resource Theory: Argues that attention is a shared resource and can be allocated to multiple tasks based on priorities and the complexity of those tasks.
Perception:

- Perceptions are a cognitive process because we often consciously and unconsciously interpret information gained through our perceptions, forming thoughts, opinions and emotional reactions.

Theories of Perception:
Bottom-up processing: Involves building perceptions from individual sensory data (e.g., colors, shapes).

Top-down processing: Involves using prior knowledge, expectations, and context to interpret sensory data.(Eg: you read a misspelled word ("bok") as "book" due to context and prior knowledge.)

Gestalt Principles: Emphasize how we perceive patterns and structures in a holistic manner (e.g., proximity, similarity, continuity).

Remembering and Forgetting:

- It is a critical component in the learning process and allows people to retain knowledge about the world and their personal histories.

Theories of Memory:

- **Atkinson and Shiffrin's Multi-store Model**: Suggests that memory is composed of three stores: sensory memory, short-term memory, and long-term memory.(Eg: A phone number you just saw is briefly stored in short-term memory before being forgotten or transferred to long-term memory.)

- **Baddeley and Hitch's Working Memory Model**: Focuses on short-term memory as an active system involved in processing and manipulating information.(Eg: Solving a math problem involves using both verbal and visual memory systems.

- **Levels of Processing Theory**: Proposes that the depth of processing influences memory retention, with deeper processing leading to better memory encoding.

Forgetting:

- Forgetting or disremembering is **the apparent loss or modification of information already encoded and stored in an individual's short or long-term memory**.
- Forgetting information from **short term memory (STM)** can be explained using the **theories of trace decay and displacement**.
- Forgetting from **Long term memory (LTM)** can be explained using the **theories of interference, retrieval failure and lack of consolidation**.

Theories:

Decay Theory: Suggests that information fades over time if it is not rehearsed. (Eg: you learned a new phone number last week, but now, after not using it or rehearsing it, you can no longer remember it because it has "decayed" from your memory over time).

Interference Theory: Proposes that forgetting occurs because new or old information interferes with memory retrieval. (Eg: You recently changed your email password, and now you keep mixing it up with your old password because the old password interferes with remembering the new one. This is **retroactive interference**

Retrieval Failure Theory: Suggests that forgetting is due to the inability to access stored information, often due to insufficient cues. (**Eg**: you walk into a room and forget why you went in).

Knowledge and Expertise:

- Knowledge is essential for the competent functioning of most mental processes, not only in memory, language and thought , but also in perception and attention.
- Expertise refers to the psychological processes that underlie the superior achievement of experts, who are typically defined as those who have acquired special skills in, or knowledge of, a particular subject through professional training and practical experience.

Theories of Knowledge and Expertise:

Schneider and Shiffrin's Automaticity Theory: Proposes that through practice, cognitive tasks become automatic and require less cognitive effort.

(**Eg:** After practicing driving for years, you can navigate familiar routes without consciously thinking about every step, demonstrating how tasks become automatic with practice).

Expertise and the Role of Mental Representation: Experts develop intricate mental models or schemas that allow them to process information faster and more efficiently than novices.

(**Eg:** A chess grandmaster quickly recognizes complex patterns on the board because they have developed mental schemas from years of experience).

Cognitive Load Theory: Suggests that experts can handle more complex information due to their well-organized mental structures, whereas novices are limited by cognitive load.

(**Eg:** A beginner learning to solve a Rubik's Cube struggles to remember all the steps, while an expert can solve it effortlessly because their cognitive load is lower due to well-organized knowledge).

CHAPTER NINE

PRINCIPLES AND PROCESSES OF PERCEPTION

INTRODUCTION

Perception is the process through which individuals interpret and make sense of sensory information. It is a complex cognitive function that allows humans to understand their environment and respond appropriately. Perception is influenced by both physiological and psychological factors, and it involves various principles and mechanisms that shape the way people experience the world. Understanding perception is crucial in fields like psychology, neuroscience, marketing, and artificial intelligence, as it determines human behavior and decision-making.

PRINCIPLES OF PERCEPTION

Perception is governed by several fundamental principles, which help in organizing and interpreting sensory data. These principles include:

1. Gestalt Principles of Perception

Gestalt psychology emphasizes that humans perceive objects as whole entities rather than as a sum of individual parts. The major Gestalt principles include:

- **Figure-Ground Relationship**: The ability to distinguish objects (figures) from their background (ground).
- **Proximity**: Objects that are close together are perceived as belonging to the same group.
- **Similarity**: Objects with similar characteristics (such as shape, color, or size) are perceived as part of the same group.
- **Continuity**: The human eye prefers to see continuous lines and patterns rather than disjointed elements.
- **Closure**: The mind tends to complete incomplete figures to form a recognizable image.
- **Common Fate**: Objects moving in the same direction are perceived as part of a group.

2. Perceptual Constancy

Perceptual constancy allows individuals to recognize objects as stable despite variations in sensory input. This includes:

- **Size Constancy**: Objects are perceived as the same size regardless of changes in distance.
- **Shape Constancy**: Objects maintain their shape perception despite changes in orientation.
- **Color Constancy**: The perceived color of objects remains stable despite changes in lighting.
- **Brightness Constancy**: The brightness of an object is perceived as unchanged even in varying light conditions.

3. Depth Perception

Depth perception enables individuals to judge distances and perceive three-dimensional space. It relies on:

- **Binocular Cues**: Depth cues that require both eyes, such as retinal disparity and convergence.

- **Monocular Cues**: Depth cues that can be perceived with one eye, including linear perspective, texture gradient, interposition, and shadowing.

4. Selective Attention
Selective attention refers to the brain's ability to focus on specific stimuli while ignorng others. It is influenced by:

- **Bottom-Up Processing**: When perception is driven by external stimuli.
- **Top-Down Processing**: When perception is influenced by prior knowledge, expectations, and experiences.

5. Perceptual Set
A perceptual set is a mental predisposition to perceive things in a particular way based on past experiences, emotions, and cultural background.

BEHAVIOURISTIC LAWS OF PERCEPTION
Behaviorism focuses on observable behavior and the ways stimuli shape responses. These laws explain how behavior can be influenced by perception, which is relevant in shaping the responses of farmers to new agricultural practices.

1. **Law of Contiguity**

   - This law states that when two events or stimuli are paired together, they will be associated in the mind, leading to a learned response.
   - **Example**: Associating a new farming technique with positive outcomes (e.g., higher crop yield) can lead farmers to adopt it.
   - **Reference**: Pujari and Laxmi Lal (2004).

2. **Law of Frequency**

   - Repeated exposure to a stimulus increases the likelihood of the stimulus eliciting a response.
   - **Example**: Repeated demonstrations of a new farming method increase its adoption by farmers.
   - **Reference**: Ray (2014).

3. **Law of Effect**

   - Responses followed by positive outcomes are more likely to be repeated.
   - **Example**: If farmers observe that adopting a new irrigation technique results in better crop yield, they are more likely to continue using it.
   - **Reference**: Umesh (2017).

TYPES OF PERCEPTION
Perception can be categorized into various types based on the sensory input and cognitive processes involved:
1. Visual Perception

- The ability to interpret visual stimuli such as shapes, colors, and movements.
- Involves processes like depth perception, motion detection, and object recognition.

2. Auditory Perception

- The interpretation of sound waves and auditory stimuli.

- Involves distinguishing pitch, tone, and speech patterns.

3. Tactile Perception

- The sense of touch, including temperature, texture, and pain perception.

4. Olfactory Perception

- The ability to detect and interpret smells.
- Closely linked to memory and emotions.

5. Gustatory Perception

- The sense of taste, influenced by chemical composition and individual taste preferences.

6. Social Perception

- The process of interpreting and understanding social cues and behaviors in interpersonal interactions.

PROCESSES OF PERCEPTION

Perception follows a sequence of cognitive processes, which include:

1. Sensation

The initial stage where sensory organs detect stimuli from the environment (e.g., light, sound, pressure).

2. Attention

The process of focusing on specific stimuli while filtering out others.

3. Interpretation

The brain organizes and assigns meaning to sensory information based on past experiences and cognitive frameworks.

4. Recognition

Identifying and categorizing stimuli based on memory and learned knowledge.

5. Response

The final step where perception leads to action or reaction based on the interpreted stimuli.

HALF FULL
HALF EMPTY

CHAPTER TEN

CONSCIOUSNESS – MEANING, TYPES, SLEEP AND DREAMS

Consciousness refers to the state of being aware of and able to think about one's own existence, thoughts, feelings, and surroundings. It is the experience of being conscious, where individuals are aware of both their internal mental processes and external stimuli. Consciousness allows us to process sensory input, reflect on experiences, make decisions, and navigate through daily life.

Philosophers, neuroscientists, and psychologists have explored the nature of consciousness in depth, and while many aspects remain mysterious, it is commonly described as:

- **Self-awareness**: The ability to recognize oneself as distinct from others and to be aware of one's thoughts and emotions.
- **Perception**: The capacity to interpret sensory information from the environment, such as sights, sounds, and touch.
- **Attention**: The mental process of focusing on certain stimuli while ignoring others.
- **Intentionality**: The ability to form goals and take action in pursuit of them.

There are also different levels of consciousness, such as being awake, in a dream state, or under anesthesia, each representing a different degree of awareness.

In a more philosophical context, the "hard problem" of consciousness, introduced by philosopher David Chalmers, questions how and why subjective experiences arise from neural processes in the brain. Despite extensive research, the exact mechanisms behind consciousness remain one of the most profound mysteries in science and philosophy.

TYPES OF CONSCIOUSNESS:

Consciousness can be understood in different ways, and researchers often categorize it into various types based on levels of awareness, states of mind, and experiences. Here are some common types of consciousness:

1.WAKING CONSCIOUSNESS

- This is the everyday state of being awake, aware, and alert. It involves being conscious of one's thoughts, feelings, sensory experiences, and the external environment. In this state, individuals are able to think clearly, make decisions, and interact with others.

2. SLEEP CONSCIOUSNESS

- While we are asleep, we often experience different levels of consciousness, ranging from deep sleep with little awareness to more vivid dreaming states (REM sleep). Although we may not be consciously aware of our surroundings, our brains are still active in processing information and consolidating memories.

3.ALTERED STATES OF CONSCIOUSNESS (ASC)

- These are states where the normal waking consciousness is changed, often due to external influences or practices. Examples include:

  - **Meditation**: A mental state achieved by focusing the mind, often leading to relaxation and a deeper sense of awareness or altered perception.
  - **Hypnosis**: A trance-like state of heightened suggestibility and focused attention.
  - **Drug-Induced States**: Certain substances like alcohol, cannabis, or hallucinogens can alter perceptions, thoughts, and awareness.
  - **Dreams**: Both lucid and non-lucid dreams represent altered states where the mind operates in a different way compared to waking life.

4. SELF-CONSCIOUSNESS

- This refers to a heightened awareness of oneself, both in terms of one's physical appearance and internal thoughts. Self-consciousness involves reflecting on one's identity, actions, and how others perceive them. It can sometimes lead to feelings of self-awareness and social anxiety.

5. UNCONSCIOUSNESS

- This is the state where a person is not aware of themselves or their surroundings, typically due to injury, illness, or anesthesia. In this state, a person cannot consciously interact with their environment or process sensory information.

6. SUBCONSCIOUS

1. This refers to the part of the mind that is not fully conscious but still affects thoughts, behaviors, and emotions. It holds memories, desires, and experiences that influence actions without full awareness. Freud and other psychoanalysts believed that the subconscious plays a significant role in shaping our behaviors and mental states.

7. COLLECTIVE CONSCIOUSNESS

- A concept introduced by sociologist Émile Durkheim, this refers to the shared beliefs, ideas, and moral attitudes that operate as a unifying force within society. It's the consciousness held collectively by a group of people or society, influencing cultural norms and social behavior.

8.MINIMAL CONSCIOUSNESS

- A state where an individual exhibits some awareness of their environment but is not fully conscious. This can be seen in cases of brain injury, where people may have limited responses or awareness, such as responding to pain or sound, but are not fully conscious or able to communicate.

9.HIGHER CONSCIOUSNESS (TRANSCENDENTAL OR SPIRITUAL CONSCIOUSNESS)

- This type of consciousness involves a deeper awareness of life, existence, and the universe, often associated with spiritual or philosophical enlightenment. It's characterized by a sense of oneness, connectedness, and the perception of a higher reality beyond the individual self.

10. FLOW STATE

- A highly focused mental state often experienced during activities that require intense concentration and skill, such as sports, music, or creative endeavors. When in a flow state, individuals feel immersed in the activity and lose awareness of time and surroundings, performing at their peak.

These types of consciousness highlight the complexity and variety of human awareness, from everyday wakefulness to altered mental states and deep introspective experiences.

SLEEP:

The **consciousness of sleep** refers to the various levels and states of awareness that occur during sleep. While sleep is often associated with a lack of consciousness (or reduced consciousness), it is a dynamic state with various stages that feature different degrees of awareness. Understanding the consciousness of sleep involves exploring how our mind transitions from full wakefulness to unconsciousness and how it functions during sleep.

Key Aspects of Consciousness of Sleep:

- **Transition from Wakefulness to Sleep:**

  - When we fall asleep, our conscious awareness gradually fades, but we don't immediately lose consciousness entirely. The process of falling asleep includes stages where we become less aware of external stimuli, and our brain activity changes. This transition can involve a **hypnagogic state** where you may still have some awareness of your thoughts, sensations, or surroundings but are starting to drift off to sleep.

- **Levels of Consciousness in Different Sleep Stages:**

  - **Non-REM (NREM) Sleep:**

    - **Stage 1 (Light Sleep):** This is the initial stage of sleep where consciousness begins to fade. You may experience a brief sense of drifting or floating, and your body starts to relax. During this stage, you are still somewhat aware of external stimuli, like sounds or movements, but you are already on the edge of sleep.
    - **Stage 2 (Deeper Sleep):** As you enter deeper sleep, consciousness is reduced further. At this point, you are not aware of your surroundings, and it becomes harder to wake you up. The brain's electrical activity shows a pattern of sleep spindles (bursts of brain activity) and K-complexes (sharp waves), which are thought to aid in memory consolidation and blocking external disturbances.
    - **Stages 3 & 4 (Deep Sleep):** These are the deepest stages of NREM sleep. Consciousness is almost fully absent in these stages, and it is extremely difficult to wake a person during this period. The brain activity is slow, and the body focuses on physical restoration, growth, and immune function.

  - **REM Sleep (Rapid Eye Movement Sleep):**

    - During REM sleep, the brain shows patterns of activity similar to wakefulness, and most vivid dreaming occurs. However, although the brain is active, the body is paralyzed (a phenomenon called REM atonia) to prevent acting out dreams. Consciousness during REM sleep is different from waking consciousness in that the person is not aware of their surroundings but may have intense, vivid experiences in their dreams.
    - **Lucid Dreaming:** This is an interesting phenomenon where a person becomes aware they are dreaming while still in the dream. During lucid dreaming, individuals can have some control over their dream environment, blending elements of waking consciousness with the dream state. While the person is technically asleep, their consciousness is partially awake, which creates a unique intersection of the two states.

- **Awareness During Sleep:**

- In general, during deep stages of sleep, awareness of the environment is significantly reduced, and we are not consciously aware of our surroundings. However, in lighter stages of sleep, external stimuli, like noise or movement, can sometimes awaken us or influence our dreams.
- **Sleep Disorders and Consciousness**:

  - **Sleepwalking** (somnambulism): In this state, a person is partly asleep but may perform actions like walking or talking. The person is not fully conscious, but their body functions are active. They are unaware of what they are doing and have no memory of it once they wake up.
  - **Sleep Paralysis**: This occurs when a person is either falling asleep or waking up, and they temporarily experience an inability to move, sometimes accompanied by vivid hallucinations. During this time, consciousness is partially active, but the body remains in a sleep-like state, often resulting in feelings of fear and helplessness.
  - **Night Terrors**: These are intense episodes of fear or panic that occur during deep NREM sleep. The person is not conscious during the event, but it may cause them to scream or move in ways that resemble being awake. These experiences are typically forgotten once the person wakes up.

- **Dreaming and Consciousness**:

  - Dreaming is an essential aspect of sleep consciousness, primarily occurring during REM sleep. While dreaming, we may experience vivid visual and emotional sensations, and our minds create scenarios that may feel very real.
  - **Consciousness in Dreams**: Most dreams occur without the dreamer being aware they are dreaming. However, in lucid dreams, the dreamer becomes aware of the fact that they are in a dream and can sometimes control the dream's content. This state is a unique form of partial consciousness during sleep.

- **Sleep and Brain Activity**:

  - Brainwaves during sleep vary across the different stages of sleep. For example, in **deep sleep** (stages 3 and 4), **slow-wave** brain activity dominates, which is associated with restorative processes and little to no conscious awareness.
  - In **REM sleep**, the brain's electrical activity is similar to that of wakefulness, but the person's consciousness is disconnected from the external world, and they experience dreams. The brain may "seem awake," but the conscious awareness that governs our interactions with reality is inactive.

- **The Role of Sleep in Restoring Consciousness**:

  - Sleep plays a crucial role in restoring both physical and mental health. Although our conscious mind rests during sleep, the brain is actively working to consolidate memories, process emotions, and maintain various cognitive functions. Proper sleep improves waking consciousness by enhancing memory, attention, mood regulation, and overall cognitive performance.

Dreams:

The **consciousness of dreams** refers to the level of awareness and experience a person has while they are dreaming. While dreaming, the mind creates vivid and sometimes bizarre scenarios, but the consciousness within the dream is often not fully aware of the fact that it is a dream. However, in some cases, people can become conscious of their dreaming, which leads to a different state of awareness.

Here's an overview of the **consciousness of dreams** and how it manifests in different types of dreams:

1. Lucid Dreaming (Awareness During Dreams):

- **Lucid Dreams** are the most direct example of consciousness in dreams. In a lucid dream, the dreamer is aware that they are dreaming while the dream is still ongoing. This awareness allows the dreamer to have some control over the events, environment, and characters in the dream.
- **Consciousness in Lucid Dreaming**: The person experiences a blend of conscious awareness (similar to waking) while their body is asleep. In this state, their mind may continue to operate as it would during wakefulness, but with the added freedom to shape the dream's narrative. Some lucid dreamers can even train themselves to control the dream, fly, or change the surroundings.
- Lucid dreaming occurs during **REM sleep**, when the brain is highly active, but the person's external consciousness (their awareness of the physical world) is still dormant.

2. Non-Lucid Dreams (Ordinary Dreams):

- **Ordinary Dreams** occur when the dreamer is unaware that they are dreaming. The person may experience a wide range of emotions, settings, and actions, but they do not have the conscious realization that what they are experiencing is not real.
- **Consciousness in Non-Lucid Dreams**: In these dreams, consciousness is much more passive, and the dreamer simply experiences the events without questioning the reality of the situation. The mind may create scenarios based on thoughts, memories, or external stimuli, but the dreamer doesn't reflect on the fact that it's a dream while experiencing it.
- Most dreams fall into this category, and although they might seem vivid, emotional, or real at the time, the dreamer typically cannot exert control over the events or recognize that it's a product of the subconscious mind.

3. Dream Consciousness and Brain Activity:

- Dreaming occurs primarily during **REM (Rapid Eye Movement) sleep**, when brain activity is high and resembles wakefulness. The conscious mind is temporarily disengaged from the external world, but the brain continues to function and process information. The brain during REM sleep is highly active, which is why we experience vivid dreams, but the body is paralyzed (a state called **REM atonia**) to prevent physical movement that could result from acting out dreams.
- **Neural Activity in Dreams**: During REM sleep, the **prefrontal cortex**, the area of the brain responsible for higher-level reasoning and self-awareness, is less active. This may explain why we often lack critical thinking or full awareness during dreams. On the other hand, regions of the brain that deal with emotions and sensory experiences (such as the **amygdala** and **visual cortex**) are more active, making dreams vivid and emotionally charged.

4. Dream Recall and Conscious Reflection:

- Many people can remember some aspects of their dreams upon waking, which brings a level of **consciousness** to the experience. The degree to which someone can recall their dream may vary, and some people are better at remembering dreams than others.
- **Conscious Reflection on Dreams**: After waking, individuals often engage in reflection or interpretation of their dreams. This allows the conscious mind to engage with the dream experience, making connections to waking life, thoughts, and emotions. This kind of conscious processing can help people better understand their unconscious desires, fears, or unresolved issues, as dreams often reflect deeper aspects of the mind.

5. Dreams and Self-Awareness:

- **Self-Consciousness in Dreams**: Occasionally, a person may experience self-awareness within a dream, where they realize that something in the dream does not fit with reality or that they are dreaming. However, this level of self-consciousness is different from lucid dreaming in that the person may not have full control over the dream. Instead, they might simply have a moment of clarity about the unreality of the situation.
- **Dreams as a Reflection of Consciousness**: In some theories of psychology, especially in Freudian and Jungian interpretations, dreams are seen as a form of **unconscious expression**. The conscious mind may suppress or filter emotions, desires, and thoughts, but the dream state can reveal these subconscious elements, offering a glimpse into the unconscious mind's workings.

6. Nightmares and Consciousness:

- **Nightmares** are a type of dream that is often associated with negative or terrifying emotions. In these dreams, the person is usually not conscious of the fact that it's a dream, and the fear or distress feels very real. However, because of the emotional intensity of nightmares, some people might experience a brief moment of lucidity or self-awareness during the dream (especially if the nightmare becomes overwhelming), though they are still unable to control or change the situation.

7. Theories of Dream Consciousness:

- **Activation-Synthesis Theory**: This theory suggests that dreams are a result of the brain's attempt to make sense of random electrical activity during REM sleep. The theory posits that the conscious mind weaves together random neural signals into a coherent story, which we experience as a dream.
- **Freudian Theory**: Sigmund Freud believed that dreams were a form of unconscious wish fulfillment, where repressed desires and thoughts were expressed symbolically. According to this view, the consciousness of a dream reveals the unconscious mind's desires, fears, and conflicts.
- **Jungian Theory**: Carl Jung believed that dreams are a form of **collective unconscious**, a shared reservoir of experiences and archetypes common to all humans. In this view, dreams can provide insight into the deeper layers of the psyche and reflect not just personal but universal elements of human experience.

CHAPTER ELEVEN

LEARNING AND MEMORY –MEMORY MEANING TYPES AND MECHANISMS OF STORAGE AND RETRIEVAL OF MEMORIES IN THE HUMAN BRAIN

LEARNING

According to Hergenhahn, 1988 learning is a relatively permanent change in behaviour or in behavioural potentially that results from experience and cannot be attributed to temporary body states such as these induced by illness, fatigue or drugs.

MEMORY

Since the 1960s, human memory from the information processing approach. The mind is visualized as a computer, with information being entered, stored and then retrieved as needed.

MEANING OF MEMORY

Memory is the power to retain and recall information and past experiences. Your brain's memory helps you recall lots of memories — like multiplication tables and bad dates. The word memory applies to both the individual facts and experiences you remember as well as the brain's ability to contain it all.

WORKING MEMORY

According to Salthouse,1992 Working memory with it's definite limits, is considered by many researchers to be a potential important mediator of the relations between age and cognition.

TYPES OF MEMORY

LONG TERM MEMORY

Long term memory (LTM) is the brain's ability to store and retrieved information for a long time. Three major differences have surfaced in Long- term memory for older versus younger learners, changes in the encoding or acquisition of material , the retrieval of information and the speed of memory.

Long-term memory (LTM) is the stage of the Atkinson–Shiffrin memory model in which informative knowledge is held indefinitely. It is defined in contrast to sensory memory, the initial stage, and short-term or working memory, the second stage, which persists for about 18 to 30 seconds. LTM is grouped into two categories known as explicit memory (declarative memory) and implicit memory (non-declarative memory). Explicit memory is broken down into episodic and semantic memory, while implicit memory includes procedural memory and emotional conditioning.

STORES

The idea of separate memories for short- and long-term storage originated in the 19th century. One model of memory developed in the 1960s assumed that all memories are formed in one store and transfer to another store after a small period of time. This model is referred to as the "modal model", most famously detailed by Shiffrin.

The model states that memory is first stored in sensory memory, which has a large capacity but can only maintain information for milliseconds. A representation of that rapidly decaying memory is moved to short-term memory.

Short-term memory does not have a large capacity like sensory memory but holds information for seconds or minutes. The final storage is long-term memory, which has a very large capacity and is capable of holding information possibly for a lifetime.

The exact mechanisms by which this transfer takes place, whether all or only some memories are retained permanently, and even to have the existence of a genuine distinction between stores, remain controversial.

LTM encodes information semantically for storage, as researched by Baddeley.In vision, the information needs to enter working memory before it can be stored into LTM. This is evidenced by the fact that the speed with which information is stored into LTM is determined by the amount of information that can be fit, at each step, into visual working memory. In other words, the larger the capacity of working memory for certain stimuli, the faster will these materials be learned.

Synaptic consolidation is the process by which items are transferred from short- to long-term memory. Within the first minutes or hours after acquisition, the engram (memory trace) is encoded within synapses, becoming resistant (though not immune) to interference from outside sources.

As LTM is subject to fading in the natural forgetting process, maintenance rehearsal (several recalls/retrievals of memory) may be needed to preserve long-term memories. Individual retrievals can take place in increasing intervals in accordance with the principle of spaced repetition. This can happen quite naturally through reflection or deliberate recall (also known as recapitulation), often dependent on the perceived importance of the material. Usingtesting methods as a form of recall can lead to the testing effect, which aids long-term memory through information retrieval and feedback.

In LTM, brain cells fire in specific patterns. When someone experiences something in the world, the brain responds by creating a pattern of specific nerves firing in a specific way to represent the experience. This is called distributed representation. Distributed representation can be explained through a scientific calculator. At the top of the calculator is an opening in which the numbers typed in show up. This small slot is compiled by many blocks that light up to show a specific number. In that sense, certain blocks light up when prompted to show the number 4, but other blocks light up to show the number 5. There may be overlap in the blocks used, but ultimately, these blocks are able to generate different patterns for each specific situation. The encoding of specific episodic memories can be explained through distributed representation. When you try to remember an experience, perhaps your friend's birthday party a year ago, your brain is activating a certain pattern of neurons. If you try to remember your mother's birthday party, another pattern of neurons is fired but there may be overlap because they are both birthday parties. This kind of remembering is the idea of retrieval because it involves recalling the specific distributed representation created during the encoding of the experience.

TYPES OF LONG-TERM MEMORY

Long-term memory (LTM) is divided into two main types: declarative memory (explicit memory) and nondeclarative memory (implicit memory):

DECLARATIVE MEMORY

Also known as explicit memory, this type of memory stores facts, events, and locations that you can consciously recall. Declarative memory can be further divided into episodic memory (specific events) and semantic memory (knowledge about the world).

Semantic memory is the ability to store and recall general knowledge about the world, including facts, words, and concepts. It's a type of declarative memory that's based on experiences and culture, and it's the basis for many human activities. Examples:

- General knowledge: Knowing what a car is, how an engine works, or the definition of the word "restaurant"
- Historical knowledge: Who won the Civil War
- Scholastic concepts: Reading and math
- Geographical knowledge: Where the University of Michigan is located
- Vocabulary: The meaning of a word, like the longest word in the English language

Episodic memory is the ability to recall specific past events, along with the details of the time and place they took place. It's a crucial part of daily life, helping us remember where things are and contributing to our sense of self.

Examples :

- Where you parked your car this morning
- The dinner you had with a friend last month
- The details of a recent holiday gathering

NONDECLARATIVE MEMORY

Also known as **implicit memory**, this type of memory stores learned skills, habits, or relationships that you aren't consciously aware of. Implicit memory includes procedural memory, which involves memories of body movement and how to use objects in the environment. Emotional conditioning is another type of implicit memory.

SENSORY MEMORY

Sensory Memory also called the sensor register, "holds incoming information long enough can undergo preliminary cognitive processes " (Omrod,1996).primarily through the senses of vision, hearing, and touch, images, sounds and vibration are entered into our memory systems. Sensory memory has a very brief storage time of only milliseconds before it either enters our working system or is lost.

TYPES OF SENSORY MEMORY

ECHOIC MEMORY

Echoic memory is a sensory memory that stores and briefly retains auditory information. It's the earliest stage of auditory memory formation, and it allows people to recall sounds that have been heard. Examples of echoic memory include sounds you've just heard and are able to refer back to for several seconds.

HAPTIC MEMORY

Haptic memory is a type of sensory memory that allows you to retain information about touch, such as pressure, pain, itching, or pleasant sensations. It's used for many things, including:

- Gripping and interacting with objects: Haptic memory helps you assess the forces needed to grip and interact with familiar objects. It can also influence how you interact with new objects that are similar in size and density.
- Playing an instrument: Haptic memory helps you feel where your fingers are so you can play the right notes.
- Typing on a computer: Haptic memory helps you find the correct keys.

ICONIC MEMORY

Iconic memory is a type of short-term memory that allows you to briefly recall visual images after the physical image has disappeared:

Duration: Iconic memory is a very brief memory store that lasts less than a second.

Capacity: Iconic memory is a high capacity memory store.

Function: Iconic memory retrieves visual signals from the outside world and either transfers it to other forms like short-term memory, or discards it.

Examples: You might experience iconic memory when you glance at a friend's phone and spot something as she quickly thumbs past it. You can close your eyes and visualize an image of the item very briefly.

GUSTATORY MEMORY

Gustatory memory, also known as taste sensory memory, is the ability to remember tastes and associate them with other memories. It's closely related to olfactory memory.

Here are some ways gustatory memory works:

Identifying foods

Gustatory receptor cells on the tongue help identify the five basic tastes: salty, sweet, bitter, sour, and umami.

Associating tastes with other memories

Tastes can trigger memories of the past, such as when a dish makes you nauseous because it previously made you sick.

Anticipating tastes

After acquiring gustatory memories, you can anticipate the taste of food by looking at it.

Conditioned taste aversion

This is a survival tactic where you associate the taste of food with an unpleasant consequence, such as feeling sick.

OLFACTORY MEMORY

Olfactory memory is the ability to recognize and remember smells. It's a complex process that involves the brain's neural network, which includes the olfactory cortex, amygdala, and hippocampus:

Olfactory cortex: Relays information to the amygdala and hippocampus

Amygdala: Involved with emotional memory

Hippocampus: Related to short-term and working memory

Olfactory bulb: Part of the brain responsible for processing smells

Olfactory memory is different from other types of memory in a few ways:

Persistence: Olfactory memories are highly resistant to forgetting.

Emotional connection: Smells are particularly evocative of emotional memories. For example, the smell of grass and rubber cleats might bring back memories of childhood soccer games.

Formation: A single exposure to an odor can be enough to form a long-term memory.

SHORT TERM MEMORY

Short-term memory (STM) is the ability to hold a small amount of information in an active state for a short period of time. It's typically estimated to last seconds.

Duration

The limited duration of short-term memory (~18 seconds without rehearsal)[20] suggests that its contents spontaneously decay over time.[21][citation needed] The decay assumption is part of many theories of short-term memory. The most notable one is Baddeley's model of working memory. The decay assumption is usually paired with the idea of rapid covert rehearsal: to retain information for longer, information must be periodically repeated or rehearsed, either by articulating it out loud or by mental simulation. Another type of rehearsal that can improve short-term memory is attention-based rehearsal. Information is mentally searched in a particular sequence.Once recalled, the information re-enters short-term memory and is then retained for a further period.

Capacity

STM can typically hold five to seven items, like a phone number or license plate. However, the capacity can vary depending on the individual. Younger people or those with poor mental abilities may only be able to hold five items, while adults or those with trained memories can hold nine or more.

Decay

Without rehearsal, STM decays rapidly and probably lasts less than 30 seconds.

Memory consolidation

The brain converts short-term memories into long-term memories through a process called memory consolidation. Rehearsing or recalling information strengthens neural networks in the brain.

Memory tools

Mnemonics, like songs, rhymes, and acronyms, can help you remember things more effectively.

Attention

The main problem with STM is attention. Items that are attended to are remembered, while those that aren't are lost.

Position

The position in which information is received can also affect STM. Information received first or last is processed fully, but information in the middle is often lost.

MECHANISMS OF STORAGE AND RETRIEVAL OF MEMORIES IN THE HUMAN BRAIN

Memory is one of the brain's foundational elements. It guides us through life by helping us learn from experiences and shaping our sense of self. It keeps us safe—like remembering not to touch a hot stove—and forms the stories that define who we are. But how exactly does the brain hold onto cherished memories or recall forgotten details with such precision?

The process of memory Is extraordinary. Our brains can capture, store, and retrieve vast amounts of information, from familiar faces to facts learned in school. The science behind memory reveals how the brain organizes and manages these experiences. But what exactly is happening in our brains when we create a memory?

The simplest explanation Is that the brain rewires itself each time a new memory is formed. This happens through synapses—tiny gaps between brain cells or neurons. Neurons communicate via an intricate electrochemical system. A change in one neuron's electrical charge releases chemicals called neurotransmitters across synapses, which are picked up by a neighbouring neuron. This communication strengthens the connection between neurons over time, making it easier for them to interact and solidify the memory. Conversely, when neurons rarely communicate, their bond weakens, and sometimes they stop transmitting altogether. At its core, memory is built by reinforcing these connections between networks of neurons.

HOW DOES THE BRAIN STORE MEMORIES?

At its core, memory is the brain's way of encoding, storing, and retrieving information. The brain's ability to store memories is a dynamic process that involves several regions working together, most notably the hippocampus, amygdala, and prefrontal cortex.

1.ENCODING: THE FIRST STEP IN MEMORY FORMATION

Memory formation begins with this encoding process, as our sensory systems relay information to the brain. Encoding is transforming sensory input into a format the brain can interpret and store. This involves external stimuli—such as sight, sound, touch, taste, and smell—being converted into neural signals. These signals are then transmitted to various regions of the brain, particularly the hippocampus, a seahorse-shaped structure deep within the brain that plays a crucial role in forming explicit memories.

The **hippocampus** Is essential in converting short-term experiences into long-term memories. For example, when you meet someone new, your brain captures their face, voice, and name, temporarily holding this data in short-term memory. Short-term memory can store only a limited amount of information for a brief period. However, if that person becomes significant in your life, the brain strengthens the neural connections associated with them, transferring the memory into long-term storage. This reinforcement of neural pathways ensures that important information is retained for future recall.

2.STORAGE: STRENGTHENING NEURONS

Once a memory is encoded, it needs to be stored. At the biological level, memories are stored by strengthening connections between neurons (brain cells). Neurons communicate with each other through tiny gaps called synapses. This process, called synaptic plasticity, involves the release of neurotransmitters that strengthen the bond between neurons.

When you repeatedly recall or use a particular memory, the synapses associated with that memory become stronger. Over time, this reinforcement creates a more robust neural pathway, making it easier for the brain to access that memory in the future. This is why practicing something repeatedly—like playing a musical instrument or studying for an exam—helps solidify it in long-term memory.

3.RETRIEVAL: ACCESSING STORED INFORMATION

Retrieving a memory involves reactivating the same neural pathways used during the initial encoding and storage processes. This is where the brain retrieves stored information and brings it back into consciousness. Depending on the complexity and emotional significance of the memory, different parts of the brain, including the hippocampus and prefrontal cortex, are engaged during retrieval.

For example, when trying to remember where you left your keys, your brain retrieves the stored memory of that event, possibly using cues (such as visualizing the last place you saw them) to aid in the retrieval process. This demonstrates how the brain uses associations to retrieve information.

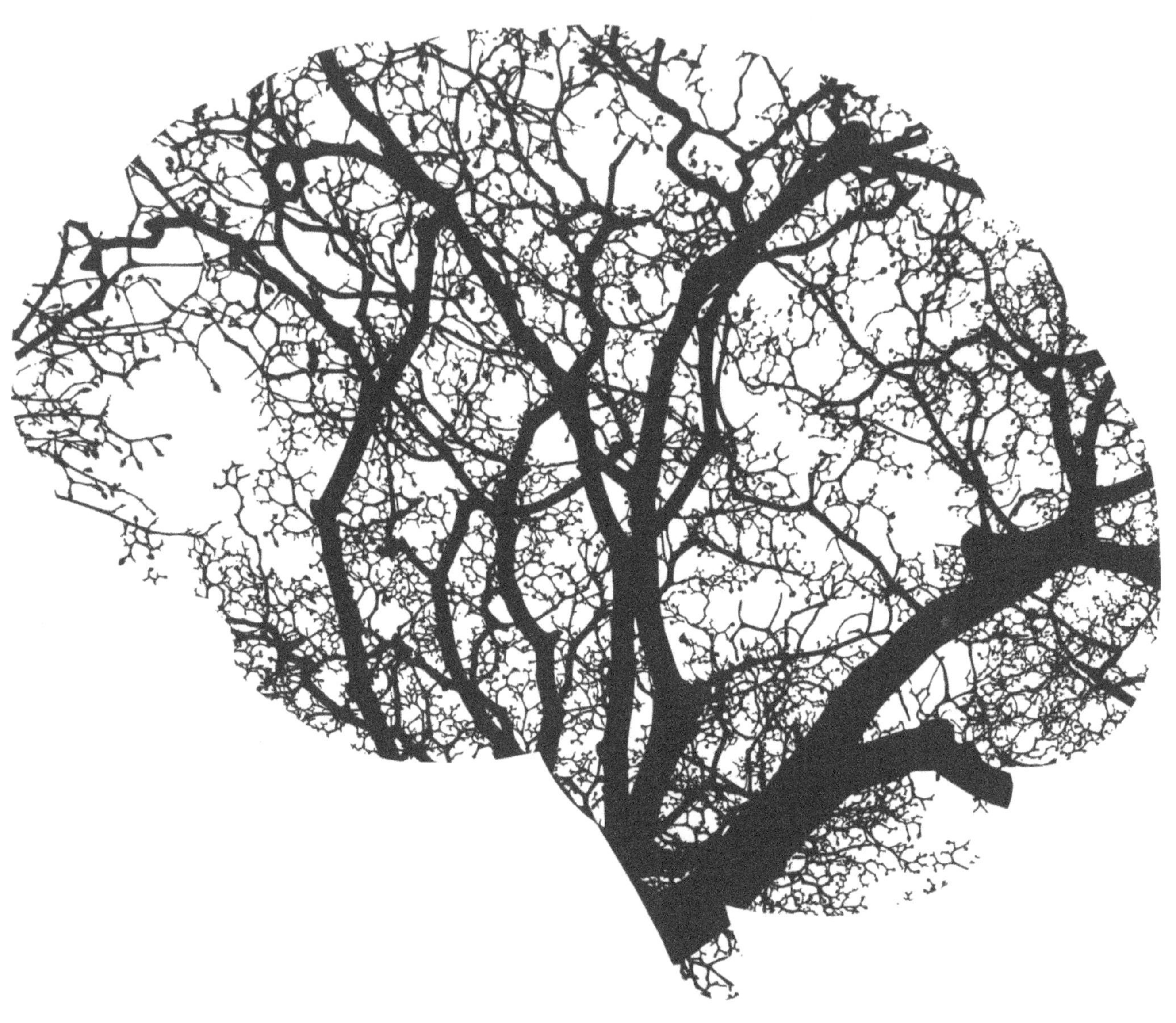

CHAPTER TWELVE

COMPLEX COGNITIVE PROCESSES – CONCEPT FORMATION, THINKING, PROBLEM SOLVING AND TRANSFER- FOUNDATIONS, THEORIES AND APPROACHES

COMPLEX COGNITIVE PROCESS

- Complex cognitive process is defined as all mental processes that are used by individuals for deriving new information out of given information, with the intention to solve problems, make decision, and plan actions.
- Complex cognitive processes are those processes that lead to understanding; the ability to transform and use knowledge in appropriate settings

- Woolfolk (2005)

Example: concept learning, problem – solving, metacognition,critical thinking, knowledge transfer learning and reasoning, memory, perception,attention

CONCEPTUAL UNDERSTANDING

- It helps to understand the main concepts in a subject rather than just memorizing isolated facts
- Through concept learning, students build connections between what they know and what they are learning by putting information into categories
- **Concepts** are broad topics under which students classify more detailed examples
- When students encounter new experiences, they attempt to make sense of new examples by associating them with a category
- For example, a student is able to make assumptions about the characteristics of various living things by classifying them as plants, animals, or insects

CONCEPTS

- Concepts are categories that group objects, events and characteristics on the basis of common properties
- It is an element of cognition that help to simplify and summarize information
- These are formed through direct experiences with objects or through symbols (e.g., words, formulas, graphs and pictures).

FORMATION OF CONCEPTS

1. **Comparison :**

In order to form concepts about an object, the first step is to observe the characteristics of the objects of the same class.
Then comes analysis of the qualities of each of them .
The points of their of their similarity and their points of differences are noted .
2. Abstraction:
In this stage, the concrete details of sense perception is eliminated and general features of objects are separated.

1. **Generalisation :**

The idea that the special features which have been separated through analysis will be found in each of the object of the class is called generalization .

3. **Naming :**

Lastly , for the expression of the concept we need naming the object. That is the creature which has two wings, two legs and one beak is a bird. Naming completes of concept.
THINKING:
Thinking, also known as 'cognition', refers to the ability to process information, hold attention, store and retrieve memories and select appropriate responses and actions. The ability to understand other people, and express oneself to others can also be categorised under thinking.
1. Critical Thinking
Critical thinking involves asking questions and probing the underlying validity and assumptions behind statements or ideas. Critical thinking is very concerned with investigating the origins of claims and how they come about, and whether they come from hearsay or misinformation.

2. Creative Thinking

Creative thinking is always engaged with coming up with something new: new ideas, new theories, new solutions. The impetus for this way of thinking therefore, is to use ideas and information as a springboard for entering the creative process, always pushing towards the innovative and the new.

3. Analytical Thinking

Analytical thinking is one of the most common ways of thinking. Analytical thinking is about breaking ideas and solutions incot component parts and creating methods for categorizing and examining those parts using evidence and logic.
The most well known examples of analytical thinking come from science and math.

4. Abstract Thinking

Abstract thinking is also useful in puzzle-solving, since abstract thinking has no problem dealing with figurative language and symbols. So on teams they make very good problem solvers who can easily see something from multiple perspectives and find the connections between different ideas.

5. Concrete Thinking

concrete thinking is also known as practical thinking. In contrast to abstract thinking, concrete thinking looks at ideas and problems very literally and pointedly. Concrete thinking doesn't get carried away with context, analysis, or brainstorming. Its goal is to find the simplest solution as quickly as possible.

6. Divergent/Lateral Thinking

Divergent thinking and convergent thinking are two types of thinking that are more concerned with how you find solutions and answers. With divergent thinking, the method is to find as many different solutions as possible in order to spark new ideas. Sometimes you even stray far away from the original problem in order to look for inspiration. This type of thinking is therefore often connected with creative and abstract thinking

7. Convergent/Vertical Thinking

convergent thinking, or vertical thinking is about finding one single path forward by combining ideas or eliminating them, through logic and analysis. Convergent thinking is very organized and focused on efficiency, but there is also some elegance and artfulness to it, since it does require combining and merging different ideas together.

TWO MORE TYPES OF THINKING: SEQUENTIAL & HOLISTIC

There are also two more types of thinking that are sometimes placed with the other types of thinking on this list. However, I chose to place them separately because I think they are a little bit different. For one, they are more about overall viewpoint and process, and so they might be better called "categories" instead of types, since they could include many of the types listed above.

8. Sequential Thinking (Linear Thinking)

Sequential thinking deals with problems step by step. So it encompasses many of the types on this list that are more logical—such as analytical thinking, convergent thinking, etc. But even more creative personalities may use sequential thinking when it comes to breaking larger processes up into smaller steps (e.g. brainstorm→outline→create→edit/review→final product).

9. Holistic Thinking

holistic thinking is about looking at the big picture and seeing how each component part fits into the larger whole. This is often attributed to management, or leaders. However, I would argue that all team members need at least some holistic thinking abilities in order to see how their actions fit in with and benefit the rest of the team.

PROBLEM – SOLVING

According to skinner (1968) , problem – solving is a process of overcoming difficulties that appear to interfere with the attainment of a goal. It is a procedure of making adjustment. Inspite of interferences.

APPROACH OF PROBLEM – SOLVING

1. Trial and error

In the trial and error Behaviour ,an organism is set for a certain goal. It explores the situation, find certain leads and tries them one after another , fails several times, and, finally, finds a good lead and reaches the goal.

2.Insight

The gestalt psychologists emphasise the importance of perception of total situation. The classical experiments of kohler on chimpanzees show that solution of problem is achieved all of a sudden through insight into the situation.

STEPS IN PROBLEM – SOLVING

1. Understanding of the problem
2. Collection of the relevant information
3. Formation of hypothesis
4. Verification of the hypothesis

Transfer

According to H.C Ellis Transfer of learning means that experience or performance an one task influences performance on some subsequent task.

THEORIES OF TRANSFER
THEORY OF MENTAL DISCIPLINE

1. **Faculty psychology** :

According to faculty psychology our mind is composed of a large number of faculties such as intelligence, memory, imagination,reasoning,thinking and soon.

" The faculties of our souls are improved and made useful to us just after the same manner as our bodies are".

2. **Formal discipline** :

The Basic premise of formal discipline was that vigorous exercise would enhance faculties . If the faculty of memory of a person could be strengthened by learning long poems, he would be able to memorise the dates of different incidents in history and difficult mathematical formulae .

The formal discipline theory emphasized that form of the matter should be difficult and vigorous execise of the different matter would increase mental powers.

3.Criticism:

Most of the educational thinkers of the present day do not subscribe to the theory of mental discipline or faculty theory at present mind is never thought to be composed of several faculties.

APPROACH OF TRANSFER

1. William james's experiment :

William james (1890) was the first psychologist who attacked the theory of mental discipline . He practiced learning 158 lines & 132 minutes from victor hugo's satyr.

2. E.L.Thorndike's experiment : E.L.thorndike (1923) conducted experiments on 8,000 students and the time over which it was spread was one year . one group studied latin and the other group studied physical education.

CHAPTER THIRTEEN

INFORMATION PROCESSING MEANING, PRINCIPLES; MODELS OF INFORMATION PROCESSING WAUGH AND NORMAN MODEL OF PRIMARY AND SECONDARY MEMORY

INTRODUCTION:

Cognition as a psychological area of study goes far beyond simply the taking in and retrieving information. Neisser (1967), one of the most influential researchers in cognition, defined it as the study of how people encode, structure, store, retrieve, use or otherwise learn knowledge. The information processing approach to human cognition remains very popular in the field of psychology.

Information processing is the change (processing) of information in any manner detectable by an observer. Within the field of cognitive psychology, information processing is an approach to the goal of understanding human thinking. It arose in the 1940s and 1950s. The essence of the approach is to see cognition as being essentially computational in nature, with mind being the software and the brain being the hardware.

One of the primary areas of cognition studied by researches is memory. By the 1960s research in memory had reached a high state of activity, and it was about this time that some formalised comprehensive theories of memory were beginning to be formulated. There are many hypotheses and suggestions as to how this integration occurs, and many new theories have built upon established beliefs in this area. Currently, there is widespread consensus on several aspects of information processing; however, there are many dissentions in reference to specifics on how the brain actually codes or manipulates information as it is stored in memory. This section considers a few of the more viable memory theories of that time.

PRINCIPLES OF THE INFORMATION PROCESSING:

There are few principles of the information processing system by Huitt (2000). Based on these principles various researchers do their research. These principles are as follows:

- The limited capacity of a mental system
- The requirement of the control mechanism
- Two-way flow of information
- Genetic preparation of the human organism

Explanation of above:

The limited capacity of a mental system: As per this principle our mind can process only limited information at a particular period. Our mind has its capacity.

For Example-We stored water in a bottle but when we take out the water from the bottle it depends on the size of a bottleneck. We can't take out the whole water in a single go, water comes at its speed at a time. Similarly, our brain process limited information at a time.

The requirement of control mechanism: According to this principle Human are not using his whole capacity or capability all the time. When any person learning a new skill he is leaming it with full concentration and doing it with higher capacity as compared to the one who is doing that task for so long. This principle is required to oversee the encoding, transformation, processing, storage, retrieval, and utilization of the information.

For Example, A person who knows how to chive a car is simultaneously doing lots of things at a time without even realizing like turning to steer, changing the gear, pressing the clutch, checking the rare view, and side-view matter but when a person is at a learning stage, he is doing all the things with more consciousness and with its 100% potential. As per the new leamer driving a car is not a piece of cake. It uses its whole brain with 100% potential at a time, it requires his whole attention on a single task

Two-way flow of information: In a two-way flow of information, we have two ways of processing the information. First is Bottom-Up Processing and second is Top-Down Processing. Bottom-Up Processing means we gather the information with the help of our senses. Our senses perceive the information and we store it in our mind and use it as per the requirement. Top-Down Processing means the information which is already stored in our memory like the way of our thinking style.

For Example- Few people always think about positivity whether the situation is good or it's bad and sortie find the negativity in good situations also. It all depends on our thinking style, how we perceive things.

Genetic preparation of human organism: As per this principle every human being is born with basic abilities and instincts whether that person is living in India or any country of the world inspective of the cultures also. Few things are common in everybody.

For Example, The initial sounds or the crying sound of new born babies are similar, whether they are born in India or anywhere in the world, they behave in a same manner. This principle shows that few genetic features are common in everybody during Initial days of birth, after leaming from the culture and environment everyone's thinking becomes different and they start behaving differently.

MODELS OF INFORMATION PROCESSING:

Waugh and Norman model of primary and secondary memory:

The Waugh and Norman model of memory (1965) is an influential framework in cognitive psychology that provides a dual-process explanation of how humans store and retrieve information. It categorizes memory into two distinct systems: primary memory (short-term) and secondary memory (long-term). This model emphasizes the processes of encoding, rehearsal, and retrieval, and highlights the factors influencing memory retention and loss.

Key Features of the Model

1. Primary Memory (Short-Term Memory)

Primary memory refers to the immediate and temporary holding area for information.

Characteristics:

Capacity: Limited to 7±2 items (Miller's Law).

Duration: Retains information for about 15–30 seconds unless rehearsed.

Function: Acts as a workspace for active processing, such as reasoning, problem-solving, and decision-making.

Accessibility: Information is readily accessible while it is being processed.

Examples:

- Remembering a phone number immediately after hearing it.
- Holding an address in mind while navigating to it.

2. Secondary Memory (Long-Term Memory)

Secondary memory refers to the storage of information over longer periods, from hours to a lifetime.

Characteristics:

Capacity: Vast and potentially unlimited.

Duration: Permanent storage of information.

Function: Houses knowledge, experiences, and skills not currently in use.

Accessibility: Retrieval depends on cues or effort.

Examples:

- Remembering your first day at school.
- Recalling facts for an exam.

The Transfer from Primary to Secondary Memory,

Waugh and Norman proposed that information moves from primary memory to secondary memory through processes like rehearsal and encoding. This transfer depends on several factors:

Attention: Focusing on the information improves encoding.

Rehearsal: Repeating the information increases the likelihood of retention in secondary memory.

Interference: Competing information can disrupt the transfer process.

Supporting Evidence:

1. Serial Position Effect:

Primacy Effect: Items at the beginning of a list are better remembered because they are encoded into secondary memory.

Recency Effect: Items at the end of a list are remembered due to their presence in primary memory.

2. Forgetting:

Forgetting in primary memory is attributed to interference, where new information replaces old, rather than simple decay over time.

Applications of the Model

1. Education:

Techniques like chunking, mnemonics, and spaced repetition leverage the principles of primary and secondary memory to improve learning.

2. Workplace Training:

Enhancing focus and rehearsal can improve information retention.

3. Clinical Psychology:

Understanding memory systems helps in diagnosing and treating conditions like amnesia and dementia.

Criticisms of the Model

Simplicity:

The model is considered too simplistic, as it does not account for sensory memory or the dynamic processes involved in encoding and retrieval.

Overshadowed by Later Models:

The Atkinson and Shiffrin model (1968) introduced sensory memory and a more comprehensive multi-store framework, which expanded upon Waugh and Norman's ideas.

The Waugh and Norman model of primary and secondary memory is a foundational theory that provides a clear distinction between short-term and long-term memory systems. While its simplicity has been critiqued, it remains a pivotal concept in understanding the mechanisms of memory storage, transfer, and retrieval. It laid the groundwork for further advancements in cognitive psychology and memory research.

ATKINSON AND SHIFFRIN'S STAGE MODEL OF MEMORY:

The Atkinson and Shiffrin stage model of memory (1968), also known as the multi-store model, is a foundational framework in cognitive psychology. It describes memory as a linear process consisting of three distinct stages: sensory memory, short-term memory (STM), and long-term memory (LTM). The model explains how information is encoded, stored, and retrieved over time.

Key Stages of the Model

1.Sensory Memory

Definition: Sensory memory is the initial stage of memory, where sensory information is briefly stored in its raw form.

Characteristics:

Duration: Very short, lasting about 0.25 to 2 seconds.

Capacity: Large, as it stores vast amounts of sensory input.

Function: Acts as a buffer, allowing information to be processed or discarded.

Types:

Iconic Memory: Visual sensory memory, lasting about 0.5 seconds.

Echoic Memory: Auditory sensory memory, lasting about 3–4 seconds.

Example: Seeing a lightning flash and briefly holding its image in your mind.

2. Short-Term Memory (STM)

Definition: Short-term memory temporarily holds and processes information for immediate use.

Characteristics:

Duration: About 15–30 seconds without rehearsal.

Capacity: Limited to 7±2 items (Miller's Law).

Function: Provides a workspace for active cognitive tasks such as problem-solving and decision-making.

Processes:

Rehearsal: Repetition of information to maintain it in STM or encode it into LTM.

Chunking: Grouping information into meaningful units to increase capacity.

Example: Remembering a phone number long enough to dial it.

3. Long-Term Memory (LTM)

Definition: Long-term memory is the stage where information is stored indefinitely for future retrieval.

Characteristics:

Duration: Potentially unlimited.

Capacity: Virtually infinite.

Function: Houses knowledge, experiences, and skills.

Types:

Declarative Memory (Explicit): Memories that can be consciously recalled, such as facts and events.

Episodic Memory: Personal experiences (e.g., your last vacation).

Semantic Memory: General knowledge (e.g., the capital of France).

Non-Declarative Memory (Implicit): Unconscious memories, such as skills and habits (e.g., riding a bike)

Processes in the Stage Model

1. Encoding:

The process of converting sensory input into a form that can be stored in memory.

Example: Listening to a lecture and taking notes to remember the content.

2. Storage:

Maintaining information over time.

Example: Memorizing historical dates for a test.

3. Retrieval:

Accessing stored information when needed.

Example: Recalling the answer to a question during an exam.

Strengths of the Model

1. Clear Structure:

Provides a simple and intuitive explanation of memory processes.

2. Empirical Support:

Evidence from studies like the serial position effect (primacy and recency effects) supports the model.

3. Practical Applications:

Useful in education, helping to design strategies for improving memory retention (e.g., chunking, spaced repetition).

Limitations of the Model

1. Oversimplification:

The model treats memory as linear and passive, ignoring interactions between the stages.

2. Lack of Focus on Active Processes:

It does not adequately explain the active role of attention and the dynamic nature of memory.

3. Neglect of Implicit Memory:

The model primarily focuses on explicit memory, overlooking implicit memory processes.

4. Later Theories:

Models like Craik and Lockhart's Levels of Processing Theory and Baddeley and Hitch's Working Memory Model addressed these limitations.

Applications of the Model

1. Education:

Encourages strategies such as repeated rehearsal and chunking to enhance memory.

2. Therapy:

Helps in understanding memory loss and developing interventions for memory disorders.

3. Artificial Intelligence:

Provides a basis for designing memory storage and retrieval systems in AI.

The Atkinson and Shiffrin stage model of memory provides a foundational framework for understanding how information is processed, stored, and retrieved. Despite its limitations, it has significantly influenced cognitive psychology and inspired further research on memory systems. It remains a valuable tool for teaching, learning, and understanding human memory.

LEVELS OF PROCESSING MODEL OF MEMORY (CRAIK AND LOCKHART, 1972)

The Levels of Processing Model of Memory, proposed by Craik and Lockhart (1972), challenges traditional stage-based models of memory (e.g., Atkinson and Shiffrin) by suggesting that memory is not a product of distinct stores but rather the result of depth of processing. According to this theory, the deeper and more meaningful the processing of information, the better it is encoded and retained in memory.

Key Concepts of the Levels of Processing Model

1. Depth of Processing

The model focuses on the quality of mental engagement rather than the quantity of time spent rehearsing. Processing occurs at different levels, from shallow to deep:

Shallow Processing: Involves superficial engagement with information.

Focuses on physical or perceptual features.

Example: Recognizing the font or color of a word.

Deep Processing:

Involves meaningful analysis and elaboration.

Focuses on semantic content (meaning)

Example: Thinking about how a concept relates to prior knowledge.

Focuses on semantic content (meaning).

Example: Thinking about how a concept relates to prior knowledge.

2. Types of Processing

Craik and Lockhart proposed three levels of processing:

1. Structural Processing (Shallow)

Focus: Physical features of the information (e.g., how a word looks).

Example: Identifying whether a word is written in uppercase or lowercase.

Result: Weak memory trace, leading to poor recall.

2. Phonemic Processing (Intermediate)

Focus: Sound properties of the information (e.g., how a word sounds).

Example: Thinking about whether two words rhyme.

Result: Moderate memory trace, leading to better recall than structural processing.

3. Semantic Processing (Deep)

Focus: Meaning and connections of the information.

Example: Relating a concept to your personal experiences or generating examples.

Result: Strong memory trace, leading to excellent recall.

Supporting Evidence

1. Craik and Tulving (1975) Experiment:

Participants were asked to process words at different levels (structural, phonemic, and semantic) and later recall them.

Result: Words processed semantically were remembered significantly better than those processed at shallow levels.

2. Elaboration and Encoding:

Studies show that creating associations or applying knowledge enhances retention, consistent with deep processing.

Applications of the Model

1. Education and Learning:

Encourages strategies such as elaboration, making connections, and applying concepts to real-life situations to improve memory.

Example: Using mind maps to link concepts.

2. Effective Note-Taking:

Highlighting meaningful content and summarizing it in your own words helps with deep encoding.

3. Exam Preparation:

Using practice questions that require critical thinking rather than rote memorization ensures deeper processing.

Strengths of the Model

1. Focus on Quality Over Quantity:

Emphasizes meaningful engagement with information rather than time spent rehearsing.

2. Practical Implications:

Provides actionable strategies for enhancing learning and memory retention.

3. Empirical Support:

Research consistently demonstrates better recall with semantic processing.

Limitations of the Model

1. Lack of Clear Definition for "Depth":

The concept of deep vs. shallow processing is somewhat subjective and difficult to quantify.

2. Overemphasis on Depth:

Neglects other factors influencing memory, such as individual differences, emotional significance, and context.

3. Ignores the Role of Memory Systems:

Does not consider the distinctions between short-term and long-term memory.

A CONNECTIONIST (PARALLEL DISTRIBUTED PROCESSING) MODEL OF MEMORY: RUMELHART AND MCCLELLAND

The **Connectionist Model of Memory**, also referred to as the **Parallel Distributed Processing (PDP) Model**, was developed by **David E. Rumelhart** and **James L. McClelland** in the 1980s. This model represents a significant departure from traditional, symbolic models of memory and cognition, emphasizing distributed representations and parallel processing. It is foundational to understanding modern neural networks and artificial intelligence.

Overview of the Connectionist (PDP) Model

The model posits that memory and cognitive processes arise from the interactions of numerous simple, interconnected units (analogous to neurons) operating in parallel. These interactions are governed by weighted connections, which encode information.

Key characteristics of the model:

1. **Distributed Representation:**

   - Information is not stored in a single location but is distributed across a network of nodes.
   - Each unit in the network represents only a small part of the overall information.

2. **Parallel Processing:**

   - Multiple processes occur simultaneously across the network.
   - Unlike serial processing models, which process one item at a time, the PDP model can handle complex computations faster and more flexibly.

3. **Learning through Adjustment:**

   - Learning occurs by adjusting the strength of connections (synaptic weights) between nodes based on experience.
   - The model uses algorithms such as **backpropagation** to fine-tune these weights.

4. **Nonlinear Activation:**

   - Each unit in the network has an activation level determined by a combination of inputs and connection weights.
   - These activation levels influence the activity of other connected units.

Components of the PDP Model

1. **Units (Nodes):**

   - Represent the smallest processing elements in the network.
   - Analogous to neurons in the brain.
   - Can take on varying activation values, often between 0 and 1.

2. **Connections:**

   - Represent the pathways linking units.
   - Each connection has a weight that determines the strength and direction of influence between units.

3. **Activation Functions:**

   - Determine how the input to a unit is transformed into its output (activation).
   - Common functions include linear, sigmoid, or threshold-based activation.

4. **Input and Output Layers:**

   - **Input layer:** Receives external stimuli or information.
   - **Output layer:** Produces the model's response or behavior.

- Hidden layers between these two allow for more complex transformations and representations.

5. **Weight Adjustment (Learning):**

   - The model adapts through experience by adjusting connection weights.
   - This is achieved using rules such as the **Hebbian learning rule** ("cells that fire together wire together") or more advanced algorithms like **backpropagation**.

Processes in the PDP Model
1. Encoding:

- Information is represented by patterns of activation across the network.
- Input patterns lead to specific activation states in the network.

2. Storage:

- Memory is stored in the connection weights rather than in isolated locations.
- Knowledge is embedded in the overall structure of the network.

3. Retrieval:

- When partial input is presented, the network can reconstruct the full pattern through a process called **pattern completion**.
- This enables the model to fill in gaps in incomplete or noisy data.

4. Learning:

- Connection weights are modified through repeated exposure to stimuli.
- Errors between the desired and actual outputs guide the adjustment of weights.

Applications of the PDP Model

1. **Modeling Cognitive Processes:**

   - The PDP model has been used to simulate various cognitive phenomena, including language acquisition, pattern recognition, problem-solving, and categorization.

2. **Memory Research:**

   - Explains how memories are formed, stored, and retrieved through distributed processes.
   - Accounts for phenomena like generalization (applying learned knowledge to new situations) and interference (difficulty in retrieving specific memories due to overlapping representations).

3. **Artificial Neural Networks (ANNs):**

   - The PDP model is the foundation of modern ANNs used in machine learning and AI.
   - Deep learning systems are extensions of the PDP framework, incorporating multiple hidden layers and advanced learning techniques.

4. **Addressing Cognitive Disorders:**

   - The model has been used to study how disruptions in network connectivity or weight adjustment might lead to cognitive deficits, such as those seen in amnesia or dyslexia.

Strengths of the PDP Model

1. **Biological Plausibility:**

   - Mimics the parallel and distributed nature of information processing in the brain.
   - Reflects the neural architecture and mechanisms of learning.

2. **Robustness:**

   - The distributed representation allows the model to function effectively even when some units are damaged (graceful degradation).

3. **Flexibility:**

   - Adapts to new information through weight adjustments, enabling learning and generalization.

4. **Handling Incomplete/Noisy Data:**

   - Can reconstruct patterns from partial or degraded inputs, similar to how humans recognize incomplete visual or auditory stimuli.

Criticisms of the PDP Model

1. **Lack of Symbolic Representation:**

   - Critics argue that the model struggles to explain abstract reasoning or rule-based behavior that relies on symbolic manipulation.

2. **Oversimplification:**

   - While biologically inspired, the model oversimplifies actual neural processes and structures.

3. **Interpretability:**

   - The distributed nature of representations makes it challenging to interpret how specific information is stored and processed.

4. **Learning Challenges:**

   - Algorithms like backpropagation require large amounts of data and computational resources, making them less efficient for certain types of learning.

The **Connectionist (PDP) Model** introduced by Rumelhart and McClelland represents a paradigm shift in understanding memory and cognition, emphasizing distributed representations, parallel processing, and adaptive learning. Its principles underpin modern neural network research and have contributed significantly to fields like artificial intelligence, cognitive psychology, and neuroscience. However, it is complemented by other approaches to account for symbolic reasoning and other cognitive phenomena that remain difficult to model with purely connectionist frameworks.

BLOOM'S TAXONOMY:

Bloom's Taxonomy is a framework designed to classify educational goals, learning objectives, and outcomes into different levels of cognitive complexity. Originally created by Benjamin Bloom and his colleagues in 1956, it has since been revised and widely used in education to design curricula, assessments, and instructional strategies.

The Original Bloom's Taxonomy (1956)

The original taxonomy is structured into six hierarchical levels, representing increasing cognitive complexity:

1. **Knowledge**: Recall of facts, terms, basic concepts, or answers.

   ◦ Example: Memorizing definitions or historical dates.
   ◦ Verbs: Define, list, name, identify, describe.

2. **Comprehension**: Understanding the meaning of information.

   ◦ Example: Explaining a concept in your own words.
   ◦ Verbs: Explain, summarize, interpret, paraphrase.

3. **Application**: Using knowledge in new situations.

   ◦ Example: Solving mathematical problems or applying a scientific principle to a real-world scenario.
   ◦ Verbs: Apply, demonstrate, use, calculate.

4. **Analysis**: Breaking information into components to understand its structure.

   ◦ Example: Identifying patterns, examining relationships, or recognizing assumptions.
   ◦ Verbs: Analyze, differentiate, compare, contrast.

5. **Synthesis**: Combining elements to create something new.

   ◦ Example: Writing an original essay or designing a product.
   ◦ Verbs: Create, design, formulate, assemble.

6. **Evaluation**: Making judgments based on criteria and standards.

   ◦ Example: Assessing the validity of an argument or deciding the best course of action.
   ◦ Verbs: Evaluate, justify, critique, argue.

Revised Bloom's Taxonomy (2001)

In 2001, a group of cognitive psychologists, led by Anderson and Krathwohl, revised Bloom's Taxonomy. The revision modernized the framework by:

1. **Renaming the levels**: Verbs replaced nouns to emphasize actions.

2. **Reordering the hierarchy**: Synthesis (now "Create") became the highest level.
3. **Adding a knowledge dimension**: It integrates factual, conceptual, procedural, and metacognitive knowledge.

The revised levels are:

1. **Remember**: Retrieving relevant knowledge from memory.

   - Example: Reciting facts, dates, or formulas.
   - Verbs: Recall, recognize, list, name.

2. **Understand**: Explaining ideas or concepts.

   - Example: Summarizing a lecture or interpreting a graph.
   - Verbs: Explain, summarize, classify, infer.

3. **Apply**: Using information in real-world scenarios.

   - Example: Implementing a formula or using a theory in practice.
   - Verbs: Implement, execute, use, solve.

4. **Analyze**: Breaking information into parts to explore relationships.

   - Example: Identifying trends in data or distinguishing between causes and effects.
   - Verbs: Differentiate, organize, attribute, examine.

5. **Evaluate**: Making judgments based on criteria and standards.

   - Example: Critiquing an argument or assessing a project's success.
   - Verbs: Check, critique, validate, defend.

6. **Create**: Producing something original or innovative.

   - Example: Writing a novel, designing an experiment, or inventing a solution.
   - Verbs: Design, construct, develop, formulate.

Knowledge Dimensions in the Revised Taxonomy

1. **Factual Knowledge**: Basic elements, such as terminology or specific details.
2. **Conceptual Knowledge**: Interrelationships among concepts, such as theories or models.
3. **Procedural Knowledge**: Processes and methods of doing something.
4. **Metacognitive Knowledge**: Awareness of one's own learning and cognitive processes.

Applications in Education

Bloom's Taxonomy is widely used for:

1. **Curriculum Development**: Ensuring objectives span various levels of cognitive complexity.
2. **Instructional Design**: Creating lesson plans that move from basic recall to critical thinking and creativity.
3. **Assessment Design**: Crafting questions and assignments targeting specific cognitive levels.

By aligning teaching strategies with Bloom's Taxonomy, educators can foster deeper learning and help students develop higher-order thinking skills.

STERNBERG'S INFORMATION PROCESSING APPROACH:

Sternberg's Information Processing Approach, developed by psychologist Robert Sternberg, is a framework that explains human intelligence and cognitive processes through the lens of information processing. It emphasizes how individuals encode, store, retrieve, and apply information to solve problems and adapt to their environment. Sternberg's approach is best exemplified in his **Triarchic Theory of Intelligence**, which integrates analytical, creative, and practical aspects of cognition.

Core Principles of Sternberg's Information Processing Approach

1. **Cognitive Mechanisms:**

   - Sternberg emphasized the **mental processes** involved in problem-solving rather than focusing solely on the outcomes of intelligence tests.
   - He identified **three key components** of cognitive processing:

     1. **Encoding**: Recognizing and interpreting information.
     2. **Storage**: Retaining information for later use.
     3. **Retrieval**: Accessing stored information for application.

2. **Componential Subtheory** (Analytical Intelligence):

   - This part of Sternberg's theory is directly tied to information processing and involves three types of components:

     1. **Metacomponents**: High-level executive functions that plan, monitor, and evaluate problem-solving strategies. For example, deciding how to approach a complex math problem.
     2. **Performance Components**: Processes used to execute tasks, such as reading, calculating, or drawing conclusions.
     3. **Knowledge-Acquisition Components**: Processes that involve learning and storing new information, such as recognizing patterns or categorizing information.

3. **Focus on Practicality:**

   - Unlike traditional IQ tests that emphasize static, abstract problem-solving, Sternberg's approach emphasizes how individuals apply their knowledge in real-life situations, bridging the gap between theoretical intelligence and practical functionality.

THE TRIARCHIC THEORY OF INTELLIGENCE

The Triarchic Theory, a cornerstone of Sternberg's work, categorizes intelligence into three interconnected domains:

1. **Analytical Intelligence:**

   - Relates to academic problem-solving and logical reasoning.
   - Involves critical thinking, analyzing relationships, and evaluating arguments.
   - Example: Solving a mathematical equation or understanding complex theories.

2. **Creative Intelligence:**

   - Involves generating novel ideas, adapting to new situations, and thinking divergently.
   - Focuses on how people deal with unfamiliar problems and develop innovative solutions.
   - Example: Writing a unique story or devising a creative marketing strategy.

3. **Practical Intelligence:**

   - Centers on real-world problem-solving and the ability to adapt to one's environment.
   - Known as "street smarts," it involves using past experiences and contextual knowledge to achieve goals.
   - Example: Negotiating a raise or navigating a social situation effectively.

Information Processing Model in Sternberg's Theory

Sternberg's approach aligns closely with the broader **Information Processing Theory** in cognitive psychology, which views the mind as analogous to a computer. The steps include:

1. **Input (Sensory Perception):**

   - Information is perceived through the senses, such as reading a word or hearing a sound.
   - Involves selective attention to relevant stimuli.

2. **Processing (Cognition):**

   - Information is analyzed, categorized, and interpreted using working memory.
   - Involves Sternberg's components like metacomponents and performance components.

3. **Output (Response):**

   - Decisions are made and actions are taken based on processed information.
   - Could involve answering a question, solving a problem, or performing an action.

4. **Feedback Loop:**

   - Results of the output are evaluated and may influence future information processing strategies.

Applications of Sternberg's Approach

1. **Education:**

   - Sternberg advocated for teaching strategies that integrate all three types of intelligence (analytical, creative, and practical).
   - Encourages diverse assessments beyond standardized tests to evaluate students' abilities.
   - Example: Designing a curriculum that includes problem-solving tasks, creative projects, and real-world applications.

2. **Problem-Solving:**

- Focuses on understanding how individuals process information to solve problems, which is critical for fields like engineering, programming, and management.
- Tailors problem-solving approaches to individual strengths.

3. **Intelligence Testing:**

- Sternberg argued that traditional IQ tests fail to capture the full range of human intelligence.
- His model influenced the development of alternative assessments that measure practical and creative skills.

4. **Career Development:**

- Practical intelligence plays a vital role in workplace success, emphasizing adaptability and situational problem-solving.
- Helps in identifying career paths aligned with an individual's strengths in the triarchic model.

Strengths and Criticisms
Strengths:

- Holistic view of intelligence that goes beyond traditional IQ.
- Practical applications in education, career development, and real-world problem-solving.
- Emphasizes the dynamic nature of intelligence and its adaptability.

Criticisms:

- Difficulty in empirically testing the triarchic model.
- Overlap between the three types of intelligence, making them hard to distinguish in practice.
- Limited applicability to certain domains, like purely theoretical sciences.

CHAPTER FOURTEEN

ATTENTION, PERCEPTION– MEANING, TYPES THEORIES AND MODELS; CONSCIOUSNESS

ATTENTION

In psychology, **attention** refers to the mental process of focusing cognitive resources on certain information while ignoring other stimuli. It allows individuals to prioritize specific tasks, stimuli, or thoughts over others, enabling effective perception, memory, and decision-making. Attention is fundamental to many cognitive processes, such as learning, problem-solving, and language comprehension.

MEANING OF ATTENTION:

Attention involves the selective concentration on a specific object, event, or task, at the expense of other stimuli. It is a limited resource; a person can only focus on a certain amount of information at one time. The effectiveness of attention influences various aspects of cognitive performance, such as memory retention, problem-solving ability, and the execution of tasks.

DEFINITION OF ATTENTION GIVEN BY AUTHORS:

- According to Stout, attention is connation determining cognition.
- Ross defines attention is the process of getting an object or thought clearly before the mind.
- Kulpe says that attention as a state of consciousness.
- Bently says that attention is a name for attribute of clearness.

CONDITIONS THAT DRAWS MORE ATTENTION:

- **INTENSITY:** Loud noise and bright colors attract more attention.
- **SIZE:** Full moon attract more attention that a small star
- **NOVELTY:** Something new and innovate attracts more attention.
- **MOVEMENT:** Objects that move attracts more attention.
- **REPETITION:** Some stimulus the repeated emphasized draws more attention.
- **ISOLATION:** When some objects kept isolated form other objects attracts more attention.
- **CHANGE:** Some stimulus that is dynamics attracts attention.
- **CONTRAST:** Some factor that is distinct from the rest is attracted by the receiver.
- **DEFINITE FORM:** Something that lacks a form will note draw attention instead the one with definite form draws attention.

TYPES OF ATTENTION

1. **SELECTIVE ATTENTION:**

- This is the ability to focus on a specific stimulus or task while ignoring other irrelevant or distracting stimuli.
- **Example**: Focusing on a conversation in a noisy room, filtering out background sounds.

2. **SUSTAINED ATTENTION** (also known as **Vigilance**):

- The ability to maintain attention and concentration over a prolonged period of time.
- **Example**: Staying focused on a task like reading or watching a lecture for an extended duration without losing concentration.

3. **DIVIDED ATTENTION**:

- This refers to the ability to attend to multiple tasks or stimuli simultaneously.
- **Example**: Driving while having a conversation or cooking while listening to music.

4. **ALTERNATING ATTENTION**:

- The ability to shift attention between tasks or stimuli that require different cognitive processes.
- **Example**: Switching between studying and answering phone calls.

5. **EXECUTIVE ATTENTION**:

- This involves the ability to control and manage cognitive processes, such as decision-making, problem-solving, and error correction. It also includes inhibiting impulses and distractions.
- **Example**: Deciding which task to focus on first in a multitasking situation, or controlling one's reaction to distractions while working.

KINDS OF ATTENTION ACCORDING TO ROSS (1951)
ATTENTION
Volitional Attention Non-Volitional Attention
Implicit Explicit Enforced Spontaneous
VOLITIONAL ATTENTION (VOLUNTARY):

- It involves a conscious effort of will or volition.
- It can involve mental strain and effort, and can be directed at various things.
- **IMPLICITLY VOLITIONAL:** When a single effort is required, attention is called implicitly volitional. For example, when a teacher warns a student that coming late to class leads to punishments. The situation leads the student's will power to come to class on time.
- **EXPLICITLY VOLITIONAL:** When more than one effort of will is required attention is said to be explicitly volitional. For example, during preparatory days of an examination, one has to struggle hard for keeping oneself attentive.

NON-VOLITIONAL ATTENTION (Involuntary attention)

- It is spontaneous and does not involve an effort of volition.
- It is not a matter of choice and does not involve any role of will.
- It can be aroused by instincts or produced spontaneously by sentiments.
- **ENFORCED ATTENTION:** The attentions that are aroused by our instincts are enforced attention. For example: Mother' attention towards a crying child.

- **SPONTANEOUS ATTENTION:** It is aroused by our sentiments. We pay spontaneous attention to the objects around which our sentiments have already been formed. For example: when we attend to a patriotic song, it becomes spontaneous non-volitional attention

THEORIES AND MODELS OF ATTENTION
1. FILTER THEORY (BROADBENT, 1958)

- This theory suggests that attention acts as a filter, selecting which information gets processed based on its physical characteristics (such as loudness or pitch) before higher cognitive processing occurs.
- Information that does not meet the criteria for attention is filtered out at an early stage.

Are you paying attention? – The Emotional Learner

Example: In a noisy room, you may only focus on the conversation in front of you and ignore other background noise.

2. ATTENUATION THEORY (TREISMAN, 1964)

- Treisman expanded on Broadbent's theory by proposing that attention does not act as an all-or-nothing filter, but rather as an attenuator.
- Unattended information is weakened (not completely blocked) and may still be processed to some extent. The theory suggests that when attention is directed to a particular stimulus, other stimuli are still processed at a lower level.

Are you paying attention? – The Emotional Learner

Example: You might hear your name in a loud conversation even when you are focusing on another conversation.
3. COGNITIVE RESOURCE THEORY (KAHNEMAN, 1973)

- According to this theory, attention is a limited resource. The brain has a finite amount of cognitive resources available at any given time, and how we allocate these resources determines how effectively we can perform different tasks.

- Tasks that require more cognitive effort use more resources, and if multiple tasks demand resources beyond the available capacity, performance on one or more tasks may be impaired.

Lab 2: Attention: A Limited Resource – Laboratory in Cognition
Student Manual

Example: You might struggle to drive while also trying to read a map, because both tasks demand significant attention.

4. SPOTLIGHT THEORY (ERIKSON & St. JAMES, 1986)

- The "spotlight" model compares attention to a spotlight that can be focused on different parts of the visual field. The spotlight can be moved or shifted across a scene, and it enhances perception of the selected area while leaving other parts of the field less processed.
- Attention is not static; it is dynamic and can be directed toward different stimuli or areas in the environment.

It is more useful for teachers to see
attention as an effect not a cause |
Research Communities by Springer
Nature

Example: When searching for a friend in a crowd, your attention shifts as your "spotlight" moves across the crowd.

5. LATE SELECTION THEORY (DEUTSCH & DEUTSCH, 1963)

- In contrast to Broadbent's early-selection model, the late-selection theory suggests that all incoming information is processed to a certain degree, and the selection happens later in the process, after meaning and interpretation have occurred.
- Even information that is not attended to is analyzed for meaning, but only the most relevant information is selected for further processing.

17.9 Late Selection Theory of Attention

Example: You may not initially notice the background noise in a room, but if someone mentions a topic you are interested in, your attention shifts toward it even if you didn't consciously attend to it before.

6. FEATURE INTEGRATION THEORY (TREISMAN&GLADE, 1980)

- This theory explains how we combine different features of an object (such as color, shape, and size) into a unified perception. The theory posits that attention is required to bind these features together to form a complete representation of an object.
- Attention serves as glue that holds together the different features of an object, and without attention, objects are perceived as disconnected features.

Feature Integration Theory In Powerpoint And Google Slides Cpb

Example: When you look at a red car, you notice its color, shape, and size, but attention is required to integrate these features into the perception of a single object (the car).

7. RESOURCE ALLOCATION THEORY (PASHLER, 1994)

- Attention is viewed as a limited-capacity resource, and how individuals allocate these resources affects their performance on various tasks.
- The theory emphasizes that individuals have finite cognitive resources, and multitasking or performing multiple tasks at once can lead to decreased performance due to the sharing of these resources.

Example: Trying to text while driving might reduce your ability to focus on the road and lead to errors in judgment.

8. MULTIPLE RESOURCE THEORY (WICKENS, 1984)

- This theory suggests that attention is not a single, undifferentiated resource but consists of multiple pools of resources; each specialized for different types of tasks (e.g., visual processing, auditory processing, etc.).

- When tasks require the same type of resource (e.g., two visual tasks), performance will suffer more than when they require different types of resources.

Cognition: Memory, Attention,
and Learning | SpringerLink

Example: Listening to a podcast while driving is easier than trying to talk on the phone while driving because the two tasks draw on different cognitive resources.

9. INATTENTIONAL BLINDNESS THEORY (SIMONS & CHABRIS, 1999)

- This theory suggests that when we focus on one task, we often fail to notice other stimuli in our environment, even if they are quite obvious.
- Our attention is limited, and when focused on one thing, we might miss other important visual or auditory information.

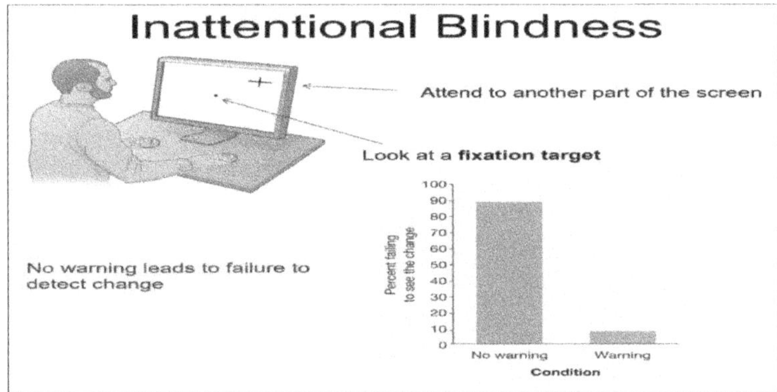

Example: In a well-known experiment, participants were asked to watch a video of people passing a basketball and were asked to count the passes. Many people failed to notice a person in a gorilla suit walking across the scene because they were focused on counting the passes.

10. DUAL-TASK INTERFERENCE THEORY

- This theory focuses on how performing two tasks simultaneously can lead to performance deficits, depending on the types of tasks involved.
- When two tasks require the same type of cognitive resource (e.g., both involve visual processing), performance on one or both tasks is impaired due to interference.

Example: Trying to watch a movie and read a book at the same time often leads to difficulty understanding either task because both require cognitive processing resources.

PERCEPTION

In psychology, **perception** refers to the process by which individuals organize and interpret sensory information from their environment to make sense of it. It is how we interpret and understand the world around us based on the sensory input we receive (e.g., visual, auditory, tactile, etc.).

MEANING OF PERCEPTION

Perception involves not just the raw data we receive from our senses, but also how we interpret it based on past experiences, beliefs, expectations, and other cognitive processes. It is a complex process that allows individuals to recognize objects, people, and events, interpret meaning, and respond accordingly. It is influenced by various factors, including biological, psychological, and social influences.

DEFINITION OF PERCEPTION BY AUTHORS:

- Perception is the process by which impressions, opinions, feelings about an object are formed by means of a sensory operation. **(Kuppusamy)**
- Perception is theinterpretation of sensory information, as a constructing creative process which endows sensory experience with meaning. **(Kumble, Germerz and Zinger, 1985)**
- Perception is the process of becoming aware of situations and adding meaningful associations to sensations. **(B.H. Gilmer)**

STAGES OF PERCEPTION:

1. **SENSATION:** Meaningful awareness of an object
2. **ATTENTION:** It is perceptual readiness.
3. **UNDERSTANDING:** Getting the meaning of the object.
4. **RELATING TO PAST EXPERIENCE:** Relating an object at present to the past experience.
5. **PERCEPTION:** Finally Perceives

DETERMINANTS OF PERCEPTION

1. **INTENSITY AND CONTRASTS:** Intensity of the stimulus is the important factor when it comes to perceiving a stimulus. Contrast of the object demand and get our attention.
2. **CHANGE AND MOVEMENT:** Things in movement and objects in motion are perceived quickly.
3. **NUMBER AND ARRANGEMENTS:** The objects one arranged orderly rather than randomly arranged are perceived easily.
4. **STRUCTURES AND PATTERNS:** The objects with orderly arrangement and definite forms are quick to be perceived.

TYPES OF PERCEPTION

1. **VISUAL PERCEPTION:** This refers to the ability to interpret and make sense of visual stimuli, such as light, color, shape, size, and depth. Visual perception helps us recognize objects, judge distances, and perceive motion. Examples include depth perception and facial recognition.
2. **AUDITORY PERCEPTION:** This involves the interpretation of sounds. Auditory perception enables individuals to recognize speech, music, environmental sounds, and other auditory stimuli. This type of perception is critical for communication and environmental awareness.
3. **TACTILE PERCEPTION (TOUCH PERCEPTION):** Tactile perception is the ability to interpret sensations from the sense of touch. This includes recognizing textures, shapes, temperatures, and pressure. It allows us to interact physically with the environment and recognize objects through touch.
4. **OLFACTORY PERCEPTION (SMELL PERCEPTION):** This type of perception deals with the ability to interpret smells. Smell perception is essential for detecting hazards (e.g., smoke), recognizing food, and influencing emotions and memories.
5. **GUSTATORY PERCEPTION (TASTE PERCEPTION):** Gustatory perception is the ability to interpret tastes, such as sweet, sour, salty, bitter, and umami. This sense plays an important role in eating behavior and overall survival (e.g., avoiding spoiled or harmful foods).
6. **PROPRIOCEPTION (KINESTHETIC PERCEPTION):** Proprioception refers to the ability to sense the position and movement of our body parts in space. It helps us coordinate physical activities and maintain balance without necessarily relying on visual cues.

7. **SOCIAL PERCEPTION (SOCIAL COGNITION):** This type of perception refers to how we interpret and understand other people's behaviors, emotions, and intentions. It involves the ability to read social cues, such as facial expressions, body language, and tone of voice.

8. **MULTIMODAL PERCEPTION:** This is the integration of information from multiple sensory modalities (e.g., sight, sound, and touch) to form a cohesive understanding of the environment. For example, watching a person speak while hearing their voice and seeing their lips move creates a unified perception of their speech.

FACTORS INFLUENCING PERCEPTION:

- **PAST EXPERIENCE:** Previous encounters or knowledge can affect how we interpret new sensory information.
- **CULTURAL INFLUENCES:** Cultural background can shape how people perceive certain objects, events, or behaviors.
- **CONTEXT:** The context in which stimuli occur can influence how they are perceived. For example, a person may perceive an ambiguous gesture differently depending on the social situation.
- **EXPECTATIONS:** What we expect to perceive can alter how we interpret sensory information (e.g., expecting a certain outcome).
- **ATTENTION:** The focus of our attention can determine what aspects of our environment we perceive most clearly.

In summary, perception in psychology is the process of interpreting sensory input, and it can be categorized into several types based on the sensory modality being used, each contributing to how we experience and understand the world around us.

THEORIES AND MODELS OF PERCEPTION

Perception refers to the process by which we interpret and make sense of sensory information from the environment. Various theories have been developed to explain how we perceive the world around us. These theories can be grouped into several categories, each offering different perspectives on the mechanics of perception. Below are the main theories of perception:

1. THE BOTTOM-UP THEORY

Bottom-up processing is a data-driven approach in which perception starts with the sensory input. The brain interprets raw sensory data from the environment, and this information is built up to form a perception.

- Perception begins with sensory stimuli.
- There is no prior knowledge or expectations influencing the process.
- The process is like assembling a puzzle piece by piece.

Example: When you look at a new object, your brain first processes the basic elements such as color, shape, and size before recognizing it as something meaningful.

2. THE TOP-DOWN THEORY

Top-down processing is a concept in which perception is influenced by prior knowledge, expectations, or experiences. Instead of starting with raw sensory data, the brain applies pre-existing knowledge or hypotheses to interpret incoming information.

- Perception is guided by higher cognitive processes (such as memory, experience, and expectations).
- Sensory data is interpreted through the lens of existing knowledge.

Example: When you read a sentence, you don't process each letter and word individually. Instead, your brain uses context and experience to understand the meaning quickly.

3. GESTALT THEORY OF PERCEPTION

Gestalt psychology emphasizes the idea that the whole is greater than the sum of its parts. According to this theory, our perception of objects is not just based on the individual sensory elements but on how these elements are grouped and organized into unified wholes.

- The brain tends to organize stimuli into patterns or wholes.
- Principles like proximity, similarity, closure, and continuity help explain how we perceive visual patterns.

Example: If you see a group of dots arranged in the shape of a triangle, your brain will perceive the dots as a triangle, even though they are separate points.

4. DIRECT PERCEPTION THEORY (GIBSON'S ECOLOGICAL THEORY)

James J. Gibson's direct perception theory emphasizes the idea that perception is a direct process that doesn't rely heavily on cognitive processes like interpretation or inference. According to this view, our sensory systems are directly tuned to the environment, providing us with all the information we need for perception.

- We perceive the environment directly through our senses without needing to process or analyze the information.
- Information from the environment is "affordances," meaning it offers opportunities for action.

Example: If you are walking on a rocky path, you don't need to actively think about how to navigate around rocks. Your sensory systems immediately guide you based on the terrain.

5. CONSTRUCTIVIST THEORY

Constructivist theories propose that perception is an active, constructive process. According to this view, the brain actively constructs an understanding of the world by combining sensory information with prior knowledge and expectations.

- Perception involves integrating sensory data with previous knowledge and experiences.
- The brain uses past experiences and memories to interpret incoming sensory data.

Example: When you look at a face, your brain doesn't just register its individual features like eyes and nose. It constructs an image of a familiar person based on your experiences with faces.

6. INFORMATION PROCESSING THEORY

This theory compares the brain to a computer, processing information in a series of steps. Perception, in this view, is the result of encoding, storing, and retrieving sensory data.

- Information is processed in stages: encoding (sensory input), storage (memory), and retrieval (recognition).
- Perception is influenced by the capacity and limitations of the mind, similar to computer processing.

Example: You see a red apple, and your brain processes the color, shape, and texture. Once this data is stored, you can recognize it as an apple when you encounter it again.

7. THEORY OF PERCEPTUAL SET

A perceptual set is a mental predisposition to perceive things in a particular way based on experiences, expectations, emotions, and cultural influences. This theory explains how our perceptions can be biased by factors other than sensory input.

- Our expectations or prior experiences influence how we interpret sensory stimuli.
- Perception is not objective but shaped by context, culture, and personal experiences.

Example: If you're told that a certain object is a rare, expensive artifact, you may perceive it as more valuable, even if it is just a common object

1. MULTIMODAL THEORY

The multimodal theory of perception suggests that perception involves multiple senses working together to form a more complete understanding of the environment. This theory highlights how sensory modalities (vision, hearing, touch, etc.) influence each other in perception.

- Sensory systems don't work in isolation but interact with one another to provide a richer perceptual experience.
- Our understanding of the world is shaped by combining information from different sensory sources.

Example: When you listen to someone speaking while watching their lips move, your brain integrates the auditory and visual signals to better understand the speech.

CONSCIOUSNESS

MEANING OF CONSCIOUSNESS:

Consciousness refers to the state of being aware of and able to think about one's own existence, thoughts, surroundings, and experiences. It involves the ability to perceive and interpret the world and to be aware of one's own thoughts and feelings. Consciousness is a central aspect of human cognition and psychology, and it plays a critical role in how we interact with the world.

TYPES OF CONSCIOUSNESS

1. WAKING CONSCIOUSNESS:

- This is the state in which an individual is fully awake and aware of their environment and internal thoughts. It is characterized by active thinking, awareness, and engagement with external stimuli.
- In this state, individuals can think logically, reason, make decisions, and perform tasks with full awareness of their surroundings.

2. SLEEP CONSCIOUSNESS:

- During sleep, consciousness is altered. There are stages of sleep where consciousness is reduced or absent, such as during deep sleep or dreaming.
- Sleep consciousness is divided into:

  - **REM (Rapid Eye Movement) Sleep**: This is the stage where most dreaming occurs, and consciousness is fragmented but still present.
  - **Non-REM Sleep**: In this stage, the brain is less active, and consciousness is largely absent.

3. ALTERED STATES OF CONSCIOUSNESS (ASC):

- These are states where an individual's awareness or perception is different from the normal waking state. Altered states can be induced by various means such as meditation, hypnosis, drugs, or extreme physical or mental stress.
- **Examples** include:

- **Hypnosis**: A trance-like state of heightened focus and concentration.
- **Meditation**: A practice often used to calm the mind and achieve a heightened sense of awareness.
- **Psychoactive drug use**: Such as alcohol, marijuana, or hallucinogens, which alter perception and cognition.
- **Flow States**: A highly focused, immersive mental state where a person is fully engaged in an activity.

4. SUBCONSCIOUS AND UNCONSCIOUS:

- These are states where awareness and perception are less accessible or absent from conscious thought.
- The **subconscious** includes thoughts, memories, and desires that are not actively thought about but can influence behavior and decision-making.
- The **unconscious** refers to mental processes that are not directly accessible to conscious awareness, often linked with Freudian theory (e.g., repressed memories and desires).

5. MINIMAL CONSCIOUSNESS:

- This refers to a state where there is a minimal awareness of the self or environment, such as in cases of low brain activity or during certain forms of brain injuries.
- People in a minimally conscious state may show some signs of awareness, like eye movement or responding to stimuli, but they are not fully aware of their surroundings or able to think consciously.

6. SELF-CONSCIOUSNESS:

- This type of consciousness involves an awareness of oneself as an individual separate from others and the environment.
- It is the ability to reflect on one's own thoughts, feelings, and actions, and to be aware of how one is perceived by others.
- This is also associated with a sense of identity and self-awareness.

LEARNING – FOUNDATIONS, APPROACHES AND THEORIES; COGNITIVE APPROACHES OF LEARNING – MEANING, PRINCIPLES, THEORIES AND MODELS

LEARNING:

Learning is the relatively lasting change in behaviour that is the result of experience. It is the acquisition of knowledge, information and skills. Learning occupies a very important place in our life. Learning, therefore, provides a key or structure of one's personality and behaviour.

DEFINITION:

Training is the process by which behaviour (in the broad sense) is originated or changes through practice or training. **Kingslay and Garry (1957).**

Learning is an episode in which a motivated individual attempts to adopt his behaviour so as to succeed in a situation which he perceives as requiring action to attain a goal. **Pressy, Robinson and Horrocks (1967)**

The term learning covers modification in behaviour to meet environmental requirements. **Gardener Murphy (1968)**

FOUNDATIONS OF LEARNING:

Foundation of learning is the basic skill of literacy and numeracy along with transferrable skills like socio-emotional skills. The 7 foundations of learning are

i. Prior knowledge
v. Knowledge organisation
v. Motivation
v. Mastery
v. Goal directed practice and targeted feedback
v. Climate
v. Self-Directed learning

APPROACHES TO LEARNING:

The approaches to learning domain focuses on how children learn. There are many approaches to learning including learning theories, pedagogical approaches and skills and behaviours used to learn.

LEARNING THEORIES:

The three basic types of learning theory are **behaviourist, cognitive constructivist and social constructivist.**

PEDAGOGICAL APPROACHES:

v.   The Constructivist approach.
v.   The Collaborative approach.
v.   The Reflective approach.
v.   The Integrative approach.
v.   The Inquiry based approach.

SKILLS AND BEHAVIOR:
SOCIAL SKILLS:
Developing positive relationships and collaboration skills.
SELF MANAGEMENT SKILLS:
Managing time and tasks and developing mindfulness, perseverance and resilience.
EMOTIONAL, BEHAVIORAL AND COGNITIVE SELF-REGULATION:
Incorporating initiative, curiosity and creativity.
THEORIES OF LEARNING:

v.   Behaviourist learning theory.
v.   Cognitive learning theory.
v.   Constructivist learning theory.
v.   Social learning theory.
v.   Experiential learning theory.
v.   Humanism learning theory.
v.   Connectivism learning theory.
v.   Transformative learning theory.
v.   Operant conditioning.
v.   Classical conditioning.

MAJOR THEORIES OF LEARNING
BEHAVIOURIST LEARNING THEORY:
Behaviourism concentrates on the notion that students learn behaviours and information through external forces like positive and negative reinforcement rather than internal ones. Few behavioural strategies are:

v.   Drills.
v.   Guided practice.
v.   Regular reviews.

COGNITIVE THEORY:
While behaviourism concentrates solely on how people learn through external forces, cognitive theory focuses on how both internal and external forces can influence student's ability to learn. Cognitive learning strategies are :

v.   Discussions.
v.   Reflections.
v.   Visualization.

CONSTRUCTIVISM THEORY:
Constructivism learning theory states that learners create an understanding of new concepts based on prior knowledge. Few constructivist theory strategies are :

v. Research projects.
v. Field trips.
v. Experiments.

CONNECTIVISM THEORY:

This theory of learning relies on utilizing those digital networks to increase a student's learning mostly independently. Strategies for using connectivism theory includes:

v. Students centered activities.
v. Readily available technology.
v. Social networks.

HUMANISTIC THEORY:

Humanistic theory concentrates on the ideas that students benefit from education when teachers focus on ways to teach all aspects of a child by engaging their social skills, intellect, practical skills and feelings as part of education. Some other humanistic learning strategies includes:

v. Cooperative learning.
v. Choice boards.
v. Differentiated learning.

TRANSFORMATIVE LEARNING THEORY:

v. It focuses on the idea that learners can adjust their thinking based on new information.
v. This theory is a good approach for young adult and adult education.

EXPERIENTIAL LEARNING THEORY:

v. This theory focuses on learning by doing.
v. Using this theory,people are encouraged to learn through experiences that can help them retain information and recall facts.

SOCIAL LEARNING THEORIES:

v. This theory focuses on the concepts of children learning from observing others by acting on or not acting on what they see exhibited by their classmates .
v. The four elements of social learning theory are **attention,retention,reproduction and motivation.**

OPERANT CONDITIONING:

A type of associative learning that involves using reinforcement or punishment to strengthen or weaken a behavior.It focuses on voluntary behavior.

CLASSICAL CONDITIONING:

v. In classical conditioning,learning occurs by forming associations between natually occuring stimuli and a previously neutral stimulus .
v. The neutral stimulus must occur immediatelybefore the naturally occuring one.
v. Focuses on automatic,naturally occurring behaviors.

COGNITIVE APPROACHES OF LEARNING:

Cognitive learning is an active style of leaning that focuses on helping you learn how to maximize your brain's potential. It focuses on understanding information and concepts through mental activity such as thinking, remembering and using languages.

It makes it easier for you to connect new information with existing ideas hence deepening your memory and retention capacity.

The ability of the brain's mental processes to absorb and retain information through experience, senses, and thought is known as **cognition**.

MEANING:

A cognitive approach to learning focuses on understanding information and concepts by breaking down information, rebuilding information with logical connections between concepts using the brain more effectively and engaging fully in the learning process. By applying cognitive approach to learning students can

- v. Deepen their memory and retention capacity
- v. Make it easier to connect new information with existing ideas
- v. Improve their problem solving skills.

PRINCIPLES OF COGNITIVE APPROACH:

<u>Cognitivism</u> principles intend to optimize how adult learners can understand, think about, integrate and <u>process new information</u>. The new knowledge adds to the familiar knowledge in the memory of adult learners. The five principles of cognitive approach of learning are :

Learner Experiences: Experiences play a critical role in an individual's learning process. New learning is built upon the learner's prior experiences, making these experiences vital for understanding new information.

Cognition in Learning: Learners actively use cognition to make sense of their experiences. These mental processes are central to how learners process and internalise new information.

Knowledge Construction: Through cognition, learners construct knowledge by interpreting and integrating new information with what they already know. This construction of knowledge is an active, ongoing learning process.

Existing Knowledge: Learners build new knowledge on the foundation of their existing ideas. Prior knowledge shapes how new information is understood and assimilated, making it easier to learn related concepts.

Social Context: Learning is often more effective in a social setting that facilitates interaction, discussion, and collaboration. Social environments provide opportunities for learners to share and refine their understanding through communication and collective problem-solving.

THEORIES OF COGNITIVE APPROACH

THEORIES OF COGNITIVE DEVELOPMENT:

The first cognitive theory was presented by psychologist Jean Piaget in 1936. His theory are the four stages of cognitive development.

- v. **Sensorimotor stage** – Gaining experience through exploration.
- v. **Preoperational stage** – Creating knowledge through engagement.
- v. **Concrete operational stage** – Consolidating knowledge through elaboration.
- v. **Formal operational stage** – Using knowledge through application.

These stages describe how individuals progress from basic sensory experiences in infancy to complex abstract thinking in adolescence and adulthood. Piaget's cognitive learning theory also emphasises how internal and external factors, like thoughts, reasoning and social interaction, shape our understanding of the world.

COGNITIVE BEHAVIORAL THEORY:

Cognitive Behavioural Theory applies Albert Ellis's Cognitive Behavioural Therapy to a learning environment. It explains how our thoughts and beliefs about experiences influence our emotions and behaviours. The cognitive psychology theory, known as the ABC model, focuses on three central facets:

v. Activating events (experiences)
v. Beliefs (thought processes regarding activating events)
v. Consequences (our behaviour)

This model proposes that how and what we think about experiences has a greater influence on our behaviours than the experiences themselves. When applied to cognitive learning, this means that we perform tasks rationally by first logically understanding them.

SOCIAL COGNITIVE THEORY:

The Social Cognitive Theory of Learning was given by Albert Bandura in 1986, building on his earlier <u>Social Learning</u> Theory. Bandura suggests that students learn by observing the behaviours of others and adjusting their own actions based on the positive and negative reinforcement those behaviours receive.

According to his Social Cognitive Theory, learning depends on both social observation and cognitive processes during these observations.

For example, if a person notices that certain behaviours are rewarded, they are more likely to imitate them.

MODELS OF COGNITIVE APPROACHES:

MODELS OF COGNITIVE APPROACHES:

v. **Memory Models: Atkinson-Shiffrin, Baddeley & Hitch** emphasize how information is processed, stored, and retrieved.
v. **Developmental Models: Piaget, Vygotsky** focus on how cognition evolves through different stages or social interactions.
v. **Learning Models: Schema Theory, Cognitive Load Theory** concentrate on how learners process new information and manage mental resources.

ATKINSON-SHIFFRIN MODEL(MULTISTORE MODEL OF MEMORY):

This was proposed by Richard Atkinson and Richard Shiffrin in 1968, this model describes memory as a system of three stages: sensory memory, short-term memory (STM), and long-term memory (LTM).

v. **Sensory Memory:** Holds sensory information for a very short time (milliseconds to a few seconds).
v. **Short-Term Memory:** Temporarily holds information that we are currently thinking about or processing, with limited capacity
v. **Long-Term Memory:** Stores information for extended periods, with a theoretically unlimited capacity.

BADDELEY AND HITCH's WORKING MEMORY MODEL:

It is developed by Alan Baddeley and Graham Hitch in 1974, this model refines the concept of short-term memory by introducing the idea of *working memory*, which is a more dynamic system for manipulating and processing information.

v. **Central Executive:** The control system that directs attention and coordinates information from the two subsystems.

v. **Phonological Loop:** A system for processing verbal and auditory information.

v. **Visuospatial Sketchpad:** A system for processing visual and spatial information.

v. **Episodic Buffer:** Integrates information from the phonological loop, visuospatial sketchpad, and long-term memory into coherent episodes.

This model suggests that working memory is critical for tasks like problem-solving, comprehension, and learning, particularly when new information needs to be integrated with existing knowledge.

VYGOTSKY's SOCIOCULTURAL THEORY OF LEARNING:

Lev Vygotsky's theory emphasizes the role of social interaction and cultural tools in cognitive development. He argued that cognitive development is socially mediated and that learning is best achieved through collaborative activities.

Key Concepts:

v. **Zone of Proximal Development (ZPD):** The difference between what a learner can do independently and what they can achieve with guidance or collaboration.

v. **Scaffolding:** The support provided by a more knowledgeable other (teacher, peer) to help a learner accomplish a task within their ZPD.

Vygotsky's model stresses the importance of social interaction, language, and cultural tools (such as writing or mathematics) in learning. Teachers can scaffold learning to guide students through tasks just beyond their current abilities.

SCHEMA THEORY:

This was proposed by Frederic Bartlett (1932) and later expanded by others like Jean Piaget, schema theory posits that individuals organize knowledge into mental frameworks, or "schemas," that help them understand and interpret new information.

Key Concepts:

v. **Schemas:** Mental structures that represent categories of information and guide cognitive processing.

v. **Assimilation:** Incorporating new information into existing schemas.

v. **Accommodation:** Modifying existing schemas to incorporate new information.

IMPLICATIONS FOR LEARNING: Learning involves the process of fitting new experiences into existing schemas or adjusting schemas when new information doesn't fit. Teachers can help students by activating relevant schemas to facilitate learning.

COGNITIVE LOAD THEORY:

This was proposed by John Sweller in the 1980s, cognitive load theory is concerned with the limitations of working memory and how instructional designs can optimize learning by managing the cognitive load imposed on learners.

TYPES OF COGNITIVE LOAD:

v. **Intrinsic Load:** The inherent difficulty of the material being learned.

v. **Extraneous Load:** The cognitive load imposed by poorly designed instruction.

v. **Germane Load:** The cognitive load dedicated to processing and understanding the material.

Teachers should minimize extraneous load (e.g., avoid unnecessary distractions) and structure learning tasks in a way that supports the learner's cognitive capacity.

INFORMATION PROCESSING THEORY:

Overview: This theory compares the mind to a computer, with an emphasis on how information is encoded, processed, stored, and retrieved. It focuses on how learners actively construct mental representations and solve problems.

Key Concepts:

v. **Attention**: The ability to focus mental resources on relevant information.
v. **Encoding**: The process of converting sensory input into a form that can be stored in memory.
v. **Storage**: The retention of information over time.
v. **Retrieval**: The process of accessing stored information.

Implications for Learning: Information processing theory emphasizes the role of attention, memory, and problem-solving in learning. Effective instructional strategies can help learners encode information more efficiently and retrieve it when needed.

CONSTRUCTIVISM:

Constructivist learning theory, associated with Piaget and Vygotsky, posits that learners actively construct their own understanding through experience and reflection.

CHAPTER SIXTEEN

MEMORY FOUNDATION AND TYPES

Whatever we learn or experience should be somehow retained in the mind so that it can be used in future. This faculty of mind to store the past experiences and to review them when we need is known as memory.

RYBURN (1956) considers memory as a faculty to store experiences in our mind. He says "The power that we have to store our experiences and to bring them to the field of consciousness sometime after the experience have occurred is termed memory"

WATSON consider, memory as repetitive functioning of already acquired habits. But this view is too mechanical and cannot be accepted

A good memory should reflect an ideal revival. As STOUT says, "Ideal revival in which the objects of past experience are reinstated in the order and manner of their original occurrence as far as possible"

The word memory is taken sometimes in the sense of retention. But stout emphasises that it is better to confine memory to ideal revival

ROSS synthesised the different views of the psychologists thus: Memory is a complex process involving the establishment of disposition, their retention and the recalling of experiences that have left behind them.

According to Ross, "Memory cannot be viewed merely in terms of revival of past experiences

Memory is a complex process involving four factors:

1.Learning

2.Retention

3.Recall

4.Recognition

1.LEARNING- Learning is the process of forming association among ideals in the mind. We learn facts in their proper context more easily than isolated facts. Physiologically, learning consists in forming connections between neurons. Those materials which are learnt well are retained in our mind for long. Meaningful materials are not easily forgotten

2.RETENTION- Anything learnt is retained by the mind in the form of psychological or physiological dispositions.

3.RECALL- Recall is reproduction. It consists in the revival of past experiences. It is reinstatement of past experiences in the same order. What is well retained is easily recalled.

Three laws of association of ideas:

(a) The law of contiguity

(b) The law of similarity

(c) The law of contrast

4.RECOGNITION- Without recognition memory is not complete. Recognition means knowing the object again. It is the feeling of familiarity which accompanies the revival of past experiences.

TYPES OF MEMORY:

Memory has been classified by psychologists into various types according to its nature and the purpose it serves. We will discuss here some of the important types:

1.SHORT TERM AND LONG-TERM MEMORY: The material learned may be recalled immediately or after a very short time. The short-term memory of an individual can be determined from the experiment on the span of memory. It has been found that average memory span can be expressed

Unlike short-term memory, the material learned may be recalled after a lapse of time. This type of memory is called long term memory, with the help of long-term memory we store, retain and recall the most important incidents of our life at a second's notice, such as the date of marriage

2.ROTE MEMORY AND LOGICAL MEMORY:

Mechanical repetition of experience without intellectual comprehension is known as rote memory.

While logical memory depends upon understanding and assimilation. It does not depend upon mere repetition. When a student thoroughly understands a mathematical problem, he can easily retain and reproduce it on proper occasion

3.HABIT MEMORY AND PURE MEMORY:

According to Bergson, "there are two types of memory, habit memory and pure memory". Habit memory is related to the body, and pure memory to the mind. It is the result of verbal repetitions. It consists in mechanical habit formation. True memory depends on association and interest. Habit memory is rote memory, whereas true memory is logical memory

4.PHOTOGRAPHIC MEMORY:

Photographic memory stands for a kind of memory possessed by a person who can recall a scene in photographic detail. He can give a vivid description of a past incident as if he is seeing it before his eyes

5.PASSIVE MEMORY AND ACTIVE MEMORY:

When a past experience is recalled without an effort of the will, we call it passive memory.

For example, the sight of a delicious mango, spontaneously reminds us of its sweet taste. But when we remember a past incident by an effort of the will, our memory becomes active. We try to collect a forgotten incident by an effort of the will and succeed at last in recollecting it

CONDITIONS OF MEMORY:

Memorisation involves two important factors:

1) Retention

2) Recall

1)CONDITIONS OF RETENTION DEPENDS UPON:

A) PHYSIOLOGICAL CONDITION: A healthy condition of the body and the brain during the learning process is conducive to retention

B) PHYSICAL CONDITION: Intensity of stimulus, clearness and distinctness, recency of the stimulus, frequency of stimulus, duration of the stimulus, significant events, interesting episodes, amount of material, amount of learning

C) MENTAL CONDITION: Attention is a mental condition of retention. The greater attention is paid to the original experience, the greater is the power of retention. Ex: Appreciation

D)CONDITIONS OF RECALL: Recall or reproduction depends upon retention. What is well-retained is easily recalled

HOW DOES THE MEMORY CAPACITY OF A HUMAN BRAIN WORK?

- The human brain directs and accepts signals and signs all through the body. Various signals control the processes, and the brain understands each of them.
- Multiple messages are reserved within the brain. Others are communicated by the spine and the body's massive territories of nerves to length limits.
- The central nervous system depends on innumerable neurons or nerve cells. Each neuron comprises thousands of synapses, and the information a brain store is determined by the strength of networks between neurons, which is inclined by the size of synapses.
- The neurons are the formulation of three vital fragments: the soma or the spherical part comprising the nucleus, dendrites or long branching sections which attach to other cells, and an axon or long cellular segment.
- The human brain sends, receives, and eventually stores data and various information. The brain directs the information from the cortex, where the brain's nerve cells are stored, to the hippocampus to store memory.

- It wires memory, learning, direction-finding, and perception of space. It receives information from the cerebral cortex and may play a role in Alzheimer's disease.
- When we regain memories or incidents, the process works in an inverse pattern. The human brain has approximately 86 billion neurons and various neuroglia, which play a vital role as a support system for neurons.
- Connectivity between neurons is important, as every neuron can link up to around 10,000 others.

TIPS TO ENHANCE MEMORY

- Quit smoking and alcohol and limit intake of sugary and processed foods.
- Eat foods that help memory such as leafy green vegetables, nuts, berries, fish.
- Regular exercise boosts the growth of brain cells and the production of neurotransmitters enhancing memory.
- Adequate sleep. Aim for 7 to 8 hours each night.
- Keep the mind busy and challenged through lifelong learning and stimulation. Traveling, learning new languages, picking up a musical instrument, taking art or cooking classes, doing puzzles, playing board games- all promote the growth of new brain cells.
- Staying organized helps you remember information better, as does certain mental habits such as repeating a person's name as you are introduced, paraphrasing conversations and becoming a careful reader.
- Meditation, stress reduction and keeping up hood network of social relationships.

CHAPTER SEVENTEEN

BEHAVIOURAL APPROACHES OF LEARNING FOUNDATIONS AND THEORIES -CLASSICAL CONDITIONING, OPERANT CONDITIONING, APPLIED BEHAVIOUR ANALYSIS

Observable behaviours and how different types of training might alter them are the main focus of behavioural approaches to learning. These methods place a strong emphasis on how reinforcement, consequences, and outside stimuli shape human behaviour. The fundamental theories of behavioural learning—classical conditioning, operant conditioning, and applied behaviour analysis.

CLASSICAL CONDITIONING

Ivan Pavlov developed classical conditioning in the early 1900s. It is a learning process that involves making connections between a naturally occurring stimulus and an external stimulus. Pavlov's canine experiments showed how an unconditioned stimulus (food) combined with a neutral stimulus (like the ring of a bell) might produce a conditioned response (like salivation).

Elements of Classical Conditioning

1. Unconditioned Stimulus (UCS): A stimulus that spontaneously and naturally elicits a response (e.g., food causing salivation);

2. Unconditioned Response (UCR): An unlearned, natural reaction to the UCS (e.g., salivation to food);

3. Conditioned Stimulus (CS): A previously neutral stimulus that, upon association with the UCS, elicits a conditioned response (e.g., the bell);

4. Conditioned Response (CR): A learned reaction to the CS (e.g., salivation to the bell).

Classical Conditioning Processes:

- Acquisition: The first phase of learning that occurs when the CS and UCS are coupled.
- Extinction: When the CS is frequently delivered without the UCS, the CR becomes weaker.
- Spontaneous Recovery: The reemergence of an extinguished CR following a period of rest
- Generalization: Reacting to stimuli that are comparable to the CS in a similar way.
- Discrimination: Learning to differentiate the CS from other stimuli

Applications of Classical Conditioning

○ Education: To foster a supportive learning environment in the classroom, educators employ classical conditioning. For instance, children are more likely to participate in learning activities when praise is linked to effort.

◦ Therapy: By exposing patients to frightened stimuli progressively while preserving their level of relaxation, methods like systematic desensitization help treat phobias.

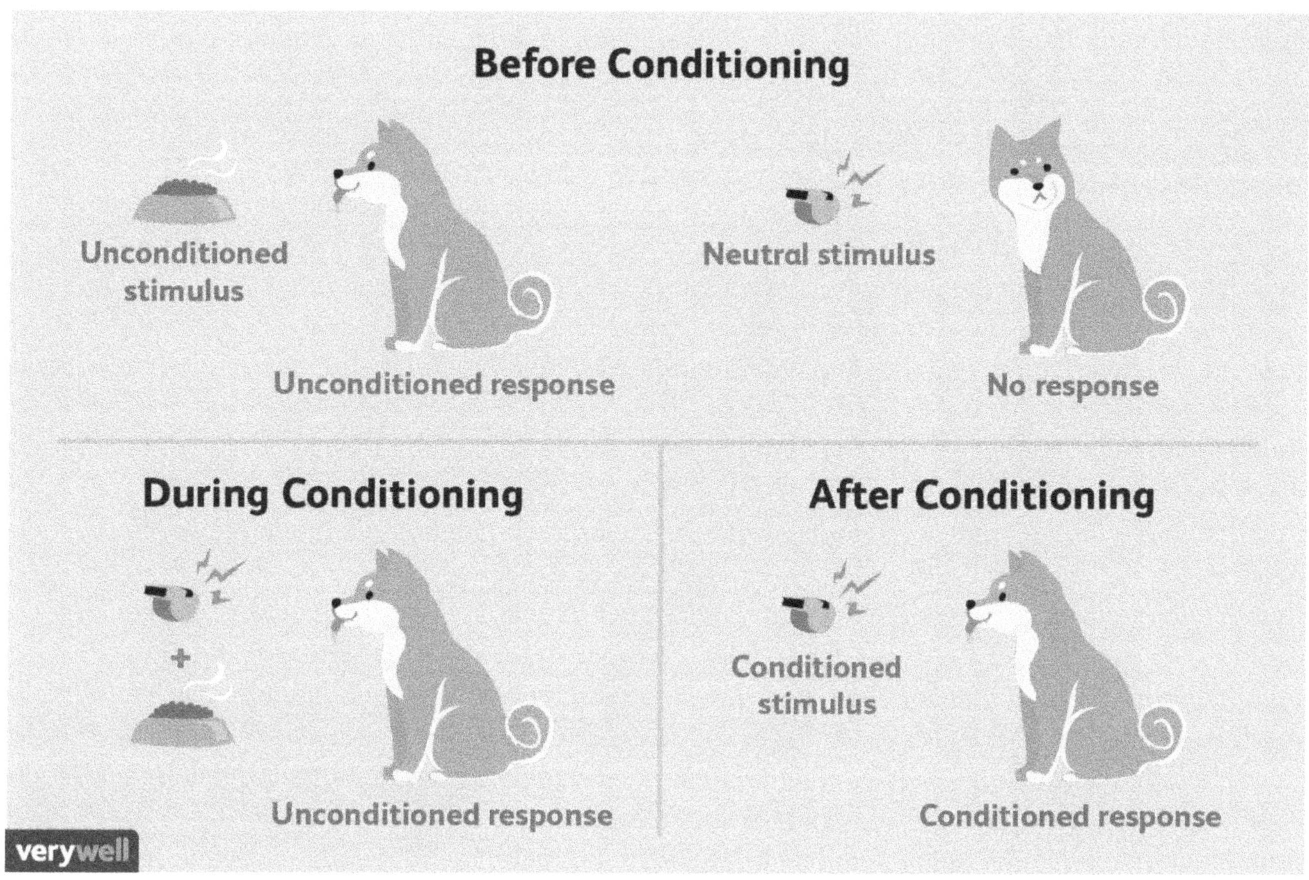

OPERANT CONDITIONING

B.F. Skinner created operant conditioning, which emphasizes the results of behaviour. It makes the argument that rewards and penalties have an impact on behaviour, making it more or less likely that an action would be repeated.

Elements of Operant Conditioning

1. Reinforcement: Makes behaviour stronger.

   Giving a youngster candy for cleaning their room is an example of positive reinforcement.
   Removing an unpleasant stimulus, such as turning off a loud alarm when a job is finished, is known as negative reinforcement.

1. Punishment: Weakens behaviour

   Including an adverse stimulus (such as reprimanding a youngster for disobedience) is known as positive punishment.
   Removing a pleasurable stimulus, such as a toy for disobeying regulations, is known as negative punishment.

Reinforcement Schedules

◦ Continuous Reinforcement: Giving praise each time a behaviour is displayed.

partial reinforcement: Intermittently rewarding behaviour that is more resilient to extinction

Types consist of:

- fixed-ratio schedule (reward every fifth response, for example).
- variable ratio schedules (such as slot machines).
- Fixed interval schedules (weekly payouts, for example).
- variable interval schedules (e.g., random pop quizzes).

Applications of Operant Conditioning

- Education: Students' participation and completion of assignments are two examples of desired behaviours that are encouraged through reinforcement. For example, positive behaviour is rewarded with stickers or points.
- Workplace: To boost productivity, employers offer incentives and bonuses.
- Parenting: Time-outs, praise, or reward systems help shape children's behaviour.
- Behaviour Modification Programs: Programs like token economies reward individuals for exhibiting target behaviours, often used in therapeutic settings.

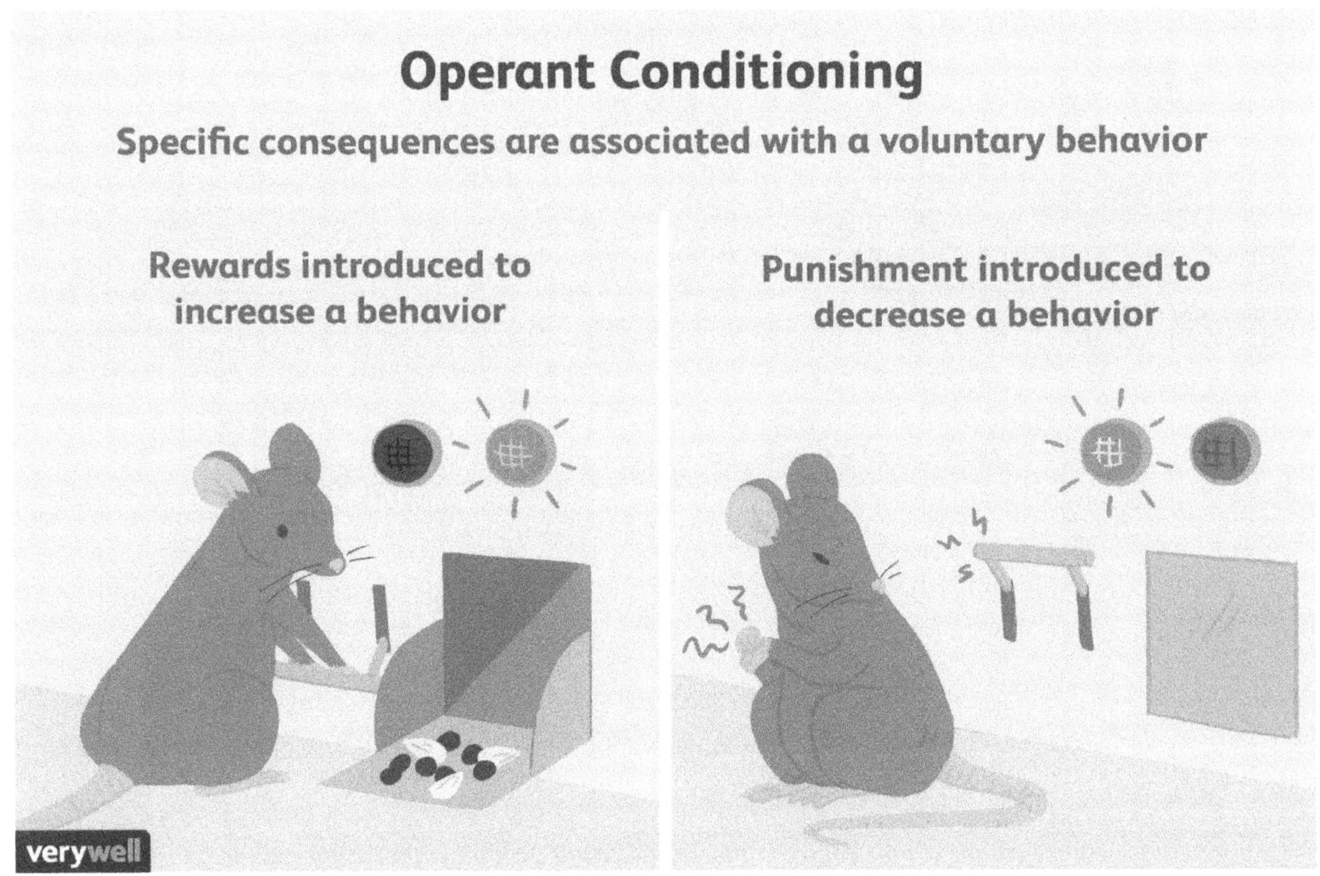

Applied Behaviour Analysis (ABA)

Based on the ideas of operant conditioning, Applied Behaviour Analysis (ABA) is a methodical approach to comprehending and changing behaviour. ABA uses data-driven techniques to assess and enhance socially significant behaviours.

Key ABA Principles:

1. Behaviour: Emphasizes observable and quantifiable actions;

2. Antecedents and Consequences: In order to understand the function of a behaviour, consider what happens before (antecedent) and after (consequence);

3. Reinforcement and Punishment: Use these strategies to increase or decrease particular behaviours; and

4. Data Collection: Constantly tracks progress using quantifiable data to modify interventions.

Uses of ABA

- Autism Spectrum Disorder (ASD): ABA is frequently used to teach social, communication, and life skills to people with ASD. Interventions are customized to meet the needs of each individual and break down difficult tasks into smaller, more manageable steps.
- Education: Teachers use ABA techniques to manage classroom behaviors and promote learning; for instance, a teacher may use a reward system to encourage participation.
- Healthcare: ABA strategies are used to treat behavioral challenges like aggression or self-harm.
- Organizational Behavior Management (OBM): ABA principles are used in businesses to enhance worker performance and workplace efficiency.

Strengths of ABA

- Highly effective for those with developmental disorders.
- Based on empirical evidence and objective data.
- Customizable for diverse contexts and individuals.

Critiques of ABA

- Critics argue that it may focus too heavily on compliance and neglect intrinsic motivation.

SOCIAL COGNITIVE AND CONSTRUCTIVIST APPROACHES TO LEARNING-FOUNDATIONS AND THEORIES-SOCIAL COGNITIVE THEORY

COGNITIVE LEARNING THEORY

i. Cognitive learning theory defines the role mental processes (also called cognition or inner thought processes) play in learning new skills, different concepts, and complex tasks.

ii. The cognitive approach to learning focuses on how attention, memory, and information processing contribute to knowledge acquisition. Cognitive learning theory explores how the thinking process itself can affect learning. That means it also explores different factors influencing our thinking, such as internal and external factors.

iii. Internal factors influencing thinking and learning include concentration, distraction, and emotions. External factors that can impact how we think include our physical surroundings and our society's value of the information itself.

COGNITIVE LEARNING THEORIES AND FRAMEWORKS

- **Theory of Cognitive Development**

The first cognitive theory was presented by psychologist **Jean Piaget** in 1936. Central to his theory are the four stages of cognitive development.

1. **Sensorimotor stage** – Gaining experience through exploration.
2. **Preoperational stage** – Creating knowledge through engagement.
3. **Concrete operational stage** – Consolidating knowledge through elaboration.
4. **Formal operational stage** – Using knowledge through application

These stages describe how individuals progress from basic sensory experiences in infancy to complex abstract thinking in adolescence and adulthood. Piaget's cognitive learning theory also emphasises how internal and external factors, like thoughts, reasoning and social interaction, shape our understanding of the world.

When exposed to new experiences in a social setting, people interpret them based on their existing knowledge and experience. This process, known as assimilation, allows individuals to expand their foundation of knowledge, facilitating growth and learning. However, the cognitive learning theory given by Piaget also emphasises the accommodation of new information. While existing knowledge provides a solid foundation, it must be adjusted to integrate new learnings and experiences effectively. Together, assimilation and accommodation are key to cognitive development, allowing individuals to continually adapt and refine their knowledge.

- **Cognitive Behavioural Theory**

Cognitive Behavioural Theory applies Albert Ellis's Cognitive Behavioural Therapy to a learning environment. It explains how our thoughts and beliefs about experiences influence our emotions and behaviours. The cognitive psychology theory, known as the ABC model, focuses on three central facets:

- Activating events (experiences)
- Beliefs (thought processes regarding activating events)
- Consequences (our behaviour)

This model proposes that how and what we think about experiences has a greater influence on our behaviours than the experiences themselves. When applied to cognitive learning, this means that we perform tasks rationally by first logically understanding them.

- **Social Cognitive Theory / Social learning theory**

The Social Cognitive Theory of Learning was given by **Albert Bandura** in 1986, building on his earlier Social Learning Theory. Bandura suggests that students learn by observing the behaviours of others and adjusting their own actions based on the positive and negative reinforcement those behaviours receive. According to his Social Cognitive Theory, learning depends on both social observation and cognitive processes during these observations.

Key factors

-Personal factors

-Environmental factors

-Behavioural factors

Example: When individuals see certain behaviors being rewarded, they are more likely to imitate thosebehaviors, demonstrating how social observation influences learning.

Bandura's Four Key Processes of Learning:

- **Attention**: The learner must be able to focus on the model's behaviour. Without attention, learning cannot take place.
- **Retention**: The learner must remember what was observed. Retention involves mental coding, which can be affected by memory and cognitive processes.
- **Reproduction**: The learner must have the ability to replicate the observed behaviour. This includes physical and cognitive skills necessary to perform the action.
- **Motivation**: Learners must be motivated to imitate the behaviour, often influenced by rewards, reinforcements, or the observed outcomes of the behaviour.

Bandura's Bobo doll experiment

The behaviors of children, as they imitate family members, friends, famous figures and even television characters. If a child perceives there is a meaningful reward for such behavior, they will perform it at some point.

Social learning theory can be used to encourage and teach desirable behaviors in the classroom through the use of positive reinforcement and rewards. For example, a student who is praised for raising their hand to speak will more than likely repeat that behavior.

Bandura's Bobo doll experiment is one of the most famous examples of observational learning. In the Bobo doll experiment, Bandura demonstrated that young children may imitate the aggressive actions of an adult model

COGNITIVE THEORY OF LEARNING CONCEPTS

1. **Attention** – Can be conscious (actively trying to pay attention) or unconscious (paying attention without realising it).
2. **Perception** – The process of grasping new concepts or forming an initial understanding of a particular subject.
3. **Memory** – The process of linking new information with our long-term memory, which consists of knowledge and experiences we've accumulated over time.
4. **Comprehension** – The construction of new knowledge based on our perception, our memory, and the connections between them.
5. **Problem Solving** – Applying new knowledge to address real-world scenarios.
6. **Decision Making** – Analysing the results of our actions and using knowledge and reasoning to make informed choices.
7. **Information Processing** – Seeing the mind as a processor that inputs, processes, stores and retrieves information.
8. **Schema** – The mental structures that help to organise and interpret information based on experiences.
9. **Constructivism** – The theory of using existing schemas to gain new knowledge.
10. **Metacognition** – The awareness and regulation of one's own learning processes, including planning, monitoring and evaluating cognitive strategies.
11. **Observational Learning (Modelling)**- Learning that occurs through observing the actions of others. People imitate behaviours observed in others, especially those who are seen as role models.
    Example: A child learns to tie their shoes by watching an older sibling do it.
12. **Self-Efficacy**- The belief in one's ability to succeed in specific situations or accomplish a task. High self-efficacy encourages greater effort and persistence, while low self-efficacy can lead to avoidance and lack of motivation.
    Example: A student who believes they can succeed in mathematics will be more motivated to persist in solving complex problems.
13. **Reciprocal Determinism**- The idea that a person's behaviour, personal factors (like cognitive skills, attitudes, and emotions), and environmental factors (such as social context or physical surroundings) all interact and influence each other.
    Example: A student's academic performance (behaviour) can be influenced by their belief in their abilities (personal factors) and the support they receive from their teachers (environmental factors).
14. **Vicarious Reinforcement**-Learning through observing the consequences (reinforcement or punishment) of someone else's behaviour. This concept emphasizes the importance of seeing others rewarded or punished as a way of influencing future actions.
    Example: A child might refrain from interrupting others after seeing another child being reprimanded for it.
15. **Outcome Expectations**-Beliefs about the likely consequences of an action. These expectations guide an individual's decisions about whether to engage in certain behaviours based on perceived rewards or punishments.
    Example: A student may choose to study more intensely for an exam, expecting that it will lead to a higher grade.

PRINCIPLES OF COGNITIVE LEARNING THEORY

The 5 principles behind cognitive theories of learning are:

1. **Learner Experiences:** Experiences play a critical role in an individual's learning process. New learning is built upon the learner's prior experiences, making these experiences vital for understanding new information.
2. **Cognition in Learning:** Learners actively use cognition to make sense of their experiences. These mental processes are central to how learners process and internalise new information.
3. **Knowledge Construction:** Through cognition, learners construct knowledge by interpreting and integrating new information with what they already know. This construction of knowledge is an active, ongoing learning process.
4. **Existing Knowledge:** Learners build new knowledge on the foundation of their existing ideas. Prior knowledge shapes how new information is understood and assimilated, making it easier to learn related concepts.
5. **Social Context:** Learning is often more effective in a social setting that facilitates interaction, discussion, and collaboration. Social environments provide opportunities for learners to share and refine their understanding

through communication and collective problem-solving.

BENEFITS OF IMPLEMENTING COGNITIVE THEORIES OF LEARNING
More Effective Training

A cognitive development in education enhances learning and reduces anxiety. Similarly, Frank L. Greitzer noted that applying cognitive principles makes training more engaging and effective, benefiting both eLearning and traditional classroom settings.

Flexible Implementation

Another benefit of cognitive learning theory is that it can be applied to a broad range of topics, employee training methods and contexts. It can easily be adapted to eLearning, in-person, or hands-on training environments. This versatility makes it a valuable approach for diverse educational and professional settings.

Self-Paced and Learner-Centric

Traditional learning methods often don't account for the active role that students play in processing, interpreting, and internalising information during training. Cognitive learning emphasises learner-centred instruction, recognising that students actively shape their learning experiences, leading to more effective self-paced and personalised learning outcomes.

Boosts Confidence

Cognitive learning empowers learners to understand their thought processes and improve their skills. This self-awareness and mastery of new concepts lead to greater confidence in their abilities, encouraging continued growth and success.

Enhances Comprehension and Knowledge Retention

Cognitive learning provides a deeper understanding of complex concepts by encouraging active learner engagement and processing of information. This allows for a more effective transfer of learning into the workplace and boosts long-term memory and retention capacity.

Improves Problem-Solving Skills

Cognitive learning emphasises critical thinking and reasoning, allowing learners to approach problems methodically. This enhances their ability to identify solutions and make informed decisions in real-world scenarios.

Boosts Creativity and Innovation

Encouraging learners to link new ideas with existing knowledge fosters creative thinking and innovation. This enables individuals to generate unique solutions and adapt to changing environments, driving organisational growth.

Promotes A Lifelong Learning Culture

A cognitive perspective of learning nurtures a mindset of lifelong learning by encouraging curiosity and self-reflection. This culture of improvement and continuous professional development leads to sustained personal and organisational growth.

COGNITIVE LEARNING EXAMPLES

Types of cognitive learning include explicit, implicit, non-associative, rote, meaningful, associative, observational and experiential. Below are some cognitive learning theory examples that illustrate how these different types are applied in practice

Explicit Learning

Explicit learning sees learners actively seeking information. It involves making a conscious effort to gain knowledge, through discovery or exploration for instance.

Example: A student actively studying a foreign language by memorising vocabulary lists and practising sentence structures.

Implicit Learning & Non-Associative Learning

Implicit learning is when the learners acquire knowledge without being consciously aware of it. It can also involve non-associative learning, in which students learn through repeated exposure without needing to act on it.

Example: A person learns the layout of their office building by walking through it daily, without actively trying to memorise the route.

Rote Learning

Rote learning focuses on memorisation through repetition, often without understanding the underlying meaning.

Example: Memorising multiplication tables or historical dates for a test.

Meaningful Learning & Associative Learning

Both meaningful and associative learning focus on creating connections between pieces of information. Associative learning links concepts by identifying similarities between them, while meaningful learning connects new information to existing knowledge by understanding the overall process.

Example: A science student learning about ecosystems by connecting the new information to their prior knowledge of the food chain (meaningful) or associating photosynthesis with plant growth (associative).

Observational Learning

In a similar way to non-associative learning, observational learning involves learning by watching others, without the need for direct reinforcement.

Example: A new employee learns how to use machinery by watching a more experienced worker operate it.

Experiential Learning

Experiential learning occurs through hands-on experience and self-reflection on that process. It involves performing actions and considering how they were conducted to gain deeper insights, improve future performance, and apply the learned skills to real-world situations.

Example: A medical student learning how to perform a procedure by practising it in a simulated environment and reflecting on their approach.

Discovery Learning

Discovery learning emphasises exploring and discovering information independently, encouraging learners to draw their own conclusions.

Example: A child learning how to solve a puzzle by trial and error without being given direct instructions.

Emotional Learning

Emotional learning focuses on understanding and managing emotions as part of the learning process.

Example: A student learns how to handle stress and anxiety in exam situations through mindfulness exercises.

Cooperative and Collaborative Learning

This applies Bandura's Social Cognitive Theory and involves learning through working together with others to achieve common goals by sharing knowledge and skills.

Example: A group of students working on a project, where each member contributes their own research to complete the task collaboratively.

APPLICATIONS OF SOCIAL COGNITIVE THEORY

- **In the Classroom:**
  Teachers can apply SCT by modelling desirable behaviours (such as academic skills or social interactions) for students. Encouraging **self-efficacy** through positive feedback and reinforcement can also motivate students to take on more challenging tasks.
- **In Media and Social Influences:**
  SCT explains how behaviours can be learned by watching media. For example, television programs, social media, and advertisements often influence viewers by showcasing behaviours and their consequences, teaching new behaviours or reinforcing existing ones.

CONSTRUCTIVIST APPROACH TO LEARNING

v. The **Constructivist Approach** to learning emphasizes that knowledge is actively built by the learner through their experiences. Rather than passively receiving information, learners **construct** their own understanding by engaging with the world around them. **Jean Piaget** and **Lev Vygotsky** are central figures in the development of constructivist theories.

v. The constructivist learning theory refers to the method of learning that allows learners to "construct" their knowledge and skills through meaningful interactions and empowers them through their own self-directed learning.

v. This educational theory leans in to the idea that each individual learner develops their own understanding through experience and reflection. Rather than memorizing facts from a teacher or external source, learners actively construct meaning for themselves.

v. At the core of constructivism is discovery—a crucial aspect of the learning process.

v. Learners take new information and internalize it, integrating it with their prior knowledge and experiences. The constructivist theory of learning emphasizes the importance of social interaction in the learning process, as learners absorb information in two ways:

Assimilation: Learners take in information from their environment and integrate it into what they already know.
Accommodation: Learners adjust their existing understanding to incorporate new knowledge or experiences.

These two methods of learning are used either interchangeably or simultaneously by all learners to better comprehend their environment and those in it.

CONSTRUCTIVIST LEARNING THEORIES

The constructivist approach to learning characterizes learners as active participants in the process who play a role in constructing their knowledge. Constructivist theories of learning were influenced by the work of psychologist Lev Vygotsky.

* **Vygotsky's sociocultural theory**

Vygotsky's sociocultural theory stressed the importance of collaboration and social interaction in the learning process.

Two important concepts of constructivist learning theories are the more knowledgeable other and the zone of proximal development:

* **More knowledgeable other**: Vygotsky described the more knowledgeable other as anyone with an understanding or ability level higher than the learner. This can often be a teacher or adult, but it can also refer to peers with more knowledge about a specific concept, task, or process.
* **Zone of proximal development**: Vygotsky described the zone of proximal development as the range of knowledge or ability that a person can display with the help of the more knowledgeable other, but that they are not yet capable of performing independently. Gradually expanding this zone is how people can learn and improve their skills over time.
* **Piaget's Stages of Cognitive Development**

Piaget proposed that children move through four stages of cognitive development: sensorimotor, preoperational, concrete operational, and formal operational. Each stage represents a different way of thinking and understanding the world. Piaget's theory emphasizes that children actively construct knowledge through their interactions with their environment.

Key Features

* **Developmental Stages:** Piaget proposed four sequential stages of cognitive development, each marked by distinct thinking patterns, progressing from infancy to adolescence.
* **Constructivist Approach to Learning**: Children actively build understanding by exploring their environment as "little scientists," rather than passively absorbing information.

- **Schemas**: Mental frameworks for organizing information, growing in number and complexity as children develop, enabling deeper world understanding.
- **Assimilation**: Integration of new information into existing schemas.
- **Accommodation**: Modifying existing schemas or creating new ones to fit new information.
- **Equilibration**: Process of balancing assimilation and accommodation to progress through cognitive stages, resolving conflicts and shifting to new thought patterns.

KEY CONCEPTS IN CONSTRUCTIVISM

1. **Schemas**
   Definition: Mental structures that help individuals organize and interpret information. Schemas are created based on prior knowledge and are modified as new information is encountered.
   Example: A child has a schema for what a dog looks like, and upon encountering a new breed of dog, they adjust their schema to include new characteristics.
2. **Cognitive Conflict (Disequilibrium)**
   Definition: A state of mental imbalance that occurs when new information challenges existing knowledge. This conflict motivates learners to resolve discrepancies by updating or modifying their schemas.
   Example: When a child sees a bird that looks different from any other bird they have seen, they experience disequilibrium and might adjust their schema of what a "bird" is.
3. **Scaffolding**
   Definition: Temporary support provided by a teacher or more capable peer to help learners achieve tasks they cannot perform independently. As learners' abilities improve, the support is gradually removed.
   Example: A teacher may help a student with a complex math problem by giving hints or breaking it down into smaller steps. Over time, the student gains the skills to complete similar problems independently.
4. **Zone of Proximal Development (ZPD)**
   Definition: Vygotsky's concept that refers to the range of tasks that a learner can perform with the help of a more knowledgeable person (teacher or peer). Learning is most effective when it takes place within this zone.
   Example: A child may struggle to complete a puzzle on their own but can do so with the guidance of a teacher or parent.

PRINCIPLES OF CONSTRUCTIVISM

The principles of constructivist learning theory revolve around facilitating meaningful learning. They are:-

1. Learners construct meaning - Learning is an active process where students build upon their existing knowledge to make sense of new information. Through constructivism, learners formulate and modify their opinions regularly.

2. Learning is inherently social-Social interaction plays an essential role in helping learners understand, evaluate, and internalize ideas and concepts. Learners are far more likely to encounter new information when they interact with others and their environment.

3. Knowledge is situated- Meaningful learning takes place when knowledge can be applied to real-world or relevant contexts. You don't just learn for the sake of learning—your education is meant to assist you.

4. Reflection plays a key role- Constructivism also stresses the importance of reflecting on one's learning process and understanding. Through reflection, learners can assess their current level of knowledge and identify areas where they need to improve or gain further insight.

5. Mistakes are part of the process- Making mistakes is an important aspect of learning, as it allows for opportunities for growth and development. Experimentation with different strategies often leads to successful outcomes later on down the line.

These aspects make up a learning theory that leaves learners with their own evolving paradigm with which to process future information.

TYPES OF CONSTRUCTIVISM

There are three main types of constructivism that have been identified, each having a significant (and slightly altered) impact on the way learners interact with their environment.

1. Social constructivism

This type of constructivism emphasizes the importance of social interaction in learning. It suggests that learners understand and internalize new concepts and ideas through collaboration, dialogue, and discourse with other people.

2. Cognitive constructivism

This type of constructivism focuses on the individual learner's ability to form meaning from their experiences. It views learning as an active process where knowledge is constructed by each individual through reflection, exploration, experimentation, problem-solving, and critical thinking.

Note: Constructivism vs. Cognitivism

Cognitive constructivism should not be confused with cognitivism—another important learning theory. While similar, the difference in cognitivism vs constructivism has to do with the theory's approach.

Cognitivism explains the internal, psychological processes that occur when information is absorbed. By contrast, constructivism explores the social and collaborative aspects of learning.

3. Radical constructivism

This type of constructivism stresses the idea that knowledge is subjective and personal. Knowledge cannot be shared or transferred between individuals because their unique perspective will cause them to interpret information differently.

APPLICATIONS OF CONSTRUCTIVISM

- **Active Learning**

  Teachers encourage students to engage in problem-solving, hands-on activities, and inquiry-based learning. This approach fosters deeper understanding and the ability to apply knowledge in various contexts.

- **Collaborative Learning**

  Group work and peer discussions allow learners to share perspectives, ask questions, and construct knowledge together. This social aspect of learning is central to the constructivist approach.

- **Problem-Based Learning (PBL)**

  PBL involves presenting students with real-world problems and guiding them to find solutions through research, collaboration, and critical thinking.

SELF-REGULATED LEARNING AND LEARNING STYLES: MEANING, TYPES, AND APPLICATIONS IN LEARNING

Learning styles and self-regulated learning are important ideas in education that influence how students learn, grow, and succeed academically. Learning styles concentrate on the various ways people process knowledge, whereas self-regulated learning highlights the learner's capacity to organize, track, and assess their learning process. With an emphasis on their importance in creating successful and individualized learning experiences, this essay examines the definition, varieties, and uses of self-regulated learning and learning styles. Self-Controlled Education Self-regulated learning (SRL) is the process by which students take charge of their education by establishing objectives, keeping track of their progress, and modifying their approach to reach desired results.

With its foundations in behaviour, motivation, and metacognition, SRL enables students to move from being passive information consumers to active learners. The idea is based on social-cognitive theories, namely Bandura's concept of self-efficacy, which highlights the importance of having faith in one's own chances of success.

Elements of Self-Regulated learning

1. Forethought Phase:

    Goal-setting: Establishing precise, quantifiable, and attainable goals.
    Strategic planning is the process of determining the tools and techniques required to achieve objectives.
    Using both internal and external motivators is known as self-motivation.

1. Performance Phase:

    Self-monitoring: Monitoring development and pinpointing areas in need of enhancement.
    Implementing strategies: Using methods to improve comprehension, such as elaboration, visualization, or summarization.

3. Phase of Self-Reflection:

    Self-evaluation: Comparing performance to predetermined objectives.
    Adaptive responses: Changing tactics or initiatives in reaction to input and outcomes
    Advantages Self-Regulated Learning

- Self-regulated learning promotes independence and self-reliance.
- Improves the ability to think critically and solve problems.
- Enhances the capacity for lifelong learning and academic success.

Self-Regulated Learning Applications

1. In the classroom: Teachers can promote SRL by incorporating self-assessment tools, teaching goal-setting strategies, and promoting reflective behaviours. Journals or progress trackers, for example, might assist students in keeping tabs on their education.

2. Online Learning Environments: Interactive tests, progress dashboards, and time management tools are examples of digital platforms that might include self-regulation capabilities. These resources enable students to monitor their progress and modify their study habits.

3. Workplace Training: Employees can define career goals, participate in ongoing learning, and adjust to shifting work settings thanks to self-regulated learning, which is crucial for professional development.

Learning styles

The preferred methods that people process, understand, and remember knowledge are referred to as learning styles. They represent the distinct cognitive, emotional, and contextual inclinations that shape an individual's preferred method of learning.

Learning Style Types

Although there are other models that classify learning styles, Neil Fleming's VARK model is the most well-known.

1.Visual learners:Diagrams, charts, films, and other visual aids are preferred by visual learners. Visual representations of information are the most effective way to learn.

2. Auditory Learners: Perform exceptionally well while learning through audiobooks, lectures, or discussions. Gain from group discussions and vocal explanations.

3. Text-based resources like books, handouts, and written instructions are preferred by reading and writing learners. Effective learning involves taking notes and summarising information.

4. Kinaesthetic Learners: Benefit from exrimentation, hands-on experiences, and physical engagement.

Applications of Learning Styles

1. Classroom Instruction: Teachers can create classes that include kinaesthetic, visual, auditory, and reading/writing exercises. For instance:

- Visual: Concepts are explained through films and infographics.
- Auditory: Including oral lectures and group discussions.
- Reading/Writing: Giving out essay assignments or offering thorough study materials.
- Kinaesthetic: Planning interactive initiatives or practical investigations. 2.

2. Personalised Learning: Teachers can create programs that are tailored to each student's abilities by having a thorough understanding of their unique learning preferences. For example, role-playing exercises may be effective for a kinaesthetic learner, whereas mind maps may be beneficial for a visual learner.

3. Online Education: To provide accessibility for all learning styles, e-learning systems can provide a variety of content types, such as text-based materials, interactive simulations, podcasts, and video courses.

Steps for Integration

1. Self-Assessment: Students evaluate their present self-regulation abilities and determine their preferred learning approaches.

2. Planning and Goal Setting: Students set objectives that suit their preferred methods of learning. A visual learner might, for instance, intend to draw diagrams to help explain difficult subjects.

3. Strategic Learning: Students use techniques based on their preferred methods of learning. For example, auditory learners may record lectures to listen to them later. Physical props or simulations may be used by kinaesthetic learners.

4. Monitoring and Reflection: While reflection aids in determining what is effective and what requires modification, regular self-monitoring guarantees that students stay on course.

5. Feedback and Adaptation: Teachers provide students feedback so they can improve their strategies and become more adaptable to various learning environments.

Challenges and Criticisms Self-Controlled learning:

Not every kid has the innate drive or aptitude for good self-control. needs constant assistance from teachers, especially for students who are younger or less experienced.

Styles of Learning: Critics contend that learning styles may oversimplify the complexity of learning processes and lack solid empirical support. The goal to create well-rounded students who can adjust to different approaches may be overlooked if there is an excessive focus on adjusting education to individual learning styles.

CHAPTER TWENTY

HUMAN JUDGEMENT- MEANING, NATURE, RANDOMNESS OF SITUATIONS, THEORIES &MODELS

Definitions of Human Judgement

i. **Daniel Kahneman:** Judgment is the process by which people make sense of information in the world around them.

ii. **Leon Festinger:** Judgment is the process of evaluating alternatives and choosing between them.

iii. **Amos Tversky:** Judgment is the process by which people assign values to events or objects in the world around them.

iv. **Herbert Simon:** Judgment is the process of reaching a decision or conclusion based on available information.

v. **Paul Slovic:** Judgment is the process of making sense of and interpreting information in a way that allows people to take action.

vi. **Edward Tolman:** Judgment is the process of using prior knowledge and experience to make predictions and decisions about the future.

vii. **Walter Mischel:** Judgment is the process of evaluating the potential consequences of different actions and selecting the best course of action based on those evaluations.

These definitions highlight the importance of judgment in a wide range of cognitive processes, including decision-making, problem-solving, and interpretation of information. They also suggest that human judgment is influenced by a variety of factors, such as prior knowledge and experience, personal values, and cognitive biases.

Nature of Human Judgement

Here are some perspectives on the nature of human judgment according to different authors:

i. **Daniel Kahneman:** Kahneman, a Nobel Prize-winning psychologist, argues that human judgment is inherently biased and flawed. He suggests that people rely on mental shortcuts, or heuristics, to make decisions quickly and efficiently, but these heuristics can lead to errors and biases.

ii. **Amos Tversky:** Tversky, a collaborator of Kahneman's, also emphasized the limitations of human judgment, but he also recognized the importance of systematic decision-making processes. He suggested that people can improve their judgment by learning to recognize and correct their biases and by using more rigorous decision-making methods.

iii. **Herbert Simon:** Simon, a Nobel Prize-winning economist and psychologist, emphasized the role of information-processing in human judgment. He argued that people use mental models, or simplified representations of the world, to make sense of complex information and that these models can be refined over time through experience.

iv. **Richard Nisbett:** Nisbett, a social psychologist, has argued that human judgment is strongly influenced by cultural and social factors. He suggests that people from different cultural backgrounds may have different ways of reasoning and making decisions, and that these differences should be taken into account in cross-cultural interactions.

v. **Gerd Gigerenzer:** Gigerenzer, a psychologist and decision theorist, has emphasized the importance of intuitive judgment in human decision-making. He suggests that people can develop and rely on simple, yet effective, decision rules, or heuristics, that are based on past experience and can help them make good decisions quickly and with minimal effort.

These perspectives suggest that human judgment is a complex and multifaceted process that is influenced by a wide range of cognitive, cultural, and social factors. While some authors emphasize the limitations of human judgment, others suggest that people can improve their judgment through experience, training, and the use of effective decision-making strategies.

Theories of Human Judgement

i. **Dual-ProcesTheory:**

- This theory was proposed by psychologist Keith Stanovich and Richard West, and further has been developed by Daniel Kahneman and Jonathan Evans.
- The "dual process theory" refers to a psychological model that proposes humans have two distinct cognitive systems for thinking: **"System 1" which is fast, intuitive, and automatic,** and **"System 2" which is slow, deliberate, and requires conscious effort;** essentially describing how we can make quick, often instinctive decisions alongside more thoughtful, analytical reasoning depending on the situation
- This theory suggests that there are two distinct systems of judgment in the brain - a fast, intuitive system that relies on heuristics and automatic processing, and a slower, more deliberative system that uses logic and controlled processing.

ii. **Information-Integration Theory:**

- This theory suggests that people combine information from multiple sources to form a judgment, and that the way in which they integrate this information depends on the context and the task at hand.
- This theory was proposed by Ward Edwards and has been further developed by other researchers such as James Shanteau and Gary Klein.

iii. **Signal Detection Theory:**

- This theory suggests that people make judgments based on their ability to detect signals (i.e. pieces of information) in a noisy or uncertain environment.
- This theory was proposed by psychophysicists and has been applied in fields such as medical diagnosis, air traffic control, and security screening.

iv. **Mental Model Theory:**

- This theory suggests that people use simplified mental models to understand and make judgments about complex systems and events. These mental models are often based on prior knowledge and experience, and can be refined over time through feedback and learning.
- This theory was proposed by cognitive psychologists Peter Johnson-Laird and Philip Johnson-Laird.

Social Judgment Theory:

- This theory suggests that people's judgments are influenced by the opinions and values of others in their social environment.
- This theory was proposed by psychologist Muzafer Sherif and has been further developed by other researchers such as Carolyn Sherif, Elliot Aronson, and Herbert Klman.

These theories highlight the complexity and diversity of human judgment, and suggest that there are many factors that influence how people form and make judgments in different contexts and situations.

Models of Human Judgement

- **Expected Utility Model:**

  ◦ This model suggests that people make decisions based on the expected value of each option, taking into account both the probability of the outcome and the value of the outcome.
  ◦ This model was proposed by John von Neumann and Oskar Morgenstern and has been further developed by other economists and decision theorists

- **Prospect Theory Model:**
- Prospect theory is a theory that explains how people make decisions when faced with risk, uncertainty, and probability.
- This model suggests that people's decisions are influenced not only by the expected value of each option, but also by the way that options are framed and presented.
- This theory was proposed by Daniel Kahneman and Amos Tversky, and has been influential in the fields of psychology and economics.
- **Heuristics and Biases Model:**
- HEURISTICS: Mental shortcuts that help people make decisions, especially when there's uncertainty. For example, people might use the availability heuristic to judge how likely an event is by how easily they can think of an example.
- BIASES: Systematic errors in thinking that can occur when using heuristics. For example, people might overestimate the frequency of events that are easy to recall.
- This model suggests that people often rely on mental shortcuts, or heuristics, to make decisions quickly and efficiently, but these heuristics can also lead to errors and biases.
- This theory was proposed by Kahneman and Tversky and has been influential in the field of cognitive psychology.
- **Social Judgment Model:**
- This model suggests that people's judgments are influenced by their attitudes and beliefs, and that these attitudes and beliefs can be changed by exposure to persuasive messages.
- Social judgment theory (SJT) is a theory that explains how people form opinions and evaluate ideas by comparing them to their current beliefs. It's used to understand how people are persuaded and how likely they are to change their minds.
- This theory was proposed by Carolyn Sherif and has been influential in the fields of social psychology and communication studies
- **Fuzzy-Trace Model:**

  ◦ This model suggests that people make judgments based on both verbatim information (i.e. specific details) and gist information (i.e. general impressions).
  ◦ The Fuzzy Trace Theory (FTT) is a cognitive theory that explains how people process and retain information, particularly in the context of decision-making and reasoning.
  ◦ Key Components:
  ◦ 1. Fuzzy traces: Mental representations of information that are fuzzy, vague, and lacking in detail.

- ◦ 2. Verbatim traces: Mental representations of information that are precise, detailed, and verbatim.
- ◦ 3. Gist: The essential meaning or essence of information.

These models reflect different perspectives on how people make judgments, and emphasize the complexity and diversity of human decision-making processes. They also highlight the importance of understanding how different factors, such as framing, heuristics, social influence, and memory processes, can influence the judgments that people make in different contexts and situations.

CHAPTER TWENTY-ONE

CHOICE – MEANING, CRITERIA FOR EVALUATING OPTIONS; THEORIES AND MODELS OF HUMAN CHOICE; CHOICE ARCHITECTURE

MEANING OF CHOICE:

Choice refers to the act of selecting between two or more possibilities, alternatives, or options. It plays a central role in decision-making processes in both personal and professional settings. Humans face choices daily, whether it's deciding what to eat, which career to pursue, or even political decisions. The concept of choice also extends to areas like economics, psychology, and behavioural sciences.

"choice" refers to the act of selecting one option from a set of available alternatives, essentially giving an individual the power to decide between different behaviours or actions, thereby promoting a sense of control and engagement; this concept is often associated with "Choice Theory" developed by Dr. William Glasser, which emphasizes that individuals actively choose their behaviours to fulfil their needs and desires.

CRITERIA FOR EVALUATING OPTIONS

When evaluating options, humans typically use certain criteria or factors to make their decisions. These include:

1. *The option is feasible / implementable with little or no risk of unintended consequences*

- Feasibility / ease of implementation, and little or no risk of unintended consequences are important
- Preference is given to options/solutions that are flexible, scalable and relatively easily reversible

1. **The option is consistent with the Authority's statutory objectives**

- The Authority's main statutory objective is "To promote competition in, reliable supply, and the efficient operation of, the electricity industry for the long-term benefit of consumers".
- The Authority's additional objective is to "protect the interests of domestic consumers and small business consumers in relation to the supply of electricity to those consumers".
- Refer to the Authority's interpretation of its original (2010) statutory objective for guidance on this criterion
- To further the Authority's statutory objectives, the benefits of an option must outweigh its costs

3. **The option promotes competitive neutrality amongst technologies / fuels**

- The option/solution should be neutral as to which technology / fuel can provide the required service/output

4. **The option signals full costs and benefits**

- The option/solution should signal the full marginal costs and benefits to participants / consumers associated with alternative technologies / fuels providing the required service/output

5. **The option is a market-based approach**

- Preference is given to market-based approaches to providing the required service/output, to promote innovation and transparency of the full costs and benefits of an option/solution

6. **The option is output-based rather than prescriptive**

- If practicable the option/solution should specify outcomes required of industry participants

THEORIES AND MODELS OF HUMAN CHOICE

Human decision-making is a complex process influenced by various factors, including cognitive limitations, emotions, social influences, and external environments. Over the years, numerous models have been developed to understand how people make choices.

1. Rational Choice Model

- The **Rational Choice Model** is one of the most classical approaches to understanding decision-making. It assumes that individuals make decisions by logically evaluating the alternatives available to them and choosing the one that maximizes their utility or satisfaction.
- This model is based on the assumption that people are **rational** actors who seek to maximize their benefit (utility) while minimizing costs.

Key Assumptions:

- **Full information**: The decision-maker has all relevant information about the alternatives.
- **Consistency**: Preferences are consistent and transitive. If a person prefers option A to B and B to C, then they should prefer A to C.
- **Maximization**: The individual will choose the option that provides the highest utility or satisfaction.

Limitations:

- **Cognitive limitations**: People often do not have the capacity to process all relevant information.
- **Emotions**: This model overlooks the role of emotions, biases, and other irrational factors that often influence choices.

2. Bounded Rationality Model (Herbert Simon)

- **Bounded Rationality**, a concept introduced by **Herbert Simon**, challenges the Rational Choice Model. It suggests that while individuals aim to make rational choices, their ability to do so is constrained by cognitive limitations, time, and available information. Instead of making an optimal choice, people often make decisions that are "good enough" based on the information available to them at the time.
- **Satisficing**: This is a key concept of bounded rationality. Instead of seeking the optimal choice, individuals look for a satisfactory solution that meets a minimum threshold of acceptability.

Key Assumptions:

- **Limited information**: Decision-makers don't have complete information or the time to fully analyze every option.
- **Cognitive limitations**: People are not equipped to process large amounts of information.
- **Satisficing**: Individuals settle for a decision that meets their basic needs or criteria, rather than maximizing utility.

Limitations:

- **Simplification**: While realistic, the model assumes decision-makers settle for the first acceptable option without truly weighing alternatives.

3. Prospect Theory (Kahneman & Tversky)

- **Prospect Theory**, developed by **Daniel Kahneman** and **Amos Tversky**, challenges the traditional economic models that assume humans are entirely rational. This theory emphasizes how people make decisions involving risk and uncertainty, focusing particularly on how people value potential gains and losses.
- One of the key insights of **Prospect Theory** is **loss aversion**: the idea that people tend to experience the pain of loss more intensely than the pleasure of an equivalent gain.

Key Assumptions:

- **Loss aversion**: Losses are psychologically more impactful than gains of the same magnitude.
- **Reference dependence**: People evaluate outcomes relative to a reference point (e.g., their current situation), not in absolute terms.
- **Risk aversion for gains and risk-seeking for losses**: People tend to avoid risk when it comes to gaining something but are willing to take more risks when it comes to avoiding losses.

Key Concepts:

- **Value function**: The value function in Prospect Theory is concave for gains and convex for losses, showing diminishing sensitivity to both gains and losses as they increase.
- **Framing effect**: People make different choices based on how a problem is framed (e.g., as a gain or a loss), even if the options are mathematically equivalent.

4. Dual-Process Theory (Kahneman)

- **Dual-Process Theory** posits that humans use two distinct systems of thinking to make decisions:

  - **System 1**: Fast, automatic, intuitive, and emotional thinking. It is effortless and based on heuristics or mental shortcuts.
  - **System 2**: Slow, deliberate, and logical thinking. It involves conscious thought, reasoning, and analysis

Key Assumptions:

- **System 1 (Intuition)**: This system is fast, automatic, and often driven by emotions and experience. Decisions made using System 1 are quick but prone to errors and biases.
- **System 2 (Reasoning)**: This system is slow, deliberate, and requires more cognitive effort. It is used for more complex decisions where careful analysis is needed.

Key Concepts:

- **Heuristics**: Mental shortcuts that often involve focusing on one aspect of a complex problem and ignoring others.
- **Cognitive biases**: Biases like availability bias, anchoring, and confirmation bias arise from System 1 and influence decision-making.

Example:

- **System 1**: When you see a friend in a crowd, you instantly recognize them without thinking much about it.
- **System 2**: If you are tasked with solving a math problem, you engage System 2, carefully analyzing the problem and working through the solution.

5.Social Choice Theory

- **Social Choice Theory** is concerned with the collective decision-making process, exploring how individual preferences can be aggregated into a collective decision. This theory is often applied in voting systems, public policy, and democratic decision-making.
- It attempts to solve problems related to how preferences should be combined in a way that reflects fairness, justice, and consistency.

Key Assumptions:

- **Collective decision-making**: The theory focuses on aggregating the preferences of multiple individuals to form a group decision.
- **Arrow's Impossibility Theorem**: This theorem proves that no voting system can perfectly translate individual preferences into a collective decision while satisfying a set of fairness criteria (e.g., non-dictatorship, unanimity).

Key Concepts:

- **Voting systems**: Different methods (e.g., plurality voting, ranked-choice voting, Borda count) are used to aggregate individual preferences into a group decision.
- **Fairness criteria**: Criteria like **Pareto efficiency, transitivity,** and **independence of irrelevant alternatives** guide the design of fair social choice systems.

Example:

- A city council voting on a new public project might use a voting system to decide on the best project. The decision-making process would consider the preferences of each member, ensuring that the final choice is a fair representation of the group.

6. The Elimination by Aspects Model (Eliot Smith & Richard T. L. Shafir)

- The **Elimination by Aspects Model** is a decision-making model where individuals eliminate alternatives based on certain features or attributes, one by one, until only one option remains.
- In this model, a person filters out options that do not meet certain criteria in a step-by-step manner.

Key Assumptions:

- **Attribute-based decision-making**: Decision-makers eliminate options based on a comparison of relevant aspects or attributes (e.g., price, quality, etc.).
- **Non-compensatory model**: If one alternative has a very poor feature, it might be eliminated from consideration even if it excels in other aspects.

Example:

- When choosing a new phone, you may eliminate phones that do not meet the minimum requirement for camera quality. You then continue narrowing down options based on battery life, price, and brand reputation until only one phone is left.

7. The Theory of Planned Behavior (Ajzen)

- **Theory of Planned Behavior (TPB)** is a psychological model that explains human decision-making based on **attitudes, subjective norms**, and **perceived behavioral control**.
- TPB is often used to understand behaviors that individuals intend to perform, especially those that involve some degree of planning.

Key Assumptions:

- **Attitudes**: The individual's positive or negative evaluation of the behavior.
- **Subjective norms**: The perceived social pressure to perform or not perform a behavior.
- **Perceived behavioral control**: The individual's perception of their ability to perform the behavior, which can include factors like resources, knowledge, or time

Example:

- If someone intends to exercise regularly, their decision to actually do so will depend on their attitude toward fitness, the social pressures (e.g., friends who work out), and their perceived ability to find time for exercise.

CHOICE ARCHITECTURE

Choice Architecture refers to the design of the environment in which people make decisions. It is about how choices are presented to influence behaviour in predictable ways without removing freedom of choice. The goal is to "nudge" people toward a particular behaviour or decision. **Richard Thaler** and **Cass Sunstein**, in their book Nudge, popularized this concept.

Elements of Choice Architecture:

1. **Defaults:**

   - People are more likely to stick with pre-set options, which is why defaults are a powerful tool. For example, many companies offer subscription services where the default option is automatic renewal, increasing the chances of retaining customers.
   - **Example:** In retirement savings plans, employees are automatically enrolled, but they can choose to opt-out. Studies have shown that opt-in rates are significantly lower than opt-out rates, increasing participation in savings programs.

2. **Framing Effects:**

   - The way a choice is framed can significantly influence decision-making.
   - **Example:** A product advertised as "90% fat-free" is more appealing than one labeled as "contains 10% fat," even though both describe the same product. This is because people are more attracted to positive framing (focusing on the benefits) than negative framing (focusing on the losses).

3. **Anchoring:**

   - The initial piece of information presented serves as a reference point (anchor) for subsequent decisions. People tend to rely heavily on the first piece of information when making judgments.
   - **Example:** If a car dealer shows you a high-priced vehicle first, a subsequent vehicle with a lower price may seem like a better deal, even if it is still expensive. This is known as the **anchoring effect**.

4. **Social Proof:**

   - People tend to conform to what others are doing, assuming that the behavior of others reflects correct or optimal behavior.
   - **Example:** Online retailers often display "Best-seller" or "Most Popular" labels on items, nudging customers to buy those products because they assume others' choices reflect quality or value.

5. **Simplification:**

   - The more options there are, the more difficult it becomes for people to make decisions. Reducing the number of choices or simplifying complex options can lead to better decision-making outcomes.
   - **Example:** Online shopping websites often filter products into categories (e.g., by price, size, rating) to make it easier for users to choose without feeling overwhelmed.

6. **Commitment Devices:**

   - A commitment device is something that helps people stick to their goals, often by making the consequences of failure more immediate or tangible.
   - **Example:** A fitness app might allow users to set a goal and then charge them a penalty if they do not meet that goal, leveraging a sense of commitment to ensure they keep up with their exercise plans.

PRACTICAL APPLICATIONS OF CHOICE ARCHITECTURE:

1. **Health and Wellness:**

- Choice architects can nudge individuals to make healthier choices by altering the way options are presented in healthcare settings or food environments.
- **Example**: In a hospital cafeteria, placing healthy food at eye level and reducing the size of unhealthy snack portions can promote healthier eating choices.

2. **Environmental Decision-Making**:

- Governments and organizations can use choice architecture to nudge people toward environmentally friendly choices.
- **Example**: By making energy-efficient products the default in homes or offices, and by promoting the benefits of these options, individuals may be nudged toward more sustainable choices.

3. **Financial Services**:

- Many banks use choice architecture to encourage savings or reduce unnecessary spending.
- **Example**: Automatically enrolling employees in a retirement savings program, where they can opt-out, encourages higher participation in savings plans.

4. **Consumer Marketing**:

- Marketers use choice architecture to influence purchasing decisions. From product placement to personalized recommendations, businesses design their marketing strategies to guide consumers toward specific choices.
- **Example**: Online retailers like Amazon or Netflix employ algorithms that suggest products based on past purchases or viewing history, making it easier for consumers to choose by reducing the number of options they need to consider.

CHAPTER TWENTY-TWO

DECISION MAKING – MEANING , PROBLEM ANALYSIS , STEPS AND TECHNIQUES OF DECISION MAKING UNDER DIFFERENT CONTEXTS

DECISION MAKING

- The process of consciously choosing courses of action from available alternatives and integrating them for the purpose of achieving the desired goal.
- According to George R. Terry, "Decision-making is the selection based on certain criteria from two or more alternatives"
- According to Mary Cushing Niles, "Decision-making takes place in adopting the objectives and choosing the means and again when a change in the situation creates a necessity for adjustments."
- According to Heinz Weihrich and Harold Koontz, "Decision-making is defined as the selection of a count of action.

CHARACTERISTICS

1. **Goal-Oriented**: Decision-making is focused on achieving specific objectives or solving a particular problem. The decision process is driven by the need to meet predefined goals or outcomes.
2. **Uncertainty**: Decisions are often made under conditions of uncertainty, where outcomes are not always predictable. This requires assessing risks and potential consequences to make informed choices.
3. **Multiple Alternatives**: Decision-making involves considering various alternatives or options. Evaluating these alternatives helps in choosing the most suitable course of action based on available information.
4. **Resource Allocation**: Decision-making often involves allocating limited resources, such as time, money, or personnel. Efficient and effective distribution of resources is crucial in making the best decisions.
5. **Impact on Stakeholders**: Decisions often have far-reaching consequences, affecting various stakeholders such as employees, customers, and investors. The potential effects on these groups must be considered when making decisions.

COMPONENTS

- Assessing the situation and identifying the problem.
- Setting objectives and prioritizing between goals.
- Making and assessing forecasts.
- Valuing options and

- Learning to utilize institution.

Decision making is ,

1. What goals are to be achieved ?
2. What means and methods are to be adopted in reaching them ?
3. What facts are available ?
4. How they are interpreted ?

Decision making is influenced by ,

- Level of knowledge
- Cost involved
- Time available
- Decision implementation

MAJOR TYPES OF DECISION MAKING

- Programmed Decision
- Rational Decision
- Bounded Rationality Decision
- Non-Programmed Decision

- **Programmed Decision** Programmed decision straight-forward, mundane, and less thoughtful everyday decisions. Decision on the kind of clothes to wear, food to eat daily, including recurring customers' complaints are example of such decision.
- **Rational Decision** Rational decision involves series of steps decision maker would consider if goal of such decisions is to maximize the decision's outcomes. Ideal method for how managers should make decision.
- **The Rational Decision Making Process** Intelligence identify problems & opportunities define objectives & criteria for success Design develop and evaluate alternatives Choice prioritize and select one or more alternatives Implement and evaluate implement the choice and monitor success
- **Bounded Rationality Decision** How decision are made under severe time and resource constraints. Helps manager in their decision making process to limit their search in a manageable way for alternatives.
- **Non-Programmed Decision** Non routine decision made in response to unusual or novel opportunities and threats.The are no rules to follow since the decision is new.

KEY PRINCIPLES OF DECISION MAKING

There are several key principles that guide effective organizational decision making. Understanding these principles can help you make better, more informed decisions that align with your overall strategy and goals.

- **Define clear objectives:** This involves understanding, with clarity, what the organization seeks to achieve.
- **Gather and analyze relevant data:** Making informed decisions requires accurate, up-to-date and relevant data.
- **Evaluate alternatives:** This involves comparing the pros and cons of each course of action.
- **Make the decision:** Based on the evaluation, the most beneficial alternative is chosen.
- **Implement the decision:** The chosen course of action is put into practice.
- **Monitor and adjust:** The impact of the decision is monitored and any necessary adjustments are made.

PROBLEM ANALYSIS

Problem analysis involves identifying the overriding problem and establishing the causes and effects related to that problem.

- Identify the problem : Define the problem and make a goal statement.
- Discover the root cause : Determine the extent of the problem.
- Gather information : Collect the relevant information.
- Identify alternatives : Brainstorm to generate ideas.
- Evaluate alternatives : Consider the likely outcome ease of implementation and potential negative side effects.
- Choose a solution : Select the best option from the alternatives.
- Take action : Develop an action plan and assign tasks with milestones.
- Review the decision – Evaluate the results and process and make any necessary adjustments.

STEPS IN DECISION MAKING

STEP 1 – Diagnosing , defining , identifying , the source of the problem.

STEP 2 – Information gathering and analysis of the facts required to solve the problem

STEP 3 – Developing and evaluating alternative solutions to the problem.

STEP 4 – Choosing the best decision from the alternatives.

STEP 5 - Communicating the decisions.

STEP 6 – Implementing the decisions.

STEP 7 – Review of key factors

These are all the steps involved in decision making.

TECHNIQUES OF DECISION MAKING UNDER DIFFERENT CONTEXTS

QUALITATIVE TECHNIQUES

- Cost benefit analysis
- Decision tree
- Risk analysis

COST BENEFIT ANALYSIS

This method aims at comparing total benefits derived from a project with the total costs incurred for the same.

DECISION TREE

It is a graphic representation of various alternative solutions that are available to solve a problem.

RISK ANALYSIS

It is a process that helps you identify an manage potential problems that could undermine key business initiatives and projects.

QUANTITATIVE TECHNIQUES

- Brainstorming
- Delphi techniques
- Nominal group

BRAINSTORMING

It is a combination of group problem solving and discussions . It works on the belief that the more the no. of ideas , greater the possibility of arriving at a solution to the problem that is acceptable to all .

DELPHI TECHNIQUE

The Delphi method is a forecasting process framewok based on the results of multiple rounds of questionnaires sent to a panel of experts.

NOMINAL GROUP

Nominal group techniques is defined as a structured method of group brainstorming . Team members begin by writing down their ideas , then selecting which idea they feel is best.

OTHER TECHNIQUES

1. **SWOT Analysis**: A strategic planning tool used to identify and evaluate a project's or organization's Strengths, Weaknesses, Opportunities, and Threats. It helps in understanding internal and external factors that may affect decision-making and planning.
2. **Game Theory**: A mathematical framework for analyzing strategic interactions between rational decision-makers. It is used to predict the outcome of competitive situations where the actions of one participant affect the others, such as in economics and political science.
3. **Multi-Criteria Decision Analysis (MCDA)**: A decision-making process that evaluates and prioritizes multiple conflicting criteria when making a choice. It helps to assess different options by considering various factors and assigning them weights based on importance.
4. **Pareto Analysis**: A decision-making technique that applies the Pareto Principle (80/20 rule), which suggests that 80% of effects come from 20% of causes. It helps prioritize issues or problems based on their impact, allowing focus on the most significant factors.
5. **Cost-Effectiveness Analysis**: A method used to compare the relative costs and outcomes of different courses of action. It assesses whether the benefits of an intervention justify the cost, often used in healthcare or project evaluation.
6. **Decision Matrix**: A tool used to evaluate and prioritize different options or alternatives by assigning scores based on defined criteria. It helps decision-makers systematically compare choices and make informed decisions.
7. **Electronic Meeting**: A form of communication where participants engage in discussions and decision-making through digital platforms, enabling virtual collaboration. This is commonly used in remote work environments.
8. **Multi Voting**: A technique used to prioritize options by allowing participants to vote multiple times on the alternatives they prefer. It helps identify the most favored choices in group decision-making processes.
9. **Linear Programming**: A mathematical technique used for optimization problems, where the goal is to maximize or minimize a linear objective function subject to constraints. It's widely used in operations research and resource allocation.
10. **Network Analysis**: A method used to model and analyze complex systems represented as networks, such as supply chains or communication systems. It focuses on identifying the most critical elements and understanding the flow within the system.

CHAPTER TWENTY-THREE

ATTITUDES – MEANING, ASSUMPTIONS, TYPES, THEORIES AND MODELS OF ATTITUDE FORMATION; METHODS OF CHANGING ATTITUDES.

ATTITUDES

Attitudes refer to a psychological construct representing an individual's degree of like or dislike for an object, person, idea, or situation. Attitudes influence behavior, perception, and interactions, serving as a key concept in psychology, sociology, and behavioral sciences.

MEANING OF ATTITUDES

1. An attitude is a predisposition or a learned tendency to evaluate things in a certain way.
2. It can be positive, negative, or neutral and includes emotions, beliefs, and behavioral tendencies.

ASSUMPTIONS ABOUT ATTITUDES

1. Learned Behavior: Attitudes are acquired through experience, social interactions, and cultural influences.

2. Subject to Change: Attitudes are dynamic and can evolve over time due to new experiences or information.

3. Influence Behavior: While attitudes shape behavior, the relationship isn't always linear or direct.

4. Three Components: Attitudes involve:

- Affective: Emotional reactions.
- Cognitive: Beliefs or thoughts.
- Behavioral: Tendency to act in a certain way.

TYPES OF ATTITUDES

1. Positive Attitude: Involves optimism and enthusiasm (e.g., admiration for teamwork).

2. Negative Attitude: Reflects pessimism, dislike, or disapproval (e.g., prejudice against certain groups).

3. Neutral Attitude: Indifference toward a topic, object, or person.

4. Ambivalent Attitude: Mixed feelings or contradictory attitudes toward the same subject.

THEORIES OF ATTITUDE FORMATION

1. Classical Conditioning:

Attitudes develop through associative learning.

EXAMPLE: Pairing a product with a pleasant stimulus (e.g., music or visuals in advertising).

2. Operant Conditioning:

Attitudes are shaped by rewards and punishments.

EXAMPLE: Positive reinforcement for a particular belief strengthens the attitude.

3. Social Learning Theory:
Attitudes are learned by observing and imitating others (e.g., family, peers, media).
4. Cognitive Dissonance Theory (Festinger):
Inconsistencies between beliefs, attitudes, and behaviors create discomfort.
EXAMPLE: Changing attitudes to align with behavior reduces dissonance.
5. Functional Theory (Katz):
Attitudes serve specific functions:
Knowledge Function: Simplify complex information.
Utilitarian Function: Maximize rewards and minimize punishments.
Ego-Defensive Function: Protect self-esteem.
Value-Expressive Function: Reflect core beliefs or values.
6. Balance Theory (Heider):
People strive for harmony in their attitudes, beliefs, and relationships.
7. Elaboration Likelihood Model (Petty and Cacioppo):
Attitude change occurs via two routes:
Central Route: Based on logical arguments and evidence.
Peripheral Route: Influenced by superficial cues like attractiveness or status.
MODELS OF ATTITUDE FORMATION
1. ABC Model of Attitude:
Affective (Feelings) + Behavioral (Actions) + Cognitive (Beliefs) = Attitude.
2. Hierarchy of Effects Model:
Explains the sequence of attitude formation ?

- Cognitive Stage: Awareness and knowledge.
- Affective Stage: Emotions and feelings.
- Behavioral Stage: Decision and action.

3. Theory of Planned Behavior (Ajzen):
Attitudes, subjective norms, and perceived control predict behavioral intentions and actions.
METHODS OF CHANGING ATTITUDES
1. Persuasion:
Involves communicating compelling arguments or appeals to influence attitudes.
TECHNIQUES:

- Logical reasoning.
- Emotional appeals.
- Social proof (e.g., testimonials).

2. Cognitive Dissonance Reduction:
Create dissonance between current attitudes and new behavior, encouraging attitude change for alignment.
3. Behavioral Interventions:
Encourage new behaviors that lead to attitude shifts.
EXAMPLE: Volunteering fosters a positive attitude toward social causes.
4. Role of Credibility:
Messages from credible sources (experts, respected figures) are more persuasive.
5. Repetition and Familiarity:
Repeated exposure to a message increases its acceptance (Mere Exposure Effect).
6. Education and Awareness:

Accurate information can challenge misconceptions and change attitudes.
7. Social Influence:
Peer pressure, group norms, or leadership can reshape attitudes.
8. Incentives:
Rewards or benefits can motivate individuals to adopt new attitudes.
9. Two-Sided Arguments:
Presenting both sides of an issue can make the communicator appear fair, increasing trust and receptivity.

CHAPTER TWENTY-FOUR

RELATING TO OTHERS -LIKING,ATTRACTION,HELPING BEHAVIOUR,PREJUDICE,DISCRIMATION,AND AGGRESSION.

LIKING:

Liking refers to the tendency to have a positive attitude towards someone and feel a sense of affinity or similarity with them. It is a tool for influence, as people are more likely to comply with requests from those they like.

Liking can be established through perceived similarity and nonverbal cues such as eye contact, smiling, and leaning forward, which convey warmth and friendliness.

- **POSITIVE REINFORCEMENT:** The core principle is that when a behavior is followed by something the person likes, they are more likely to repeat that behavior in the future.
- **INDIVIDUALIZED APPROACH:** What constitutes "liking" varies greatly between individuals, so identifying personal preferences is crucial for effective behavior modification.
- **Examples:**

  ○ Praise
  ○ Access to a preferred activity
  ○ Favorite food
  ○ Toys
  ○ Social attention

ATTRACTION:

It is the force that draws people together.Attraction also encompases the feeling of liking towards friends, and having positive thoughts towards others.

Two forms of interpersonal attraction are Friendship and love.

THEORIES OF ATTRACTION:

BALANCE THEORY:

- **PROPOSED BY FRITZ HEIDER:**

This theory was developed by psychologist Fritz Heider, who suggested that people strive for "psychological balance" in their relationships, where positive and negative sentiments are aligned in a way that feels harmonious.

- **THE "TRIAD" CONCEPT:**

Balance theory often uses the idea of a "triad" - where you, another person, and an attitude object (like a shared interest) are considered. If you like someone and they like the same thing you do, it creates a balanced and positive relationship.

- **UNBALANCED SITUATIONS CREATE TENSION:**

When there is an imbalance (like liking someone but strongly disagreeing with their opinion on a key issue), it can cause discomfort and motivate individuals to change their attitude or distance themselves from the other person to restore balance.
Example scenarios:

- **Shared interests:** If you enjoy hiking and meet someone who also loves hiking, you're likely to feel a positive attraction based on the shared interest, creating a balanced relationship.
- **Friend of a friend:** If you like someone, and they are friends with another person you also like, this can strengthen your positive feelings towards the first person due to the balanced "triad".

REINFORCEMENT /REWARD THEORY:

- **POSITIVE ASSOCIATIONS:**

When someone consistently provides positive experiences (like compliments, support, laughter), we tend to develop a positive association with them, increasing our attraction towards them.

- **NEGATIVE ASSOCIATIONS:**

Conversely, if someone repeatedly causes negative feelings (like criticism, conflict), we are less likely to be attracted to them.

- **CLASSICAL CONDITIONING ELEMENT:**

This theory draws on principles of classical conditioning, where a neutral stimulus (a person) becomes associated with a positive or negative feeling through repeated pairing.

- **"REINFORCEMENT-AFFECT MODEL":**

This is the most common term used to describe the application of reinforcement theory in attraction, highlighting the link between positive affect (feeling good) and attraction.
Example: If a person consistently makes you laugh during conversations, you are more likely to find them attractive because you associate them with positive emotions like happiness.
EXCHANGE THEORY.

- **COST-BENEFIT ANALYSIS:**

People evaluate potential partners by weighing the positive aspects (like companionship, support, attractiveness) against the negative aspects (like effort required, compatibility issues).

- **MAXIMIZING REWARDS:**

The goal is to find partners who provide the most benefits for the least amount of effort or cost.

- **COMPARISON LEVEL:**

Individuals compare their current relationship to their perceived options and past experiences to determine if the rewards are sufficient.

- **EQUITY:**

Ideally, both partners in a relationship perceive a fair balance in giving and receiving, which contributes to attraction and relationship satisfaction.
Example scenarios:

- **Attraction based on shared interests:** Someone might be attracted to a person who shares their hobbies because it provides opportunities for positive interactions and shared experiences with minimal effort.
- **Attraction based on perceived compatibility:** If someone believes they can provide emotional support to a partner who needs it, they might be attracted to that person due to the potential for a mutually beneficial relationship.

EXTERNAL DETERMINANTS OF ATTRACTION:
THE POWER OF PROXIMITY: - The power of proximity in attraction" refers to the psychological phenomenon where people are more likely to be attracted to individuals, they are physically close to, meaning they frequently see and interact with them, due to the increased familiarity and opportunity to discover shared interests, essentially stating that the closer you are to someone, the more likely you are to develop a relationship with them.
KEY POINTS ABOUT PROXIMITY AND ATTRACTION:

- **MERE EXPOSURE EFFECT:**

Repeated exposure to someone, even without deep interaction, can lead to increased liking due to familiarity.

- **FUNCTIONAL DISTANCE:**

This concept goes beyond just physical proximity and refers to how often you cross paths with someone, like being in the same class or workplace.

- **EARLY STAGES OF ATTRACTION:**

Proximity is considered a crucial factor in the initial stages of forming a relationship, allowing people to get to know each other and discover potential commonalities.
Example

- **College dorm life:** Students living on the same floor are more likely to become friends because they see each other frequently.
- **Work relationships:** People who sit near each other in an office are more likely to develop a closer bond due to increased interactions.

- **Online communities:** Even in virtual spaces, proximity can play a role as people who frequently interact in the same online forums might feel more connected.

HELPING BEHAVIOUR:

Helping behaviour refers to voluntary actions intended to help others, with reward regarded or disregarded. It is a type of prosocial behaviour (voluntary action intended to help or benefit another individual or group of individuals, such as sharing, comforting, rescuing and helping).

TYPES OF HELPING BEHAVIOR

- **PROSOCIAL BEHAVIOR:** Any cooperative or friendly behavior that helps others.

ALTRUISM: Prosocial behaviour that's motivated by helping others, even if it costs the helper. For example, anonymously donating to charity.

KIN SELECTION THEORY

Kin selection theory explains altruism from an evolutionary perspective. Since natural selection screens out species without abilities to adapt to the challenging environment, preservation of good traits and superior genes are important for survival of future generations (i.e. inclusive fitness). Kin selection refers to an inheritable tendency to perform behaviors that may Favor the chance of survival of people with a similar genetic base.

SOCIAL EXCHANGE THEORY

According to the social-exchange theory, people help because they want to gain goods from the one being helped. People estimate the rewards and costs of helping others, and aim at maximizing the former and minimizing the latter.

Examples include, volunteer work, donating money, or helping a neighbor move a heavy item of furniture

The most striking type of prosocial behavior is altruism, where a person takes on a cost to help another person with no expectation or possibility of receiving a benefit in return.

PREJUIDCE:

The premise of this review is that, in general terms, prejudice needs to be viewed as a process within a set of relationships, rather than a state or characteristic of particular people (Abrams and Houston, 2006; Abrams and Christian, 2007).

That is, we need to understand the different forms prejudice might take, when it might be expressed, and what factors promote or inhibit its expression. It is as important to know about the conditions that give rise to, and can counter, prejudice, as to measure the particular amount or virulence of prejudice at a particular time.

Prejudice can be directed to a wide range of groups and, and can be expressed in a wide variety of ways. Therefore, it is necessary to think broadly about the types of 'benchmarks' that will be useful for measuring change. It is also necessary to break down the concept of prejudice into distinct components and to understand how and when these fit together to produce discriminatory outcomes and inequality. Equally important, however, is to achieve these goals within a unifying conceptual framework.

Within psychology there have been numerous attempts to define prejudice,

Crandall and Eshelman (2003) note that prejudice cannot always be described as irrational or unjustified and that it is therefore better to define it as 'a negative evaluation of a social group or an individual that is significantly based on the individual's group membership' (p. 414). This, unfortunately, leaves us slightly adrift in terms of policy because it neglects prejudice that does not involve negative evaluations.

Therefore, the approach taken in this review is to define prejudice as:

'Bias that devalues people because of their perceived membership of a social group'.

This definition allows prejudice to arise from biases in different forms. It is not assumed that all biases are harmful or particularly consequential. Some are quite favourable

(for example, the belief that Chinese people are better at maths than Europeans would be favourable towards Chinese people in Britain). Prejudice arises when such biases are potentially harmful and consequential because they reduce the standing or value attached to a person through their group memberships. This can occur when stereotypes, attitudes and emotions towards the group are directed at an individual member of the group.

It is important to distinguish awareness of group differences from bias and prejudice. Some groups are manifestly unequal: they are poorer, less well educated, have had fewer opportunities, and visibly have lower occupational positions, worse health or engage in more crime. Some groups have more power than others in society.

It is not prejudiced to be aware of, and concerned about, these differences. On the other hand, people's knowledge is often incomplete or wrong, and they may also inappropriately generalise their knowledge, resulting in bias and prejudice.

For example, it is false and clearly prejudiced to assume that every Muslim in the UK poses a terrorist threat. It is true that mothers are women, but false to assume that all women are (or should be) mothers. It is true that elderly people are generally less physically mobile than younger people but false that all people with reduced mobility are elderly.

Actions or policies intended to help certain groups of people who are assumed to be dependent or needy (for example, through free bus passes or maternity leave) involve assumptions that may well result in disadvantages to other categories of people that are assumed to be independent. These assumptions are prejudices and for particular individuals may be just as damaging as direct hostility.

So from a policy perspective, an important task is to identify which prejudices are consequential and which are harmful, and to target these.

HISTORICAL APPROACHES

The first psychological research conducted on prejudice occurred in the 1920s. This research attempted to prove white supremacy. One article from 1925 which reviewed 73 studies on race concluded that the studies seemed "to indicate the mental superiority of the white race".[9] These studies, along with other research, led many psychologists to view prejudice as a natural response to races believed to be inferior.

In the 1930s and 1940s, this perspective began to change due to the increasing concern about anti-Semitism due to the ideology of the Nazis. At the time, theorists viewed prejudice as pathological and they thus looked for personality syndromes linked with racism. Theodor Adorno believed that prejudice stemmed from an authoritarian personality; he believed that people with authoritarian personalities were the most likely to be prejudiced against groups of lower status. He described authoritarians as "rigid thinkers who obeyed authority, saw the world as black and white, and enforced strict adherence to social rules and hierarchies".[10]

In 1954, Gordon Allport, in his classic work The Nature of Prejudice, linked prejudice to categorical thinking. Allport claimed that prejudice is a natural and normal process for humans. According to him, "The human mind must think with the aid of categories... Once formed, categories are the basis for normal prejudgment. We cannot possibly avoid this process. Orderly living depends upon it." In his book, he emphasizes the importance of the contact hypothesis. This theory posits that contact between different (ethnic) groups can reduce prejudices against those groups. Allport acknowledges the importance of the circumstances in which such contact occurs. He has attached conditions to it to promote positive contact and reduce prejudices.

TYPES OF PREJUDICE

- **Nationalism**
- **Gender identity**
- **Classism**
- **Racism**
- **Scientific racism**
- **Religious discrimination**
- **Linguistic discrimination.**

DISCRIMINATION:

Discrimination means treating some people differently from others.

It isn't always unlawful - after all, people are paid different wages depending on their status and skills. However, there are certain reasons for which your employer can't discriminate against you by law.

Discrimination refers to unjustifiable negative behaviour to- wards a group or its members, where behaviour is adjudged to include both actions towards, and judgements/decisions about, group members. Correll et al. (2010, p. 46) provide a very useful definition of discrimination as 'behaviour directed towards cate- gory members that is consequential for their outcomes and that is directed towards them not because of any particular deserving- ness or reciprocity, but simply because they happen to be mem- bers of that category'. The notion of 'deservingness' is central to the expression and experience of discrimination. It is not an ob.- ejectively defined criterion but one that has its roots in historical and present-day inequalities and societal norms. Perpetrators may see their behaviours as justified by the deservingness of the targets, while the targets themselves may disagree. Thus the be- saviours, which some judge to be discriminatory, will not be seen as such by others.

The expression of discrimination can broadly be classified into two types:

- overt or direct, and
- subtle, unconscious or auto-Matic.

THEORIES OF DISCRIMINATION
-THE SOCIAL IDENTITY PERSPECTIVE

According to social identity theory, social behavior is determined by the character and motivations of the person as an individual (interpersonal behavior) as well as by the person's group membership (i.e., intergroup behavior). People generally prefer to maintain a positive image of the groups to which they belong.

AVERSIVE RACISM THEORY
SYSTEM JUSTIFICATION THEORY.

The justification theory framework analyzes situations of disagreement wherein justifications are employed to reach an agreement/outcome in non-violent and legitimate ways, among different actors (Boltanski & Thévenot, 2006).

CONSEQUENCES OF DISCRIMINATION
The consequences of discrimination are
-pervasive,
-cumulative and
-long-lasting.

AGGRESSION:
Social psychologists define aggression as behavior that is intended to harm another individual who does not wish to be harmed (Baron & Richardson, 1994).

Because it involves the perception of intent, what looks like aggression from one point of view may not look that way from another, and the same harmful behaviour may or may not be considered aggressive depending on its intent. Intentional harm is, however, perceived as worse than unintentional harm, even when the harms are identical (Ames & Fiske, 2013).

You can see that this definition rules out some behaviours that we might normally think are aggressive. For instance, a rugby player who accidentally breaks the arm of another player or a driver who accidentally hits a pedestrian would not by our definition be displaying aggression because although harm was done, there was no intent to harm.

A salesperson who attempts to make a sale through repeated phone calls is not aggressive because he is not intending any harm (we might say this behaviour is "assertive" rather than aggressive). And not all intentional behaviours that hurt others are aggressive behaviours.

A dentist might intentionally give a patient a painful injection of a painkiller, but the goal is to prevent further pain during the procedure.

The type or level of intent that underlies an aggressive behaviour creates the distinction between two fundamental types of aggression, which are caused by very different psychological processes.

EMOTIONAL OR IMPLUSIVE AGGRESSION:

It refers to aggression that occurs with only a small amount of forethought or intent and that is determined primarily by impulsive emotions. Emotional aggression is the result of the extreme negative emotions we're experiencing at the time that we aggress and is not really intended to create any positive outcomes. When Nazim yells at his boyfriend, this is probably emotional aggression—it is impulsive and carried out in the heat of the moment. Other examples are the jealous lover who strikes out in rage or the sports fans who vandalize stores and destroy cars around the stadium after their team loses an important game.

<u>INSTRUMENTAL OR COGNITIVE AGGRESSION:</u>, on other hand, is aggression that is intentional and planned. Instrumental aggression is more cognitive than affective and may be completely cold and calculating. Instrumental aggression is aimed at hurting someone to gain something—attention, monetary reward, or political power, for instance. If the aggressor believes that there is an easier way to obtain the goal, the aggression would probably not occur. A bully who hits a child and steals her toys, a terrorist who kills civilians to gain political exposure, and a hired assassin are all good examples of instrumental aggression.

Social psychologists agree that aggression can be verbal as well as physical.

Therefore, slinging insults at a friend is definitely aggressive, according to our definition, just as hitting someone is.

<u>PHYSICAL AGGRESSION</u> is aggression that involves harming others physically—for instance hitting, kicking, stabbing, or shooting them.

<u>NON PHYSICAL AGGRESSION</u> is aggression that does not involve physical harm. Nonphysical aggression includes

- <u>verbal aggression</u> (yelling, screaming, swearing, and name calling) and
- <u>relational or social aggression,</u> which is defined as intentionally harming another person's social relationships,

for instance, by gossiping about another person, excluding others from our friendship, or giving others the "silent treatment" (Crick & Trompeter, 1995).

Nonverbal aggression also occurs in the form of sexual, racial, and homophobic jokes and epithets, which are designed to cause harm to individuals.

CHAPTER TWENTY-FIVE

LIKING/AFFECT: MEANING, TYPES, AND THEORIES

Liking or **affect** refers to a person's feelings or emotional responses toward an object, person, event, or situation. It plays a crucial role in shaping behaviours, decisions, and attitudes. Liking can manifest as positive feelings, such as fondness, affection, or attraction, and is often considered a basic emotional response that influences human interactions and judgments.

MEANING OF LIKING/AFFECT

Affect refers to the experience of feeling or emotion that can influence our thoughts, behaviours, and decisions. It is an umbrella term for emotional experiences that range from simple likes and dislikes to complex emotional states such as happiness, sadness, or anger. **Liking** is a psychological state characterized by a positive evaluation of a person, object, or idea, often leading to favourable attitudes and behaviors towards that target. This feeling can stem from various factors such as familiarity, attractiveness, and similarity, which play significant roles in how people form connections and engage with others. Liking is essential in understanding social influence, as it can lead to increased persuasion and compliance when individuals feel positively about the source of a message or request.

For example:

- You might feel **liking** or **affection** for a close friend because of shared experiences or mutual respect.
- You might feel **liking** toward a product, such as a favorite brand or food, due to positive past experiences or advertising.

Liking is also influenced by **attitudes**, which are consistent patterns of positive or negative evaluation toward a person, object, or idea.

TYPES OF LIKING/AFFECT

Types of Liking in Applied Behavior Change

- **Intrinsic Liking**: When an individual enjoys a behavior for its own sake, without external rewards or pressure. This type of liking is particularly important in long-term behavior change because it is more sustainable. For instance, a person might exercise because they genuinely enjoy it, not because they are trying to lose weight or impress others.
- **Extrinsic Liking**: In contrast, extrinsic liking occurs when individuals engage in behavior because of external rewards or social pressure. For example, a person might like exercising because it leads to positive reinforcement from peers or because it results in tangible rewards, such as a fitness tracker milestone.
- **Social Liking**: This type of liking is influenced by social groups and networks. People are more likely to adopt behaviors if they are supported or encouraged by friends, family, or colleagues. This is why social networks and peer influence are central in many applied behavior change programs, such as those aimed at encouraging healthier lifestyles or promoting environmental behaviors (e.g., recycling).

Types of Affect in Applied Behavior Change

- **Positive Affect**: Positive emotions such as joy, pride, and satisfaction play a crucial role in reinforcing behavior change. If individuals feel good about a behavior, they are more likely to repeat it. For example, after achieving a goal like running a certain distance, the positive affect (pride, accomplishment) can encourage individuals to keep running.
- **Negative Affect**: Negative emotions, such as guilt, shame, frustration, or fear, can either motivate behavior change or lead to avoidance. For example, people might change their behavior to avoid negative emotional responses, such as feeling guilty about smoking or ashamed of unhealthy eating habits. However, in some cases, negative affect can be counterproductive, leading to avoidance or withdrawal from the behavior change process.
- **Emotional Contagion**: This is the spread of emotions from one individual to another, often within groups. Positive or negative affect can spread in a group setting, affecting behavior change efforts. For example, in a support group, the collective positive feelings and encouragement can motivate individual members to persist in their behavior change goals.

THEORIES OF LIKING/AFFECT

Several sociological theories help explain how **liking** and **affect** influence applied behavior change. These theories are key to understanding how emotions and social factors work together to drive behavior modification efforts.

1. Social Cognitive Theory (Albert Bandura)

- **Core Idea**: Social Cognitive Theory emphasizes the role of social influence, self-efficacy, and observational learning in behavior change. It posits that people learn from observing others and from their own experiences. The theory incorporates emotions, such as affect, as important motivators for behavior change.
- **Relevance to Liking and Affect**: Liking and positive affect can boost self-efficacy—the belief that one can achieve a behavior change. If individuals observe someone they like or admire successfully engaging in a behavior (like exercising regularly), they may develop the confidence to try it themselves. Moreover, the positive emotions they experience while engaging in the behavior (e.g., the satisfaction after a workout) further enhance their motivation to continue.
- **Behavioral Application**: Social Cognitive Theory is used in interventions like peer-led health campaigns or community-based programs, where social modeling and emotional experiences are used to inspire and maintain behavior change.

2. Theory of Planned Behavior (Ajzen)

- **Core Idea**: The Theory of Planned Behavior (TPB) posits that individual behavior is influenced by attitudes, subjective norms (social influences), and perceived behavioral control (self-efficacy). This theory suggests that individuals are more likely to engage in behaviors they perceive as beneficial and aligned with social norms.
- **Relevance to Liking and Affect**: **Liking** and **affect** directly impact attitudes and subjective norms. For example, if people develop a positive attitude (liking) toward exercise through enjoyable experiences, they are more likely to engage in it. Additionally, affective responses like pride or happiness after exercise can shape their attitude toward continuing this behavior.
- **Behavioral Application**: The TPB is commonly applied in health promotion and environmental behavior change programs. Campaigns encouraging physical activity or reducing smoking often focus on changing attitudes (e.g., creating positive feelings toward exercise), social norms (e.g., peer support), and self-efficacy (e.g., showing that quitting smoking is possible).

3. Self-Determination Theory (Deci & Ryan)

- **Core Idea**: Self-Determination Theory (SDT) focuses on motivation and the types of motivation that drive behavior, distinguishing between intrinsic and extrinsic motivation. SDT emphasizes the importance of autonomy, competence, and relatedness in fostering intrinsic motivation.

- **Relevance to Liking and Affect**: The theory suggests that behavior change is most sustainable when individuals find the behavior intrinsically rewarding (i.e., they like the behavior itself). Positive affect associated with autonomy and mastery (e.g., accomplishing a fitness goal) enhances intrinsic motivation and promotes long-term behavior change.
- **Behavioral Application**: SDT is used in interventions aimed at increasing intrinsic motivation for behaviors such as exercise, healthy eating, or learning. Programs that focus on autonomy and competence—rather than external rewards or pressures—tend to produce more lasting behavior changes. For instance, a wellness program might allow participants to choose their own fitness activities, fostering greater enjoyment and intrinsic motivation.

4. Social Norms Theory

- **Core Idea**: Social Norms Theory suggests that behaviors are heavily influenced by perceived social norms—what people believe others do or think is acceptable. Social norms guide individual behaviors based on group expectations.
- **Relevance to Liking and Affect**: Liking and affect can be influenced by social norms. If a person likes a social group that values healthy behaviors (such as exercise or sustainable consumption), they are more likely to adopt those behaviors. Positive social emotions (affection, respect) within a group can drive individuals to conform to the group's norms.
- **Behavioral Application**: Social Norms Theory is widely used in campaigns that aim to modify public behavior, such as promoting the use of seat belts, reducing alcohol consumption, or encouraging environmentally friendly practices. By highlighting that most people engage in these behaviors (e.g., "most people in your community recycle"), individuals may be influenced by the perceived norm and develop positive feelings toward adopting the behavior.

5. Emotional Intelligence Theory (Goleman)

- **Core Idea**: Emotional Intelligence (EI) refers to the ability to recognize, understand, and manage emotions—both one's own and others'. High emotional intelligence is associated with better decision-making, conflict resolution, and behavior change.
- **Relevance to Liking and Affect**: Individuals with high EI are more adept at managing their emotions, which can lead to more effective behavior change. They can better handle the emotional ups and downs that often accompany behavior change efforts. For example, the ability to manage negative emotions like frustration (when a motivated.
- **Behavioral Application**: EI is important in applied behavior change programs that require emotional regulation, such as addiction recovery or stress management programs. Teaching emotional intelligence skills can help individuals manage the negative affects associated with change and increase the likelihood of sustained behavior change.

FACTORS INFLUENCING LIKING/AFFECT

- **Reciprocity**: We tend to like people who like us. This is known as **reciprocal liking**, which builds mutual trust and positive emotional responses.
- **Proximity**: Physical closeness or frequent contact can lead to increased liking. This is closely related to the **Mere Exposure Effect**, where being around someone frequently can enhance your feelings of liking them.
- **Physical Attractiveness**: Research suggests that people are often drawn to those who are physically attractive, as we associate beauty with other positive qualities.

- **Emotional Contagion**: Our emotions can influence those around us. When others are happy, upbeat, or affectionate, we are likely to reciprocate those emotions and develop positive feelings of liking.
- **Social and Cultural Factors**: Social norms, cultural backgrounds, and shared group identities can influence the likelihood of forming connections and feeling liking toward others.

CHAPTER TWENTY-SIX

ATTRACTION- MEANING, TYPES AND TECHNIQUES

ATTRACTION:

- Attraction can be defined as a positive attitude (or) feeling one holds toward another person, which is expressed through favorable behaviors and emotions over time. This phenomenon often includes behaviors such as seeking to enhance the well-being of other person, experiencing positive emotions in their presence and a desire to maintain close proximity (or) establish stronger bonds. In its simplest form, attraction encompasses not only romantic (or) physical allure but also the draw toward friendship, familial connections and professional relationship.

TYPES:

i. Physical attraction.
v. Social attraction.
v. Task attraction.
v. Sensual attraction.
v. Emotional attraction.
v. Romantic attraction.
v. Aesthetic attraction.
v. Intellectual attraction.

SENSUAL ATTRACTION:

- Sometimes also called physical attraction, this involves a desire for closedness and physical contact that's not in sexual (or) romantic contacts it might include hugging.

EMOTIONAL ATTRACTION:

- This involves a desire for deep closeness or connection that may (or) may not include physical contact.

ROMANTIC ATTRACTION:

- This type of attraction means you are interested in a romantic or love relationship with someone. It involves a combination of physical and emotional feelings towards them. It's possible to be romantically, but not sexually, attracted to someone.

AESTHETIC ATTRACTION:

- This involves feelings of administration for a person's appearance. This attraction type often goes along with other types of attraction relationship. For example, someone's fashion sense and also be physically attracted to them.

INTELLECTUAL ATTRACTION:

- If you are attracted to someone intellectually, you admire the way they think. You may want to have a stimulating conversation with them (or) tap into the knowledge about a certain topic.

THEORY:

- **Like attracts like**: This law suggests that similar things are attracted to one another. It means that people tend to attract people who are similar to them—but it also suggests that people's thoughts tend to attract similar results. Negative thinking is believed to attract negative experiences, while positive thinking is believed to produce desirable experiences.
- **Nature abhors a vacuum**: This law of attraction suggests that removing negative things from your life can make space for more positive things to take their place. It is based on the notion that it is impossible to have a completely empty space in your mind and in your life. Since something will always fill this space, it is important to fill that space with positivity, proponents of this philosophy say.
- **The present is always perfect**: This law focuses on the idea that there are always things you can do to improve the present moment. While it might always seem like the present is somehow flawed, this law proposes that, rather than feeling dread or unhappiness, you should focus your energy on finding ways to make the present moment the best that it can be.
- The similarity attraction hypothesis explains that people tend to be attracted to people that are similar to themselves. The similarities are in the form of sad values and beliefs, attitude, cultural background and even small behaviours like posters.
- The law of attraction explains how people attract those similar to them and that they thoughts also lead to attracting similar people. It also a film that negative thinking will lead to negative experience and positive thinking leads to desirable results.

CHAPTER TWENTY-SEVEN

GROUPS- MEANING, TYPES, GROUP PROCESSES; SUSTAINABILITY OF GROUPS

Groups Meaning: When two or more people come together it is known as a group. A group is one in which people come together to attain a common goal in which people come together to attain a common goal and the relations among the members are interdependent

Definition: - According to Mill, A unit composed of two or more persons who come together to achieve a specific purpose and consider a contact meaningful is called a group.

TYPES OF GROUPS IN EXTENSION EDUCATION

1. **Formal Groups:** These groups are organized and structured with specific goals, roles, and responsibilities. They may have regular meetings and specific leadership positions. Examples include agricultural cooperatives, self-help groups, women's groups, and local committees. In extension education, these groups are often created to facilitate specific programs, such as health education, agricultural training, or skills development.

Key Characteristics:

- **Organized and Structured:** Formal groups typically have a defined leadership structure, regular meetings, and established procedures for decision-making.
- **Clear Goals and Objectives:** These groups are formed to achieve specific goals, such as promoting agricultural best practices or improving literacy.
- **Leadership Roles:** There are designated leaders, such as a group coordinator, secretary, or treasurer, who have specific responsibilities within the group.

Examples:

- **Cooperatives:** Groups that work together for the common benefit of members, especially in agricultural production and marketing.
- **Self-Help Groups (SHGs):** Groups of individuals (often women) who come together to provide mutual support in improving their economic, health, or social status.
- **Community Development Groups:** These groups focus on solving a particular local issue (e.g., water supply, sanitation, infrastructure).

1. **Informal Groups:** Informal groups are less structured and more flexible in nature. They form naturally around shared interests or goals, without formal organization or leadership. Examples include neighborhood study circles, informal learning groups, or community gatherings. Extension educators may use informal groups to

spread awareness about health, nutrition, or sustainable farming practices.

Key Characteristics:

- **Spontaneous and Flexible**: Informal groups emerge naturally, often with no specific agenda, and operate with flexibility.
- **Voluntary Participation**: Members join based on shared interests or mutual goals, without formal induction.
- **Lack of Formal Leadership**: Leadership, if present, is usually informal and may rotate or be shared among members.

Examples:

- **Study Circles**: Groups of community members who meet informally to learn about topics such as health, agriculture, or environmental issues.
- **Neighborhood Gatherings**: Informal groups in communities that come together to discuss common concerns or learn from one another.
- **Peer Support Groups**: Groups where individuals share experiences and support one another, such as farmers discussing farming techniques.

3. **Interest-Based Groups**: These groups are formed around a common interest or activity, such as gardening, literacy, or entrepreneurship. Extension education programs often target these types of groups because the

members are already motivated and have a shared passion or concern. These groups are easier to engage and can lead to more effective learning outcomes.

Key Characteristics:

- **Shared Interest or Activity**: The group is united by a common interest, such as a hobby or specific area of concern (e.g., agriculture, crafts, education).
- **Focused Objectives**: The group's objectives are often narrow, focusing on a specific topic or skill-building related to the members' interests.
- **Enthusiastic Participation**: Since members are motivated by their interest, the level of participation is usually high.

Examples:

- **Agricultural Interest Groups**: Farmers coming together to learn about new farming techniques, market trends, or sustainable agricultural practices.
- **Cultural or Heritage Groups**: Groups focused on preserving traditional crafts, art forms, or customs.
- **Health Interest Groups**: Community groups focused on learning about nutrition, sanitation, or disease prevention.

4. **Action Groups**: These groups are created for the purpose of addressing a specific issue or engaging in a particular activity. In extension education, action groups often focus on projects that require community involvement, such as building infrastructure, implementing health campaigns, or improving agricultural techniques.

Key Characteristics:

- **Project-Oriented**: These groups are formed to work on specific, often time-bound, tasks or projects.
- **Collaborative Problem Solving**: Members work together to address specific issues, using a collaborative approach to problem-solving.
- **Hands-On Activities**: Members are actively involved in implementing projects or actions rather than just discussing ideas.

Examples:

- **Disaster Relief Groups**: Formed in response to natural disasters or emergencies to organize relief efforts, collect donations, and distribute aid.
- **Environmental Action Groups**: Groups formed to address issues such as pollution, deforestation, or climate change, through activities like tree planting, cleaning up local parks, or advocating for policy changes.
- **Health Campaign Groups**: Groups working to implement health initiatives such as vaccination campaigns or awareness programs about HIV/AIDS prevention

5. **Advisory Groups**: These are groups composed of experts, stakeholders, and community leaders who provide guidance and support to extension education programs. They may help in decision-making, resource allocation, and problem-solving. Extension educators often consult these groups to ensure that programs meet the needs of the community and are culturally appropriate.

Key Characteristics:

- **Composed of Experts or Leaders**: Advisory groups often include professionals, specialists, or influential community members who can provide valuable insights.
- **Guidance and Support**: The primary role of these groups is to offer advice, evaluate programs, and provide recommendations for future actions.
- **Decision-Making Support**: Advisory groups often participate in decisions about program design, implementation, and evaluation.

Examples:

- **Agricultural Extension Advisory Committees**: Groups of agricultural experts who advise extension agencies on curriculum, training programs, and research priorities.
- **Health Advisory Boards**: Composed of health professionals who guide extension education on public health programs or initiatives.
- **Community Development Advisory Groups**: Groups that help shape the priorities and approaches of community development initiatives.

Group Processes: Argule (1969) categorized 4 stages of group processes:

- Forming
- Storming
- Norming
- Performing

Keron (1989) identified a fifth stage:

- Mourning/ Adjourning

Forming: This is when a group first gets together. People tend to find out about each other, consider purposes, brainstorm ideas and possible structures for tasks and consider their own roles within the group. This is usually a very sociable time in the life of the group.

Storming: As the group begins to settle in and individuals get to know each other, they may start competing for status and role in the group. Disagreements occur and where some members may try to assert strong opinions or leadership tactics, others may withdraw. If tensions are not mutually dealt with at this stage, they tend to disrupt group communication and activity and most importantly mutual respect for the role of members.

Norming: After the more tense stage of Storming, the group usually begins to settle as members have found a common approach to the task that all agree upon or accept (this is where unsettled conflicts can be problematic as they will probably re-occur later). Actions plans begin to emerge and people find space to begin working on tasks

Performing: This is the stage when the group achieves optimum efficiency and work gets done. At this stage it is important to know the team work strategies you are working with that will best utilize the expertise of each member. It is also useful be aware of time spent on each task through a log/ diary so that possible conflicts do not reoccur.

Mourning / Adjourning: Having satisfactorily got through the group tasks, if the group has been successful in working together, despite initial tensions and conflicts, we often see members sad to leave each other. This is where mutual respect and achievement is felt most significantly. Often sub groups form from the larger groups to continue with personal or professional development interests.

Sustainability of Groups in Extension Education:

In extension education, sustainability refers to the capacity of groups to continue their activities, fulfill their objectives, and remain functional over time, without depending on external intervention or support. For a group to be sustainable, it must be able to maintain and expand its efforts independently, ensuring that its impact persists even after the formal extension education program concludes. Sustainability in extension education is critical for achieving long-term community development and empowering participants to continue learning, solving problems, and improving their lives.

The sustainability of groups in extension education is influenced by several factors, including the group's organizational structure, leadership, resources, and the broader social, economic, and cultural context in which it operates.

KEY ASPECTS OF SUSTAINABILITY IN EXTENSION EDUCATION

1. **Leadership and Governance**

   - **Effective Leadership**: A sustainable group requires strong, capable, and committed leadership. Leaders should possess the skills to guide the group, resolve conflicts, and keep members engaged in the long term. Leadership can be formal (designated roles like president, secretary, etc.) or informal (emerging leaders within the group).
   - **Shared Leadership**: For long-term sustainability, groups often need to have a system where leadership is shared or rotated among members. This prevents over-reliance on a single leader and ensures the group can adapt to changing circumstances.
   - **Decision-Making and Governance Structures**: Clear and transparent decision-making processes and democratic governance structures are crucial for a group's long-term viability. A sustainable group ensures that all members have a voice in decisions, fostering a sense of ownership and responsibility.

2. **Member Commitment and Participation**

   - **Active Member Engagement**: For a group to be sustainable, its members must be actively involved in its activities and take ownership of its goals. Ongoing member participation ensures that the group's work is relevant to their needs and that they are committed to its success.
   - **Community Ownership**: Groups are more likely to be sustainable if they are closely aligned with the interests and needs of the community. When members feel a sense of ownership over the group's activities, they are more likely to continue participating and supporting its efforts in the future.
   - **Inclusiveness**: Sustainable groups are inclusive, ensuring that all community members—regardless of gender, age, ethnicity, or social status—are involved. Inclusivity promotes diversity of thought, which can help the group stay dynamic and relevant over time.

3. **Financial and Resource Sustainability**

   - **Resource Mobilization**: Sustainable groups must be able to mobilize financial and non-financial resources (such as time, knowledge, and materials) to support their activities. Extension educators often help groups identify funding sources, such as government grants, private donations, or income-generating activities.
   - **Income-Generating Activities**: In many cases, sustainable groups engage in income-generating activities to become financially self-sufficient. For example, a group of farmers might engage in cooperative marketing, where they pool resources to sell their produce at a better price, or a women's group might start a small-scale business.
   - **Diversified Funding Sources**: Relying on a single funding source (e.g., donor grants) can make a group vulnerable. A sustainable group diversifies its funding sources, seeking partnerships with other organizations, local businesses, or government bodies, and leveraging the skills and assets of its members.

4. **Capacity Building and Skill Development**

- **Training and Skill Development**: Sustainable groups are characterized by their ability to continuously develop the skills and knowledge of their members. Extension educators play a critical role in providing training in areas such as leadership, financial management, group dynamics, and technical expertise.
- **Building Local Capacity**: It is important to build the capacity of local leaders and members to manage and sustain group activities independently. Extension educators may conduct training sessions on project management, conflict resolution, and other relevant topics to strengthen the group's internal capacity.
- **Adaptability to Change**: A sustainable group is one that can adapt to changes in the environment, whether technological, economic, or social. Groups that are flexible and open to learning new strategies or changing their approaches when necessary are more likely to survive over time.

5.Social Capital and Networking

- **Building Social Networks**: Social capital—the networks of relationships and trust within a community—is essential for the sustainability of extension education groups. These networks help groups access resources, share information, and collaborate on common goals.
- **Partnerships and Collaboration**: Collaboration with other groups, organizations, and institutions (e.g., local government, NGOs, businesses) enhances the sustainability of extension groups. These partnerships can provide additional resources, expertise, and support.
- **External Support and Mentoring**: While sustainability aims for independence, external support in the form of mentoring and guidance from other organizations or experts can help ensure the group remains on track and continues to grow.

5. Program Relevance and Impact

- **Continuous Evaluation and Feedback**: Sustainable groups engage in ongoing evaluation to assess their activities, measure their impact, and adjust their strategies as needed. Extension educators help groups establish mechanisms for monitoring and evaluation, ensuring that the group stays relevant to its members and continues to address important community issues.
- **Flexibility and Responsiveness**: Sustainable groups must be responsive to the changing needs of their members and the community. As local contexts evolve, groups may need to revise their goals, strategies, or approaches to remain effective.
- **Long-Term Vision**: A sustainable group should have a long-term vision or mission that guides its activities, while remaining flexible enough to adapt to new challenges and opportunities. This vision helps keep the group focused on broader goals, such as community development or empowerment, rather than just short-term objectives.

6. Cultural and Contextual Sensitivity

- **Cultural Appropriateness**: Sustainability is closely tied to a group's ability to operate within its cultural context. Extension educators should work with the group to understand and respect local customs, traditions, and values. If the group's activities align with the community's cultural norms, the group is more likely to gain acceptance and sustain its work.
- **Community Empowerment**: Extension education should focus on empowering groups to take control of their own development. Groups that feel empowered are more likely to remain active and sustain their efforts over time.

7.Monitoring and Evaluation (M&E)

- ◦ **Regular Assessment**: Sustainable groups regularly assess their own performance and outcomes through monitoring and evaluation. Extension educators assist groups in establishing M&E systems to measure progress toward goals, assess impact, and identify areas for improvement.
- ◦ **Feedback Loops**: Feedback from group members, stakeholders, and beneficiaries helps groups adjust their strategies and improve their impact. This continuous learning process ensures that the group remains effective and responsive to the community's needs.

SOCIAL INFLUENCE AND GROUPS – CONFORMITY, COMPLIANCE AND OBEDIENCE.

SOCIAL INFLUENCE-

- social influence refers to the way in which individuals change their ideas and actions to meet the demands of a social group, perceived authority, social role or a minority within a group wielding influence over the majority.
- Psychologists have spent decades studying the power of social influence, and the way in which it manipulates people's opinions and behavior.

INFORMATIONAL SOCIAL INFLUENCE-
Informational social influence occurs when individuals conform to the actions or beliefs of others because they believe that others have more information or expertise.

KEY CHARACTERISTICS:

- **AMBIGUITY:** Informational social influence is most likely to occur in situations where the correct course of action is unclear or ambiguous.
- **UNCERTAINTY:** When individuals are uncertain about how to behave or what to believe, they tend to look to others for guidance.
- **EXPERTISE:** If individuals perceive others as having more knowledge or expertise, they are more likely to be influenced by them.

EXAMPLES:

- **EMERGENCY SITUATIONS:** In an emergency, such as a fire, people often look to others for cues on how to react. If others are calmly evacuating the building, individuals are more likely to remain calm and follow suit.
- **NEW SITUATIONS:** When encountering a new situation or unfamiliar social environment, individuals may observe the behaviour of others to determine appropriate behavior.
- **EXPERT OPINIONS:** People often rely on the opinions of experts, such as doctors or financial advisors, to make important decisions.

IMPACT:
Informational social influence can have a significant impact on individual and collective behaviour. It can lead to:

- **IMPROVED DECISION-MAKING:** By relying on the knowledge and expertise of others, individuals can make more informed and accurate decisions.

- **INCREASED CONFORMITY:** In some cases, informational social influence can lead to excessive conformity and a reluctance to question the judgments of others.
- **SPREAD OF MISINFORMATION:** If individuals rely on incorrect or misleading information from others, it can lead to the spread of misinformation and false beliefs.

NORMATIVE SOCIAL INFLUENCE-
Normative social influence is a type of social influence that leads to conformity. It is defined in social psychology as "...the influence of other people that leads us to conform in order to be liked and accepted by them."
KEY CHARACTERISTICS:

- **DESIRE FOR SOCIAL APPROVAL:** Normative social influence stems from the human identity as a social being, with a need for companionship and association.
- **PUBLIC COMPLIANCE:** Individuals may publicly conform to group norms to avoid rejection or gain social approval, even if they privately disagree with the group's views.
- **FEAR OF SOCIAL DISAPPROVAL:** The fear of being ostracized or ridiculed by the group can be a powerful motivator for conformity.

EXAMPLES:

- **FASHION TRENDS:** People often conform to fashion trends to fit in with their social groups and avoid being seen as "out of style."
- **PEER PRESSURE:** Adolescents may engage in risky behaviors to gain peer approval and avoid social rejection.
- **GROUPTHINK:** In group decision-making, normative social influence can lead to groupthink, where individuals suppress their own opinions to maintain group harmony.

IMPACT:
Normative social influence can have a significant impact on individual and collective behavior. It can:

- **PROMOTE SOCIAL COHESION:** By encouraging conformity to group norms, normative social influence can help to maintain social order and stability.
- **LEAD TO PUBLIC COMPLIANCE WITHOUT PRIVATE ACCEPTANCE:** Individuals may outwardly conform to group norms while privately maintaining their own beliefs.
- **SUPPRESS DISSENT AND CREATIVITY:** The pressure to conform can stifle creativity and discourage individuals from expressing dissenting opinions.

SOCIAL INFLUENCE AND CONFORMITY-

- Social influence takes a number of forms. One type of such influence is conformity, when a person adopts the opinions or behaviors of others. This often occurs in groups, when an individual conforms to the social norms respected by a majority of the group's members.
- An individual may conform to the opinions and values of a group. They express support for views accepted by the group and will withhold criticism of group norms. Behavioral conformity can also influence a group member's actions: a person will behave in a way that is similar to others in the group.

INTERNALIZATION-
INTERNALIZATION refers to the process by which individuals adopt the beliefs, values, and attitudes of others as their own, often leading to lasting changes in their behavior and thinking.
KEY ASPECTS:

- **GENUINE ACCEPTANCE:** Internalization involves a genuine acceptance of the adopted beliefs, values, or attitudes. It's not just about public conformity, but a true integration of these external influences into one's own internal framework.
- **LASTING CHANGE:** The changes resulting from internalization tend to be enduring and resistant to change.
- **MOTIVATION:** Internalization is often driven by a desire to understand and connect with others, or to gain a deeper understanding of the world.

EXAMPLES:

- **MORAL DEVELOPMENT:** Children internalize the moral values of their parents and society, which guides their behavior and decision-making throughout their lives.
- **CULTURAL NORMS:** Individuals internalize the cultural norms and values of their society, which shapes their beliefs about appropriate behavior, social roles, and relationships.
- **RELIGIOUS BELIEFS:** Religious individuals may internalize the teachings of their faith, leading to profound changes in their worldview and lifestyle.

SIGNIFICANCE:

Internalization is a crucial process in human development and socialization. It allows individuals to:

- **DEVELOP A SENSE OF SELF:** By adopting the values and beliefs of others, individuals develop a sense of identity and belonging.
- **NAVIGATE SOCIAL SITUATIONS:** Internalized norms and values provide individuals with a framework for understanding and navigating social interactions.
- **PROMOTE SOCIAL COHESION:** Shared values and beliefs contribute to social cohesion and cooperation within groups and societies.

COMPLIANCE-

- This involves a request that an individual or group complies with the instructions of another.
- Compliance frequently occurs when a person is asked by an authority figure to meet a particular set of demands. For example, drivers comply with the directions given by traffic wardens, and students comply with the requests of their teacher, who they view as holding a position of **authority**.
- Compliance may be achieved using a number of techniques known as **compliance strategies**. These are often used by salespeople to persuade potential customers to fulfill their request to place orders.
- Compliance strategies include the **foot-in-the-door technique**, which involves a person making a small initial request in order to gain compliance with another question.
- Once a person has complied with a request, they are more likely to agree to a later, more significant, request.
- For example, a car sales representative may ask a prospective customer to agree to test-drive a new car. If the person agrees, they may be able to persuade them to extend their compliance by accepting a later request to buy the car.
- The **door-in-the-face technique** is another compliance strategy which takes an opposite approach.
- An unreasonably large request is made initially, followed by the request that the subject is expected to comply with.
- A person will almost certainly reject the first request, but the second appears more reasonable when compared to it, and so they may be more inclined to comply with the second proposition.

OBEDIENCE-

Obedience is the act of complying with or following the orders or instructions of an authority figure. It involves submitting to the will or command of another person, often due to perceived legitimacy or power.

KEY ASPECTS:

- **SUBMISSION TO AUTHORITY:** Obedience involves a degree of submission to the authority figure, even if the individual may have personal reservations about the order.
- **SOCIAL HIERARCHY:** Obedience often reflects an established social hierarchy where certain individuals or groups hold authority over others.
- **SITUATIONAL FACTORS:** The level of obedience can be significantly influenced by situational factors, such as the perceived legitimacy of the authority figure, the presence of other obedient individuals, and the proximity of the authority figure.

EXAMPLES:

- **MILITARY:** Soldiers are expected to obey the orders of their superiors without question.
- **WORKPLACE:** Employees are expected to follow the instructions of their managers.
- **LEGAL SYSTEM:** Citizens are expected to obey the laws of their country.

CHAPTER TWENTY-NINE

SOCIAL JUDGEMENT MEANING, FRAME OF REFERENCE, STEREO TYPING; JUDGEMENT OF ATTITUDE MODELS

Social judgment refers to the process by which people evaluate and interpret information and ideas that are presented to them within a social context. It involves assessing the opinions, beliefs,and behaviors of others, as well as forming judgments and making decisions based on social influences and norms. Social judgment can be influenced by various factors, such as cultural background, personal experiences, social norms, and the influence of peers and authorities.

Essentially, it's about how people perceive and interpret information in light of social influences and how these judgments affect their attitudes and behaviors in social situations.

•In social judgment theory, the "frame of reference" refers to an individual's mental structure that helps them evaluate and interpret incoming information and messages from others. It consists of three main components:

1. LATITUDE OF ACCEPTANCE: This refers to the range of ideas and opinions that a person finds acceptable. Information falling within this range is more likely to be accepted and agreed upon by the individual.

2. LATITUDE OF REJECTION: This refers to the range of ideas and opinions that a person finds unacceptable. Information falling within this range is more likely to be rejected and disagreed upon by the individual.

3. LATITUDE OF NON-COMMITMENT: This refers to the range of ideas and opinions that a person neither accepts nor rejects outright. Information falling within this range is met with a neutral or ambivalent response.

The way these latitudes are structured can vary from person to person, and they form the basis for how individuals judge and evaluate persuasive messages. When a message falls within the latitude of acceptance, it is more likely to be persuasive and influence the person's attitudes or beliefs. If it falls within the latitude of rejection, it is likely to reinforce the person's existing beliefs. Understanding an individual's frame of reference is crucial for effective communication and persuasion, as it helps tailor messages to be more persuasive within the listener's accepted range of ideas.Examples for each of the three components of social judgment theory: latitude of acceptance, rejection, and non-commitment:

1. LATITUDE OF ACCEPTANCE:

- **Example:** A person who is environmentally conscious might accept information about recycling, renewable energy, and sustainable living practices. They are receptive to messages that promote eco-friendly behaviors and may actively engage with such content.

2.LATITUDE OF REJECTION:

- **Example:** Someone with strong political beliefs might reject information from a political party they strongly disagree with. No matter how well-reasoned the arguments are, they are likely to dismiss them outright because they fall outside their accepted range of political ideologies.

3. LATITUDE OF NON-COMMITMENT:

- **Example:** Imagine a person who is undecided about a specific diet plan. They might be willing to consider various options and listen to different arguments without firmly committing to any particular plan. Their latitude of non-commitment allows them to explore different ideas without forming a strong opinion.

These examples illustrate how individuals' attitudes and judgments are influenced by their specific latitudes. People tend to be more receptive to information that aligns with their existing beliefs (latitude of acceptance), reject information that contradicts their beliefs (latitude of rejection), and remain indifferent or ambivalent about information that doesn't strongly align with their attitudes (latitude of non-commitment). Social judgment theory helps explain these processes of acceptance, rejection, and non-commitment in various social contexts.

❖ Stereotyping in social judgment refers to the process of categorizing individuals or groups based on preconceived beliefs, assumptions, or generalizations about the characteristics, behaviors, or attributes of the entire group. These stereotypes are often based on societal norms, cultural biases, or personal experiences. Stereotyping can lead to unfair judgments and prejudices, as it involves making assumptions about a person or group without considering their individual differences.

Stereotyping can affect various aspects of social interactions, including decision-making, attitudes, and behavior. It can lead to discrimination and contribute to social inequality when individuals are treated differently based on these stereotypes.

It is important to recognize and challenge stereotypes to promote understanding, tolerance, and acceptance among diverse groups of people. Encouraging empathy, educating people about different cultures and backgrounds, and promoting positive inter-group interactions can help reduce stereotyping and its negative consequences in society.

Stereotyping can manifest in various forms, and it occurs for several reasons, often rooted in cognitive processes, social dynamics, and cultural influences. Here are different types of stereotyping examples along with their causes:

1. RACIAL STEREOTYPING:

- Example: Assuming that individuals of a certain race are naturally good at sports.

- Cause: Historical prejudices, lack of exposure to diverse cultures, and media representations can contribute to racial stereotyping.

2. GENDER STEREOTYPING:

- Example: Believing that women are not as competent in leadership roles as men.

- Cause: Traditional gender roles, socialization, and media portrayal of gender can lead to gender stereotyping.

3. AGE STEREOTYPING:

- Example: Assuming that older adults are technologically illiterate.

- Cause: Cultural attitudes towards aging, lack of inter-generational interactions, and limited exposure to different age groups can cause age stereotyping.

4. SEXUAL ORIENTATION STEREOTYPING:

- Example: Assuming that individuals belonging to the LGBTQ+ community possess certain personality traits or behaviors.

- Cause: Lack of understanding and exposure to diverse sexual orientations, societal biases, and misinformation can lead to such stereotypes.

5. RELIGIOUS STEREOTYPING:

- Example: Believing that people of a certain religion are inherently more moral or immoral.

- Cause: Limited knowledge about different religions, cultural biases, and historical conflicts can contribute to religious stereotyping.

6. OCCUPATIONAL STEREOTYPING:

- Example: Assuming that all artists are unconventional and disorganized.

- Cause: Limited exposure to diverse professionals, media portrayals, and societal perceptions of certain professions can lead to occupational stereotyping.

Stereotyping often occurs due to cognitive shortcuts the brain takes to process information efficiently. When people encounter unfamiliar situations or individuals, their brains might rely on stereotypes as mental shortcuts, leading to biased judgments. Education, exposure to diverse experiences, and promoting empathy can help reduce stereotyping and foster a more inclusive society.

❖ In social psychology, there are several models that describe how people form judgments about attitudes, including social judgment theory, balance theory, and cognitive dissonance theory.

1. SOCIAL JUDGMENT THEORY: Social Judgment Theory (SJT) is a persuasion theory developed by

Muzafer Sheriff and Carl Hovland in the 1960s. Social judgment theory suggests that peopleevaluate and interpret incoming information based on their existing attitudes and beliefs. Whena message aligns with their current attitudes (in the latitude of acceptance), it is more likely to be accepted and persuasive. Messages that fall within the latitude of rejection are likely to be dismissed, while those in the latitude of non-commitment might not strongly influence attitudes.

2. BALANCE THEORY: Balance theory posits that people prefer consistency and balance in their beliefs and attitudes. When there is inconsistency or imbalance between attitudes and beliefs within a social network, individuals are motivated to reduce the dissonance by changing their attitudes or beliefs to restore balance.

3. COGNITIVE DISSONANCE THEORY: Cognitive dissonance theory states that individuals experience discomfort (dissonance) when they hold conflicting beliefs or attitudes. To reduce this discomfort, they may change their attitudes or beliefs to align with their actions or find ways to justify their behavior.Cognitive dissonance theory, developed by Leon Fe stinger in 1957, is a social psychology theory that explains the discomfort individuals feel when they hold conflicting beliefs, attitudes,or values, or when their actions contradict their beliefs. This theory proposes that when people experience cognitive dissonance, they are motivated to reduce it in order to regain internal consistency and mental harmony.

The theory is based on several key principles:

1. COGNITIVE DISSONANCE: Cognitive dissonance refers to the psychological discomfort felt by an individual who holds contradictory beliefs or values or engages in contradictory actions.

2. DISSONANCE REDUCTION: When people experience cognitive dissonance, they are motivated to reduce it. They can do this by changing their beliefs, acquiring new information that supports their existing beliefs, or changing their actions to align with their beliefs.

- Example: If a person believes smoking is harmful to health but continues to smoke, they may experience cognitive dissonance. To reduce this discomfort, they might either quit smoking (change their behavior) or convince themselves that smoking is not as harmful as they previously thought (change their beliefs).

3. SELECTIVE EXPOSURE: People tend to seek information and engage in activities that support their existing beliefs to avoid cognitive dissonance. This selective exposure helps them maintain consistency in their beliefs and actions.

- Example: Someone with strong political beliefs may prefer to watch news channels that align with their political views, avoiding information that contradicts their beliefs.

4. POST-DECISION DISSONANCE: After making a decision, individuals may experience cognitive dissonance, especially if the decision was difficult. To reduce this dissonance, they may convince themselves that the chosen option was the best, overlooking the drawbacks of the alternatives.Example: After choosing a college, a student might downplay the benefits of thecolleges they didn't choose to feel better about their decision Cognitive dissonance theory is fundamental in understanding behavior change, decision-making processes, and attitudes. It helps explain why people sometimes make irrational or unexpected decisions and how they rationalize their choices to maintain psychological harmony.These models provide insights into how people judge and respond to attitudes and information within social contexts. Understanding these theories helps researchers and psychologists analyze and predict how individuals might react to persuasive messages or conflicting attitudes in various social situations.

CHAPTER THIRTY

ATTRIBUTION MEANING, THEORIES AND RATIONAL DECISION MAKING

Attribution: The Art of Explaining Behaviour

Attribution is the process by which individuals explain the causes of events, including their own behaviour and the behaviour of others. It's a fundamental aspect of social cognition, influencing how we perceive, interpret, and respond to the world around us.

THEORIES OF ATTRIBUTION

Several theories have been proposed to explain how people make attributions:

HEIDER'S ATTRIBUTION THEORY: This theory suggests that people tend to attribute behavior to either internal (dispositional) or external (situational) factors. For example, if someone fails an exam, we might attribute it to their lack of intelligence (internal) or to a difficult exam (external).theory is a foundational concept in social psychology that explores how individuals explain the causes of events and behaviors.

CORE IDEA:

- **INTERNAL VS. EXTERNAL ATTRIBUTIONS:** Heider proposed that people tend to attribute behavior to either:

  - **INTERNAL FACTORS (DISPOSITIONAL ATTRIBUTION):** These relate to the person's personality, traits, abilities, or motives.

    - Example: "She failed the exam because she's not intelligent."

  - **EXTERNAL FACTORS (SITUATIONAL ATTRIBUTION):** These relate to the environment, luck, or other people's actions.

    - Example: "She failed the exam because the questions were too difficult."

KEY CONCEPTS:

- **NAIVE SCIENTISTS:** Heider viewed people as "naive scientists" who constantly try to understand the causes of behavior in their social world.
- **LOCUS OF CAUSALITY:** This refers to whether the cause of behavior is attributed to internal or external factors.

SIGNIFICANCE:

- **UNDERSTANDING HUMAN BEHAVIOR:** Heider's theory provides a framework for understanding how people perceive and interpret the actions of others.
- **SOCIAL PERCEPTION:** It highlights the importance of attributions in shaping our impressions and judgments of individuals.

- **INTERPERSONAL RELATIONSHIPS:** Attributions can significantly influence how we interact with others and how we perceive their intentions.

LIMITATIONS:

- **OVERSIMPLIFICATION:** The theory may oversimplify the complexity of human behavior, which is often influenced by a multitude of factors.
- **FUNDAMENTAL ATTRIBUTION ERROR:** People often overemphasize internal factors and underestimate situational factors when explaining others' behavior.

JONES AND DAVIS' CORRESPONDENT INFERENCE THEORY: This theory focuses on how people infer dispositions from behavior. It suggests that people are more likely to attribute behavior to internal causes when the behavior is freely chosen, has unique effects, and is socially undesirable.

KEY CONCEPTS:

- **CORRESPONDENCE:** The theory focuses on the degree to which a person's behavior corresponds to their underlying personality traits.
- **INFERENCE:** People make inferences about others' internal states based on their observed behaviors.

FACTORS INFLUENCING CORRESPONDENT INFERENCES:

- **CHOICE:**

  - If a behavior is freely chosen, it is more likely to be attributed to internal factors.
  - For example, if someone chooses to help a stranger, we are more likely to infer that they are a kind person.

- **EXPECTEDNESS OF THE BEHAVIOR:**

  - If a behavior is unexpected or atypical, it is more likely to be attributed to internal factors.
  - For example, if a usually quiet person suddenly becomes loud and boisterous, we are more likely to infer that something unusual is happening with them.

- **SOCIAL DESIRABILITY:**

  - If a behavior is socially undesirable, it is more likely to be attributed to internal factors.
  - For example, if someone acts rudely, we are more likely to infer that they are a rude person, rather than attributing their behavior to external factors.

LIMITATIONS:

- **FOCUS ON INTENTIONAL BEHAVIOR:** The theory primarily focuses on intentional behavior and may not fully account for unintentional or habitual behaviors.
- **CORRESPONDENCE BIAS:** The theory may contribute to the correspondence bias, which is the tendency to overestimate the role of internal factors and underestimate the role of situational factors in explaining others' behavior.

KELLEY'S COVARIATION MODEL: is a significant attribution theory in social psychology that explains how individuals make causal inferences about the behaviors of others. It suggests that people systematically examine multiple pieces of information to determine whether a behavior is caused by internal factors (dispositional attribution) or external factors (situational attribution).

THREE KEY FACTORS:

The model proposes that individuals consider three key factors to make these attributions:

1. **CONSENSUS:**

   ◦ **HIGH CONSENSUS:** If many other people behave similarly in the same situation, consensus is high.
   ◦ **LOW CONSENSUS:** If few other people behave similarly, consensus is low.

2. **DISTINCTIVENESS:**

   ◦ **HIGH DISTINCTIVENESS:** If the person behaves differently in other situations, distinctiveness is high.
   ◦ **LOW DISTINCTIVENESS:** If the person behaves similarly in other situations, distinctiveness is low.

3. **CONSISTENCY:**

   ◦ **HIGH CONSISTENCY:** If the person behaves similarly in the same situation across different times, consistency is high.
   ◦ **LOW CONSISTENCY:** If the person's behavior varies across different times in the same situation, consistency is low.

   Group inference method of attribution theory based
on Dempster–Shafer theory of evidence - ScienceDirect

MAKING ATTRIBUTIONS:

- **INTERNAL ATTRIBUTION (DISPOSITIONAL):** When consensus and distinctiveness are low, but consistency is high, people tend to make internal attributions. This suggests that the behavior is caused by the person's stable, internal characteristics.
- **EXTERNAL ATTRIBUTION (SITUATIONAL):** When consensus, distinctiveness, and consistency are all high, people tend to make external attributions. This suggests that the behavior is caused by the specific situation or stimulus.

EXAMPLE:

Imagine you observe a student falling asleep in class.

- **HIGH CONSENSUS:** If many other students are also falling asleep, consensus is high.
- **HIGH DISTINCTIVENESS:** If this student only falls asleep in this particular class, distinctiveness is high.
- **HIGH CONSISTENCY:** If this student falls asleep in this class every day, consistency is high. In this scenario, you might attribute the student's behavior to an external factor, such as a boring lecture or a stuffy classroom.

LIMITATIONS:

- **COGNITIVE LOAD:** The model assumes that people have the cognitive resources and motivation to carefully analyze all three factors.
- **AVAILABILITY OF INFORMATION:** In many real-world situations, individuals may not have access to all the necessary information to make accurate attributions.

SIGNIFICANCE:

Despite its limitations, Kelley's Covariation Model provides a valuable framework for understanding how people make causal inferences about the behaviors of others. It highlights the importance of considering multiple pieces of information before drawing conclusions about the underlying causes of behaviour.

WEINER'S ATTRIBUTION THEORY:

Bernard Weiner (1985) focused his theory of attribution on how people explain success and failure. According to his theory, explanations can be based on personal factors such as ability or effort, and situational factors such as luck or task difficulty.

Attribution theory assumes that people try to determine why people do what they do, i.e., attribute causes to behaviour. A person seeking to understand why another person did something may attribute one or more causes to that behaviour. A three-stage process underlies an attribution:

(1) the person must perceive or observe the behaviour,

(2) then the person must believe that the behaviour was intentionally performed, and

(3) then the person must determine if they believe the other person was forced to perform the behaviour (in which case the cause is attributed to the situation) or not (in which case the cause is attributed to the other person).

Weiner focused his attribution theory on achievement (Weiner, 1974). He identified

• ability,

• effort,

• task difficulty, and

• luck as the most important factors affecting attributions for achievement.

Attributions are classified along three causal dimensions:

1. locus of control,

2. stability, and

3. controllability.

The locus of control dimension has two poles:

• internal versus

• external locus of control.

The Stability dimension captures whether causes change over time or not. For instance,

• ability can be classified as a stable, internal cause, and

• effort classified as unstable and internal.

Controllability contrasts causes one can control, such as skill/efficacy, from causes one cannot control, such as aptitude, mood, others' actions, and luck.

Book 2 Attribution. - ppt download

ATTRIBUTION AND RATIONAL DECISION MAKING

Attribution plays a significant role in rational decision-making by influencing our perceptions and judgments. Here's how:

SELF-SERVING BIAS: We tend to attribute our successes to internal factors (e.g., skill, effort) and our failures to external factors (e.g., luck, circumstances). This bias can lead to overconfidence and a reluctance to learn from mistakes.

FUNDAMENTAL ATTRIBUTION ERROR: We tend to overemphasize internal factors and underestimate external factors when explaining others' behavior. This can lead to misunderstandings and misjudgments.

ACTOR-OBSERVER BIAS: We tend to attribute our own behavior to external factors (situational) and others' behavior to internal factors (dispositional). This can lead to self-serving biases and blaming others.

HOW ATTRIBUTION CAN AFFECT RATIONAL DECISION MAKING:

- **PERCEIVED RESPONSIBILITY:**

When evaluating options, people might attribute responsibility for potential outcomes to different factors, influencing their choice depending on whether they perceive the responsibility to be internal or external.

- **INFORMATION PROCESSING:**

Attributions can shape how individuals interpret information, leading to biases in how they weigh evidence when making decisions.

- **DECISION-MAKING HEURISTICS:**

When under time pressure, people may rely on quick attributions as a mental shortcut to make decisions, potentially leading to suboptimal choices.

Mitigating the impact of attribution bias:

- **AWARENESS OF BIASES:**

Recognizing that attribution biases exist and actively considering alternative explanations can help individuals make more informed decisions.

- **GATHERING DIVERSE PERSPECTIVES:**

Seeking input from others with different viewpoints can provide a more comprehensive understanding of a situation and reduce the influence of personal attributions.

- **DATA-DRIVEN DECISION MAKING:**

Relying on objective data and evidence can help to counteract subjective attributions and promote more rational choices.

CHAPTER THIRTY-ONE

SOCIAL IDENTITY – MEANING, TYPES AND ASSESSMENT

SOCIAL IDENTITY MEANING:

Social identity refers to the way individuals perceive themselves and their place within social groups, such as families, communities, organizations, or cultures.

Social identity refers to people's self categorizatons in relation to their group memberships.

This concept plays a crucial role in shaping human behavior, as individuals often derive a sense of belonging, purpose, and self-esteem from their social identities.

DEFINITION:

Social identity can be defined as an individual's knowledge of belonging to certain social groups, together with some emotional and value significance of that group membership.

TYPES OF SOCIAL IDENTITY:

1.CULTURAL IDENTITY:

Cultural identity refers to the identification with a culture or society, including its values,norms and traditions.

2. ETHNIC IDENTITY:

The ethnic identity is the identification of people with an ethnic groups. Ethnic identity usually begins to emerge in adulthood.

3.GENDER IDENTITY:

Gender Identity is defined as a personal and internal sense of oneself as male,female or other .

KEY ASPECTS OF SOCIAL IDENTITY:

1. **Group Membership**: Belonging to a social group, such as a nationality, ethnicity, or profession.

2. **Self-Concept**: The way individuals perceive themselves, including their values, attitudes, and behaviors.

3. **Inter-group Comparisons**: Comparing one's own group to others, often leading to feelings of superiority or inferiority.

4. **In-group Favoritism**: Favoring one's own group over others, often resulting in biases and prejudices.

5. **Identity Salience**: Determining which aspects of social identity are most important in different contexts.

6. **Emotional Attachment & Belonging**: Assessing the significance and emotional connection a person has with their group.

7. **Impact on Behavior**: Understanding how social identity influences decision-making, communication, and social interactions.

THEORIES OF SOCIAL IDENTITY:

1. SOCIAL IDENTITY THEORY (SIT):

Proposed by Henri Tajfel and John Turner, Social identity theory was developed to explain how individuals create and define their place in society.

People's social identity indicates who they are in terms of the groups to which they belong.

Social identity theory distinguishes between three types of strategies for status improvement:

• Individual mobility,

- Social competition,
- Social creativity.

INDIVIDUAL MOBILITY:

It allows people to pursue individual position improvement irrespective of the group. It can also be an individual-level solution for overcoming group devaluation.

SOCIAL COMPETITION:

Agroup-level strategy that requires group members to draw together and combine forces to help each other improve their joint performance or outcomes.

SOCIAL CREATIVITY:

Social creativity implies that people modify their perceptions of the in-group's standing. That can be achieved by introducing alternative dimensions of comparison in order to emphasize ways in which the in-group is positively distinct from relevant out-groups. A second possibility is to reevaluate existing group characteristics to enhance in-group perceptions. A third possibility is to compare one's group with another reference group in order to make the current standing of the in-group appear more positive.

Social creativity strategies are generally characterized as cognitive strategies because they alter people's perceptions of their group's current standing instead of altering objective outcomes. Nevertheless, it has been demonstrated that these strategies can constitute a first step toward the achievement of social change. Because social creativity strategies help preserve identification with and positive regard for the in-group, even when it has low status, over time those strategies can empower group members to seek actual position improvement for their group

2. SELF-CATEGORIZATION THEORY (SCT):

Developed by John Turner and colleagues, SCT describes how individuals categorize themselves and others into groups, influencing their perceptions and behaviors.

Social categorization refers to the tendency of people to perceive themselves and others in terms of particular social categories—that is, as relatively interchangeable group members instead of as separate and unique individuals.

Implications of Social Identity on Human Behavior:

1. **Group Conformity:** Individuals often conform to group norms and expectations to maintain social identity.

2. **Prejudice and Discrimination:** Social identity can lead to biases and prejudices against out-groups.

3. **Cooperation and Competition:** Social identity influences cooperation within groups and competition between groups.

4. **Self-Esteem and Motivation:** Social identity affects self-esteem and motivation, as individuals strive to maintain a positive self-image.

ASSESSMENT OF SOCIAL IDENTITY:

An assessment of social identity involves evaluating how strongly an individual identifies with a particular social group, typically measured by examining their feelings, beliefs, and behaviors related to their group membership, including factors like the importance they place on the group, their positive or negative perception of the group, and how much they conform to group norms; this is often done through surveys or questionnaires based on Social Identity Theory (SIT) principles.

Methods for assessing social identity:

• **Self-report questionnaires:**

• **Social Identity Scale (SIS):** A widely used scale that measures the strength of identification with a particular group, including aspects like group commitment and positive evaluation of the group.

• **Group Identification Scale (GIS):** Another common scale focusing on how strongly individuals feel like they belong to a group.

• **Qualitative methods:**

• **Interviews:** Exploring individuals' experiences and perceptions regarding their social identities through open-ended questions.

• **Focus groups:** Facilitating discussions among a group of people to uncover shared perspectives on social identities.

Important considerations when assessing social identity:

• **Inter Sectionality:** Recognizing that individuals can hold multiple social identities that overlap and interact with each other, such as being female and Asian.

• **Social context:** Considering the situational factors that can influence how strongly an individual expresses their social identity.

• **Implicit bias:** Being aware of potential biases in the assessment process, including the researcher's own biases and how they might influence interpretation.

Applications of social identity assessment:

Diversity and inclusion initiatives: Understanding the social identities present within an organization to promote equity and inclusion.

Social psychology research: Studying the effects of social identity on attitudes, behaviors, and group dynamics.

Marketing research: Targeting specific social groups based on their identity and preferences.

References

Chatterjee S. K. (2000) Advanced Educational Psychology Books & Allied Pvt. Ltd., Delhi

Sharan B.Merriam,rosemary S.Caffarella,RaymondJ.Wlodkowski,P.craton "Adult Learning"Theories,Principles and Applications

JC Aggarwal, Dr. Nidhi Agarwal and Puneet Kumar, Dr. Harish Kumar and Santosh Kumar Rout, Intelligence, creativity and education. Vikas publications.

Subhash chandra, suresh kumar, kailash chandra Bairaw, An Introduction to Agricultural Social Science, Vishal's Publication.

Tomas Chamorro-Premuzic, Personality and Individual Differences, Wiley publishers.

Swanson, B. E., & Rajalahti, R. (2010). Strengthening Agricultural Extension and Advisory Systems: Procedures for Assessing, Transforming, and Evaluating Extension Systems. The World Bank

Jiggins, J., & Röling, N. G. (2000). The challenge of making decision-making processes more inclusive in agricultural extension. Agricultural Systems, 63(2), 33-54.

Heider, F. (1958). The Psychology of Interpersonal Relations. New York: Wiley.

Kelley, H. H. (1967). Attribution theory in social psychology. Nebraska Symposium on Motivation, 15, 192-238.

Weiner, B. (1974). Achievement motivation and attribution theory. General Learning Press.

Fiske, S. T., & Taylor, S. E. (1991). Social Cognition. New York: McGraw-Hill.

Kahneman, D. (2011). Thinking, Fast and Slow. Farrar, Straus and Giroux.

Brooks, J., & Brooks, M. (1993). In search of understanding: the case for constructivist classrooms, ASCD. NDT Resource Center database.

Bandura, Albert. Social Foundations of Thought and Action: A Social Cognitive Theory. Prentice Hall, 1986

S.S. Chauhan (2009) "Advanced Educational Psychology"7th edition, Vikas Publishing house,pp 201-204, 224,225.

Asoke Kumar Sannigrahi (2011) "Human Resource Development", New India Publishing Agency, pp 12-19,35-52.

Dr. J. S. Amarnath &A. P. V. Samvel (2008) "Human Resource Development" Sakthi Serial Publishing House, pp 165-173

Bandura, A. (1986). Social foundations of thought and action: A social cognitive theory. Prentice-Hall.

Piaget, J. (1973). To Understand Is to Invent: The Future of Education. Grossman Publishers.

Vygotsky, L. S. (1978). Mind in Society: The Development of Higher Psychological Processes. Harvard University Press.

Schunk, D. H. (2012). Learning theories: An educational perspective. Pearson Education.

Woolfolk, A. (2019). Educational Psychology (14th ed.). Pearson.

Bikart, J. (2019). The art of decision making: How we move from indecision to smart choices. Hachette India.

Kahneman, D. (2011). Thinking, fast and slow. Penguin Random House India.

Ariely, D. (2010). Predictably irrational: The hidden forces that shape our decisions. HarperCollins India.

Mayer, J. D., Salovey, P., & Caruso, D. R. (2002).*Mayer-Salovey-Caruso Emotional Intelligence Test (MSCEIT): User's manual.* Toronto, ON: Multi-Health Systems

Bar-On, R. (1997).*The Emotional Quotient Inventory (EQ-i): Technical manual.* Toronto, ON: Multi-Health Systems.

Bradberry, T., & Greaves, J. (2005).*The Emotional Intelligence Quick Book.* New York: Simon and Schuster

Hogg, M. A., & Vaughan, G. M. (2010). Social psychology (6th ed.). Pearson Education India.

Misra, G. (Ed.). (2009). Psychology in India: Social and organizational processes (Vol. 2). Pearson Education India.

Baron, R. A., & Branscombe, N. R. (2017). Social psychology. Pearson Education India.

Swami, V. (2016). The psychology of love and attraction. Routledge India.

Dalal, A. K., & Misra, G. (2018). Interpersonal relationships: Beyond acquaintanceship. SAGE Publications India.

Conscious Mind" by David Chalmers (1996) - a comprehensive book on the philosophy of consciousness.

"Consciousn.ess: A Very Short Introduction" by Susan Blackmore (2005) - a concise introduction to the concept of consciousness.

"The Oxford Handbook of Consciousness" edited by Susan Schneider and Max Velmans (2017) - a comprehensive handbook on consciousness, covering its meaning, types, and related topics.

"What is Consciousness?" by David Chalmers (1995) in the Journal of Consciousness Studies, Vol. 2, No. 3, pp. 200-219.

"The Types of Consciousness" by Ned Block (1995) in the Journal of Consciousness Studies, Vol. 2, No. 2, pp. 133-155.

"Sleep and Dreams" by J. Allan Hobson (2005) in the Journal of Clinical Psychology, Vol. 61, No. 2, pp. 137-145.

"Consciousness" by the Stanford Encyclopedia of Philosophy - a comprehensive online article on the concept of consciousness.

"Theories of Consciousness" by the Internet Encyclopedia of Philosophy - a detailed online article on the various theories of consciousness.

"Sleep and Dreams" by the National Sleep Foundation - a website providing information on sleep and dreams, including articles, research, and resources.

Kenneth R. Hammond, Gary H. McClelland, Jeryl Mumpower. 1981. *Human Judgment and Decision Making: Theories, Methods, and Procedures*, University of Illinois Press Vol. 94,No. 3, pp. 542-544

Michael k Lindell. 2014. *LaboratoryExperiments in the Social Sciences-chapter 18, Judgement and decision making, Academic*

press, pp. 403-431

Kenneth R Hammond. 1996. *Human*

*Judgement and Social Policy: Irreducible Uncertainty, Inevitable Error,Unavoidable Injustice, O*xford Scholarship online, pp. 11-94

Berndt Brehmer, C. R. B. Joyce. 1988. *Human Judgement,* El Sevier Science Publisher, pp. 1-86

https//:www .wikipedia. org

https//:www . Lindene. com

https//:www.verywell.com

https//:www.psychology.com

https //:www.positivepsychology.com

https//:www.scribd.com

https://en.m.wikibooks.org

www.ncbi.nlm.nih.gov

https://doi.org/10.1016/S0308-521X(99)00080-6

FAO - Agricultural Extension:

http://www.fao.org/agriculture/crops/thematic-sitemap/theme/spi/extension/en/

World Bank - Agricultural Extension:

https://www.worldbank.org/en/topic/agriculture/brief/agricultural-extension

International Food Policy Research Institute (IFPRI) - Agricultural Extension:

https://www.ifpri.org/topic/agriculture-extension

https://www.extension.org/

https://journals.sagepub.com/doi/10.1177/0731121417712492[3]https://www.simplypsychology.org/social-identity-theory.html

https://www.psychologywizard.net/social-identity-theory-ao1-ao2-ao3.html

https://www.themantic-education.com/ibpsych/2017/02/16/social-identity-theory/

https://www.britannica.com/topic/conformity/Normative-influence

https://www.rhnet.org/site/handlers/

filedownload.ashx?moduleinstanceid=5006&dataid=24349&FileName=social%20identity.pdf

https://ndl.ethernet.edu.et/bitstream/123456789/40841/1/21.pdf.pdf

https://www.sciencedirect.com/topics/social-sciences/social-judgement
https://study.com/academy/lesson/video/what-is-social-judgment-theory-definition-examples.html
https://academic.oup.com/anncom/article/6/1/304/7820288
https://www.sciencedirect.com/science/article/abs/pii/0030507381900258
https://www.researchgate.net/publication/240239746_Social_Judgement_Theory_and_Medical_Judgement
https://www.12manage.com/description_sherif_social_judgment_theory.html
https://gcwgandhinagar.com/econtent/document/1587181812CLASSICAL%20CONDITIONING.pdf
https://www.tandfonline.com/doi/full/10.1080/08924562.2022.2052776
https://www.emexmag.com/need-want-satisfaction-chain/
https://bcastudyguide.com/unit-2-perceptionattitudevalues-motivation/
https://www.simplilearn.com/theories-of-motivation-article
www.verywellmind.com
www.simplysychology.com
www.cloudaccess.com
www.elm.com
www.wgu.com
www.structurallearning.com
www.edu.com
www.verywellmind.com
www.simplypsychology.org
www.northedu.com
http://eclkc.ohs.acf.hhs.gov
www.mlearning.com
www.valamis.com
www.structurallearning.com
www.cloudaccess.com
https://www.sciencedirect.com/topics/social-sciences/liking
https://egyankosh.ac.in/bitstream/123456789/20868/1/Unit-3.pdf
https://www.crowdspring.com/marketing-psychology/liking-principle/
https://library.scotch.wa.edu.au/psychology/year11/relationalinfluences/determinantsofliking
https://study.com/academy/lesson/attraction-theory-definition-measurements-effects.html
https://thedecisionlab.com/reference-guide/psychology/choice-architecture
https://journals.sagepub.com/doi/10.1177/10690727241298688?icid=int.sj-abstract.citing-articles.6
https://opentext.wsu.edu/social-psychology/chapter/module-12-attraction/
https://pmt.physicsandmathstutor.com/download/Psychology/A-level/Notes/AQA/11-Relationships/Set-A/Psychological%20Theories%20of%20Attraction.pdf
https://www.egyankosh.ac.in/bitstream/123456789/72634/1/Unit-7.pdf
https://www.verywellmind.com/attitudes-how-they-form-change-shape-behavior-2795897
https :// en.wikipedia.org
https:// www.apexhospitals.com
https://www.sciencedirect.com
https://testbook.com
https://mskelly.weebly.com
https://www.studysmarter.co.uk
https://www.verywellmind.com/components-of-emotional-intelligence-2795438
https://positivepsychology.com/emotional-intelligence-theories/
https://www.indeed.com/career-advice/career-development/emotional-intelligence

www.ingramcontent.com/pod-product-compliance
Lightning Source LLC
Chambersburg PA
CBHW040206110726
48005CB00019B/2908